D1572058

THE STRUCTURED WORLD
OF JORGE GUILLEN

Grateful acknowledgement is made to
the University of Warwick for generous
financial assistance towards the cost
of publication of this book

LIVERPOOL MONOGRAPHS IN HISPANIC STUDIES

⁴ THE STRUCTURED WORLD OF JORGE GUILLEN

ELIZABETH MATTHEWS

A STUDY OF *CANTICO* AND *CLAMOR*

X
FRANCIS CAIRNS

Published by
Francis Cairns
The University, P.O. Box 147, Liverpool L69 3BX
Great Britain

First published 1985

British Library Cataloguing in Publication Data

Matthews, Elizabeth
  The structured world of Jorge Guillen : a study
  of Cantico and Clamor.–(Liverpool monographs
  in Hispanic Studies, ISSN 0261-1538; 4)
  1. Guillen, Jorge–Criticism and interpretation
  I. Title   II. Series
  861'.62   PQ6613.U5Z/

ISBN 0-905205-23-5

Printed in Great Britain by
Redwood Burn Ltd, Trowbridge, Wiltshire

CONTENTS

Dedication		vi
Foreword		vii
1	**Introduction**	1
2	**The Early Editions of Cántico**	14
	The 1928 edition ... 14	
	The 1936 edition ... 26	
	The 1945 edition... 50	
3	***Cántico* (1950): Six Major Poems**	78
	Introduction ... 78	
	"El diálogo" ... 86	
	"El concierto" ... 94	
	"A vista de hombre" ... 102	
	"Luz natal" ... 113	
	"Vida extrema" ... 128	
	"Las cuatro calles" ... 138	
	Conclusion ... 149	
4	***Clamor*: Six Pillar Poems**	151
	Introduction ... 151	
	"Luzbel desconcertado" ... 158	
	"La hermosa y los excéntricos" ... 173	
	"Lugar de Lázaro" ... 183	
	"Huerto de Melibea" ... 197	
	"Dimisión de Sancho" ... 208	
	"Las tentaciones de Antonio" ... 216	
	Conclusion ... 225	
5	**Conclusion**	229
	Appendix: English Versions of Twelve Major Poems	237
	Dialogue ... 238 Concert ... 241 In Sight of Man ... 244 Native Light ... 247 Extreme Life ... 255 The Four Streets ... 260 Lucifer Disconcerted ... 263 Beauty and the Eccentrics ... 275 The Land of Lazarus ... 284 Melibea's Garden ... 294 Sancho's Resignation ... 306 The Temptations of Anthony ... 312	
	Bibliography	322
	Index of Poems Analysed	326

Dedicado con toda humildad a
la memoria de Don Jorge Guillén

FOREWORD

During the last stages of the preparation of this book the Hispanic world was saddened to hear of the death of Jorge Guillén on 6th February 1984. For the author, personal regret at this loss was compounded by the necessity of revising the passages of the text in Chapter 1 concerning Don Jorge's daily life and activities. I was privileged to be able to correspond with the poet from 1976 until his death, and was welcomed at his home in Málaga on several occasions. I hope that my admiration for both the poet and the man will be clearly discerned from a reading of this book.

This study contains my translations of the Spanish quotations, so that the non-Spanish reader may gain an insight into the work of one of the greatest poets of the twentieth century. The translations are my own, and I have tried not to introduce unnecessary interpretation, seeking always to render the Spanish as directly as possible, with occasional changes in word order according to the requirements of English syntax. Complete translations of the twelve major poems from *Cántico* and *Clamor* appear in an Appendix with the aim of providing the reader who has no knowledge of Spanish with a substantial example of the scope of these first two books of poetry. I have not included translations of the titles of Guillén's five books, as the meaning of these is easy enough to remember: *Cántico*, a hymn of praise or a song of joy; *Clamor*, clamour, outcry or protest; *Homenaje*, Homage; *Y otros poemas*, And Other Poems; *Final*, end or conclusion.

Chapter 1 is a brief introduction to the life and work of Jorge Guillén. It provides biographical details in addition to outlining the major preoccupations of Guillén's five volumes of poetry. In Chapter 2 the early editions of *Cántico*, from 1928 to 1945, are studied and the thematic development of the volumes as a whole is discussed. The texts used in the chapter are from the following editions: *Cántico*, 12th edition (Paris: Centre de Recherches de l'Institut d'Etudes Hispaniques, 1962), a republication of the first edition published by Revista de Occidente in Madrid in 1928; *Cántico (1936)*, ed. J.M. Blecua (Barcelona: Labor, 1970); *Cántico* (Mexico: Litoral, 1945). As this latter edition is very difficult to obtain in the United Kingdom, a second page reference, to *Cántico* (Barcelona: Barral, 1977), is also given. In Chapter 3 six major poems from the definitive 1950 edition of *Cántico* are analysed, to show not only their structural significance but also their thematic thrust. Of particular relevance is the importance of time (the present) and space (the world) in both of which man actively participates in his relationships with reality. The edition used is *Cántico* (Barcelona: Barral, 1977). Chapter 4 studies the six major poems which are the ideological and structural pillars of *Clamor*. The analyses show that man may create his own *exempla*, from which to learn to live courageously in the world of his own making. The valiant affirmation of the earlier volume remains, although its enemy, Chaos, is clear in the form of poems which consider man in an historical dimension. The edition used is *Clamor* (Barcelona: Barral, 1977). In the concluding chapter, the significance of *Cántico* and *Clamor* within the overall structure of *Aire nuestro* is briefly considered. References to the volumes of poetry published after *Clamor* are from the following editions: *Homenaje* (Barcelona: Barral, 1978), *Y otros poemas* (Barcelona: Barral, 1979), and *Final* (Barcelona: Barral, 1981). Abbreviations used are as follows (unless otherwise indicated, texts as above):

C_1	*Cántico* 1928
C_2	*Cántico* 1936
C_3	*Cántico* 1945
C	*Cántico* 1950
CL	*Clamor*
H	*Homenaje*
OP	*Y otros poemas*
F	*Final*
AN	*Aire nuestro* (Milan: All'insegna del pesce d'oro, 1968)
AO	*El argumento de la obra* (Milan: Scheiwiller, 1961)
LP	*Language and Poetry* (Cambridge, Mass.: Harvard Univ. Press, 1961)

Where appropriate, stanza numbers of the poems quoted are included for ease of reference. In the case of the major poems discussed in Chapters 3 and 4 quotations are accompanied by page references. To avoid duplication translations have not been included in these chapters, but line references are provided to enable the reader to locate the appropriate passage in the Appendix.

Finally there are acknowledgements to be made for a great deal of help from several sources. With gratitude I thank: the University of Warwick for generous financial assistance towards the publication of this book; my colleague, Raymond Calcraft, who has been unstinting with his advice and encouragement, as well as easing my teaching commitments at no small cost to himself; and Mrs Janet Seaton, for her skilled typing. Above all I wish to thank Don Jorge's widow, Doña Irene Mochi Sismondi de Guillén, for permission to quote the poetry of her husband, for her generosity in allowing me to visit them both in Málaga, and for giving me the privilege of knowing and therefore loving Don Jorge, the man, long after I had come to know and admire the work of Jorge Guillén, the poet.

Elizabeth Matthews
University of Warwick

CHAPTER 1

INTRODUCTION

On the 18th of January 1983 Jorge Guillén celebrated his ninetieth birthday. The many tributes which were paid to him on that occasion were richly deserved recognition both of a long and fruitful life dedicated to poetry and of his status as Spain's greatest living poet.

Guillén's childhood in the sharp and clear light of Castile was extremely happy, and he was fortunate in the various formative influences on his early life. He was educated at the Instituto de Valladolid (1903-1909), spent two years after secondary school in Fribourg, Switzerland (1909-1911), was a student in the Faculty of Philosophy and Letters at Madrid University (1911-1913), and received his first degree from the University of Granada in 1913. He spent the next year in Germany, then returned to live in Spain until 1917. From 1917 to 1923 he held his first official post in the teaching profession as *lecteur d'espagnol* at the Sorbonne in Paris.

Guillén recalled with affection his native Valladolid and was grateful for the open, liberal atmosphere of the city and its cultured residents during the first decades of this century. Valladolid is the home of Spain's third oldest newspaper, *El Norte de Castilla*, founded in 1854, to which Guillén became a contributor in 1918. The liberal ambience of Guillén's early environment was reinforced by the fairness and generosity of his father and the gentleness of his mother. As a business man Julio Guillén could well have expected his son to continue in the same career, but he accepted Jorge's wish to follow a financially unrewarding profession and, instead, allowed himself the luxury of having a poet for a son. Guillén's mother, Esperanza Alvarez Guerra, to whom *Cántico* is dedicated, had a profound influence upon the young Jorge. The special relationship between mother and child was particularly fruitful for Guillén, as his mother's Christian values were communicated to him gradually and informally. There is little or nothing of conventional religious belief in Guillén's poetry, but there is, above all, a notable reverence for both the natural world and for fellow human beings. Guillén openly acknowledged his debt to his mother, and while he did not have her orthodox faith he never lost respect for what he was taught to believe. In a letter to the present author Guillén wrote, "Yo conservo mi 'conciencia cristiana' y mi amor a Jesús de Galilea – el que se expresaba en arameo" (I still retain my "Christian conscience" and my love of Jesus of Galilee, who expressed himself in Aramaic).[1] These words echo one of Guillén's constant concerns, his interest in the expressive ability of the individual whose will to communicate with his fellow men is of supreme importance.

While studying in Madrid from 1911 to 1913 Guillén lived in the famous Residencia de Estudiantes, a place influenced by the ideas of the Institución Libre de Enseñanza, founded in 1876, Spain's first school to be free from State control, and which therefore enjoyed the possibility of encouraging liberal attitudes in its students. Modern and above all humanist in its ideology, the Residencia was exceptional in Spain. While there, Guillén came to know Luis Buñuel and Salvador Dalí and was a good friend to Federico García Lorca. As did many others, Guillén recalled Lorca's magnetic personality, his vitality and the fact that he was always the centre of attention. Guillén's long and affectionate correspondence with the younger poet shows the former to have been a wise and steadying influence as well as a close friend in whom Lorca could confide.[2]

While at the Sorbonne Guillén soon began to move in French literary circles. He wrote for the Madrid paper *La Libertad* and was good friends with the writers Paul Valéry, Jean Cassou and the critic Marcel Bataillon. Guillén married Germaine Cahen in October 1921, his daughter Teresa was born at the end of the following year, and his son Claudio in 1924. In 1918 Guillén had written his first poems and the following year, while on holiday in Tregastel, Brittany, he began to envisage his first volume of poems, *Cántico*, as well as conceiving the idea of that volume as the first of a series which would form a unified work. Guillén refers to Walt Whitman's *Leaves of Grass* and Baudelaire's *Les fleurs du mal* as significant influences on this project.[3]

[1] Letter dated 30 May 1980.
[2] Their correspondence, published by Guillén, can be found in *Federico en persona: semblanza y epistolario* (Buenos Aires: Emecé, 1959).
[3] See N.T. di Giovanni, *"Cántico": A Selection* (London: Deutsch, 1965), p.5.

The conferment of a doctorate by the University of Madrid in 1924 was followed by Guillén's participation in public examinations for university positions, and in 1926 he took up his first post as Professor of Spanish Literature at the University of Murcia, a post he held until 1929. At this point in his career Guillén was well known in Spain for his short, precise and formally elegant poems, regularly published in literary reviews since the early twenties.[4] In fact the twenties in Spain were years of extraordinary creative brilliance and Guillén was one of a group of talented and prolific writers, most widely known as the "Generation of 1927". This year marked the tercentenary of the death of Spain's great Baroque poet, Luis de Góngora, and the young poets took this opportunity to show their allegiance to a writer obscured by centuries of unmerited neglect. The Group (the designation preferred by Guillén) included Rafael Alberti (b. 1903), Vicente Aleixandre (b. 1898, Nobel Prize 1977), Dámaso Alonso (b. 1898), Manuel Altolaguirre (1905-1959), Luis Cernuda (1902-1963), Gerardo Diego (b. 1896), Federico García Lorca (1898-1936), Emilio Prados (1899-1962) and Pedro Salinas (1891-1951), and, as Guillén says, they were held together more by friendship than by a formalized system of poetic method or doctrine. He stresses the unique individuality of each poet and points out that in their very different volumes of poetry they demonstrate the collective interests of the group: admiration for the wide-ranging creativity of sixteenth- and seventeenth-century Spanish writers, for example, Garcilaso de la Vega, San Juan de la Cruz, Gil Vicente, Luis de Góngora, Lope de Vega and Quevedo; and respect for their own immediate predecessors, Juan Ramón Jiménez, Antonio Machado and Miguel de Unamuno. Spain's great literary tradition was something they wished to perpetuate and many used the classic Spanish verse forms as well as those belonging to popular poetry. At the same time they were inspired by the French Symbolists and the Imagists. In short, this was a group of young men fired by enthusiasm to integrate traditional verse forms with new ideas, to avoid sentimentality, verbal exuberance (as in the Modernists) and anything trivially anecdotal.[5] In Guillén's words they believed in "a

---

[4] The earliest publications date from 1920-1923 in *La Pluma* and *España*; 1924-1926 in *Revista de Occidente, Litoral* and *La Verdad*; 1927-1928 in *Meseta, Mediodía* and *Verso y Prosa*. For details of revisions, see K.M. Sibbald, "Some early versions of the poems of *Cántico 1919-1928*: Progress towards *claridad*", *Bulletin of Hispanic Studies*, 50 (1973), 23-44.

[5] See Gerardo Diego, "La vuelta a la estrofa", *Carmen*, 1 (Dec. 1927) and J. Guillén, *Language and Poetry* (Cambridge, Mass.: Harvard Univ. Press, 1961), pp.201-16.

poetry that would be both art with all the severity of art and creation with all its genuine *élan*".[6] The poets of Guillén's generation were concerned to achieve exact forms of expression: technical ability was sought after, for it was necessary to express any idea with clarity and precision. Guillén is careful to make clear, however, that there was no "empty formalism". Their use of Spanish metres did not arise through mere imitation but was the result of detailed study and comprehension of the significance of certain verse forms, and the validity of certain literary devices. In particular, the cultivation of the metaphor was of supreme importance to these poets, and Guillén singles out this as the major unifying force amongst them. Guillén's own metaphors combine emotional intensity with intellectual control and are used to describe not only objects but ideas and emotions. They function not to draw surprise from the reader because of their startling or disparate components, nor to impress briefly with their linguistic ingenuity, but rather to enable him to perceive the truth or reality of the object or idea described. Good examples can be found in "Tránsito" (The Passing) or "Tornasol" (Iridescence), discussed in the following chapter.

In 1928 Guillén's first volume of poetry was published. *Cántico* documents a world which is "well-made". It is a highly organized and masterful display of verse forms and, above all, shows a positive attitude to the world, which contrasts strongly with some of his contemporaries, like Lorca, Cernuda and Alberti, who, at that time, found themselves forced to express with anguish the misery of the world and society around them. *Cántico* reflects little of the turbulence of the twenties and this, combined with the formal precision and elegance of the seventy-five poems of this first volume, led to Guillén being criticized as too abstract and cerebral. However, Guillén always rejected "pure poetry" in favour of "el poema con poesía y otras cosas humanas" (the poem with poetry and other human things),[7] and it is this human dimension which is characteristic of the whole of his work. The world and man within it are minutely scrutinized and Guillén's decision to begin with *Cántico*, a hymn of joy or praise, is the starting point of a carefully structured and thematically coherent five-volume work, *Aire nuestro*.

Guillén's next academic post was as *lector* at Oxford University, where he continued to write poems which would be included

---

[6] J. Guillén, op.cit., p.204.

[7] Letter from Guillén to Fernando Vela, reproduced in Gerardo Diego, *Poesía española contemporánea*, 8th ed. (Madrid: Taurus, 1979), pp.326-28.

in later volumes. The short-lived Spanish Second Republic was proclaimed in 1931 while Guillén was still in Oxford and he returned later that year to a post as Professor of Literature at Seville University. He also contributed to the numerous literary reviews that were flourishing in Spain, and his second volume of poetry was published in Madrid in 1936. It contained fifty new poems added to the original seventy-five, still with the title *Cántico*. In July 1936 the Spanish Civil War erupted, Lorca was murdered in August, and the group of poets, linked by friendship and creative enthusiasm, was irrevocably torn apart. Many went into voluntary or enforced exile, and few remained in Spain. They continued to write and to correspond with one another but those essential creative and personal links were broken as was the whole artistic impulse of the previous decade. Guillén himself found it impossible to compromise with dictatorship and began the journey north towards France, where his wife left their children with her family. She then rejoined him in Pamplona, where they were imprisoned, Guillén because he was an intellectual and a liberal and suspected of being a spy (a totally false accusation), and Germaine because she was Jewish. They were released after five days through the efforts of Guillén's father, but the Ministry of Education prevented Guillén from holding teaching posts of any kind. They stayed with friends in Seville until Guillén finally gathered all the necessary papers to enable them to leave Spain in 1938.

From this point onwards, Guillén's life changed from one based in Spain but with frequent journeys to teach in other European countries, to one as a teacher of Spanish literature in North America with equally frequent trips to South America and Europe. Like many of his contemporaries who left Spain, Guillén defined the greatest problem of exile as being denied one's native language, a particularly tragic circumstance for a poet. However, he was able to compensate for this by continuing in the teaching profession, first at McGill University in Montreal in 1939 and then at Wellesley College, Massachusetts, from 1940 to 1957, when he retired and became Emeritus Professor. During these years Guillén continued to write; a third edition of *Cántico*, now increased to 270 poems, was published in Mexico in 1945 and the final, definitive volume, containing 332 poems and two dedications, came out in Buenos Aires in 1950.

Guillén's first official activity after his retirement was as the Charles Eliot Norton Professor of Poetry at Harvard University in 1957-1958. His lectures have been preserved in the book *Language and Poetry*, which enables us to see what a fine literary critic Guillén is.[8] He considers some of Spain's greatest writers – Berceo, Góngora, San Juan de la Cruz, Bécquer and Gabriel Miró – and the overall theme of the lectures is language: how the creative writer takes something we all use every day and converts it into a very specific and expressive instrument. He discusses the various linguistic registers and styles cultivated by these writers, from the so-called "prosaic" style of Berceo, the Baroque stylization of Góngora, the struggle against the inadequacy of language of the mystic, San Juan de la Cruz, and of the Romantic visionary, Bécquer, to the clarity and precision of his near-contemporary, Miró. In each chapter we see Guillén's unshakable faith in the power of words, unities of form and meaning used by creative writers not merely to give aesthetic pleasure but to communicate, to join writer and reader in an experience or emotion which ultimately glorifies the unique quality of the human being, his powers of linguistic expression.

After this Guillén began to receive many literary prizes, awarded from both European and American centres (1957, Poetry Prize of the City of Florence; 1959, Etna-Taormina Poetry Prize, Sicily; 1961, Grand Prix International de Poésie, Belgium; 1964, San Luca Prize, Florence; 1976, Bennet Prize for Poetry, *Hudson Review*, New York; 1977, Premio Miguel de Cervantes, Madrid; Feltrinelli International Prize for Poetry, Accademia dei Lincei, Rome). He also travelled a great deal in Europe, with the occasional trips to Spain, and Latin America, accompanied by his second wife Irene Mochi Sismondi, whom he married in October 1961. He was visiting Professor in several North and South American universities including the Colegio de México (Mexico City), the University of California (Berkeley), Ohio State University, the University of the Andes (Bogotá), the University of Puerto Rico, the University of Pittsburgh and the University of California (San Diego), until a fall, at the age of seventy-seven, resulting in a broken femur, caused him to retire from his various lecturing and teaching commitments. During these years his output of poetry continued unabated. After *Cántico* he began to publish his second volume, *Clamor*, the three parts of which appeared in 1957, 1960 and 1963.[9] The very obvious

---

[8] See note 5 above.

[9] *Maremágnum*, ... *Que van a dar en la mar, A la altura de las circunstancias*, all published in Buenos Aires, by Editorial Sudamericana. These remained as separate volumes with the general title of *Clamor*, until their inclusion in *Aire nuestro* (Milan: All'insegna del pesce d'oro, 1968). *Maremágnum* means Pandemonium, the other two titles are both quotations, the first from Manrique: "Nuestras vidas son los ríos que

difference in meaning of these two titles, *Cántico* and *Clamor*, caused something of a stir and Guillén, dubbed the "optimist", was held to have recanted his early attitudes with the publication of poems which were felt to be a more "accurate" reflection of the horrors and tragedies of the real world. However, the genesis of some of the poems of *Clamor* took place in the late forties, at the same time as *Cántico* was nearing completion, and these first two volumes should be seen as complementary and reconcilable views of reality, rather than as representing diametrically opposed attitudes.

His third volume, *Homenaje*, published in Milan in 1967, was followed in 1968, on the occasion of his seventy-fifth birthday, by *Aire nuestro*, the work which includes *Cántico*, *Clamor* and *Homenaje*, with a series of expressive dedications and initial poems. The final poem of *Homenaje*, called "Obra completa" (Finished Work), testifies to the fulfilment of Guillén's aim in 1918 to produce a single organic unity, rather than a series of poems with no relation to a greater whole. However, life continued and with it the impulse to create and the long-ago envisaged organic unity is now a five-volume opus. *Y otros poemas* was first published in Buenos Aires in 1973, and *Final* in 1981 by Barral Editores in Barcelona. After 1936 all of Guillén's work was published outside Spain but with the involvement of the Barral publishing house, not only in *Final* but also in the republication of the four previous volumes of poetry, we see one aspect of Spain's final recognition of her greatest living poet. This was initiated by the award on 1st December 1976 of the prestigious Premio Miguel de Cervantes, Spain's first official homage to Guillén after the death of Franco. Three Ministers were invited to attend the ceremony but did not, Guillén's denunciation of the Civil War and of dictatorships presumably being too difficult to ignore.[10] After this there were more honours in the form of literary awards, honorary degrees and the proud and affectionate interest of the city of Málaga, Guillén's home after 1976. During the years in Málaga, Guillén was an active correspondent, the recipient of many requests to read and comment on work by young poets and critics of his own work. His

---

van a dar en la mar, que es el morir" (Our lives are the rivers *that flow to the sea*, which is death); the second from Antonio Machado: "Es más difícil estar a la altura de las circunstancias que au dessus de la mêlée" (It is more difficult *to be equal to circumstances* than to be above the conflict).

[10] See "Potencia de Pérez" (The Power of Pérez), *Clamor* (Barcelona: Barral, 1977), pp.40-53, and "Guirnalda civil" (Civil Garland), first published in Cambridge, Mass., by Halty Ferguson in 1970 and later included in *Y otros poemas* (Barcelona: Barral, 1979), pp.143-63.

days were filled with reading and writing and receiving friends, to whom he talked wittily and energetically. All were received with openness and affection. Guillén firmly maintained that the most important thing for him was the reader. Prizes, distinctions and honours were accepted with humility, pleasure and not a little surprise, but the reader remained of supreme importance, precisely because he was a friend, a companion in creative endeavour. *Aire nuestro* is dedicated to the reader, to us: "A quien leyere" (To whomever may read); and the volume moves from this general appellation to the more specific and binding "Al amigo de siempre, al amigo futuro" (To the friend of always, to the future friend) at the end of *Homenaje*.

There is a great amount of critical material available on Guillén's poetry, much of it in Spanish. The English reader cannot fail to be inspired by Guillén's introductions to N.T. di Giovanni's volume *Cántico: A Selection* and J. Palley's *Affirmation: A Bilingual Anthology 1919-1966.*[11] Incorporating some of the volume *El argumento de la obra* (The Argument of the Work), they provide an excellent summary of his aims in *Cántico* and *Clamor*. His book *Language and Poetry* gives the reader an opportunity to study poets through the eyes of a particularly acute practitioner of the art. *Luminous Reality*, the collection of essays in English published in 1969, offers a wide spectrum of critical perspectives, tributes and homages.[12] A more recent publication, *Guillén on Guillén*, was assembled out of several hours of tape recordings of Guillén reading an anthology, selected by himself, of poems from the four books then available, interspersed with commentaries by him.[13] The Spanish text, both poems and commentaries, is translated into English and the Introduction is succinct and stimulating.

The more or less chronological survey so far given offers little idea of Guillén's development as a poet. The reader may well be curious to know why the first volume of poetry, *Cántico*, took so long to complete, why Guillén retained the same title, and why, too, he should maintain that initial note of affirmation through so many years of strife and difficulty. As has been said, *Cántico* means a hymn

[11] di Giovanni, op.cit., and J. Palley, *Affirmation: A Bilingual Anthology 1919-1966* (Norman: Univ. of Oklahoma Press, 1968).
[12] I. Ivask and J. Marichal, eds., *Luminous Reality* (Norman: Univ. of Oklahoma Press, 1969).
[13] A.L. Geist and R. Gibbons, *Guillén on Guillén* (Princeton: Univ. of Princeton Press, 1979).

of praise, of joy, and the object to which Guillén directs this emotion, and which is also its impulse, is the natural world of Creation. Essentially Creation is good. The evil side of man's nature is acknowledged but deliberately kept within limits; it provides the chorus in the background over which the positive voice rises. The world offers visible shapes for man's perception, light by which to see and air by which to breathe and live, and so the relationship between the world and man is seen to be based on harmonious reciprocation. It is these simple things, which are in fact marvels or prodigies, that cause Guillén's delight in the world, make him affirm the validity of that world, and inspire him to investigate man's relationship with it. What is more simple and less considered than the physiological coordination of human lungs with the air which surrounds us? We enjoy the tremendous privilege of participating in this world; there is a "dialogue" between man and the world and man uses his senses and his intellect to participate continually and creatively in that dialogue. As Guillén says, "*Cántico* is about these moments in which nothing occurs but the extraordinary phenomenon of normality."[14]

Gradually, between 1928 and 1950, the scope and force of *Cántico* increased, but the single-minded thematic and structural development of this volume was accompanied by very varied activities on Guillén's part. He began writing poetry in 1918, but that same year he also began his career as a literary critic writing for his local paper *El Norte de Castilla*. In fact until 1925 he wrote more critical pieces than poetry. During his stay in Paris, for example, he published a variety of thoughtful articles on the state of European culture after the First World War. These appeared in the Madrid paper *La Libertad* and gave its readers, in a Spain that had been officially neutral during the war, an idea of the tragic legacy of that conflict. Many poems were published during this time but only some of them, and those considerably revised, actually appeared in *Cántico*. In addition, Guillén was very conscious of the growing cultural vitality of the twenties, and other articles cover music, the theatre, creative writers, jazz and the cinema.[15] C.B. Morris refers to the hectic, slightly hysterical activity of these years in Europe,[16] but where Guillén differs from other artists of the time is in his belief that

[14] di Giovanni, p.9.

[15] For texts of articles, see K.M. Sibbald, *Hacia "Cántico": Escritos de los años 20* (Barcelona: Ariel, 1980).

[16] See C.B. Morris, *A Generation of Spanish Poets 1920-1936* (Cambridge: Cambridge Univ. Press, 1969).

formal rigour and concern for accuracy, concision and elegance should be maintained. He believed the poet should create with words as conscientiously as the painter with colours and the sculptor with stone, that what each creates should be linked with tradition as well as striking its own authentic note of modernity or contemporaneity. In 1922 he coined the phrase "Eficacia técnica: eficacia humana" implying the vital combination of formal or technical care with human or emotional involvement.[17] In common with his contemporaries Guillén sought "Reality, not realism. And feeling – without which there is no poetry – has no need of gesticulation. Sentiment, not sentimentalism."[18] Both he and Pedro Salinas avoided the influence of Surrealism ("There is no babble quite so empty as that of the subconscious left to its triviality."[19]), although Alberti, Lorca and Cernuda were sympathetic to the freedom that Surrealism offered as it enabled them to express adequately their hostility to a cruel and chaotic world at a particular time, the late twenties and early thirties. Much later, in 1965, Guillén published an article, "Poesía integral", in which he accepts that one cannot ignore the potential horrors of the atomic age.[20] He states that "nuestra moral se resume en el nuevo imperativo: ¡angústiate!" (our ethic is summarized in this new imperative: be anguished!"), but goes on to say that to surrender to despondency would be the easiest way out and the worst. The role of poet is that of "portavoz y porta-conciencia" (spokesman and conscience-bearer); in fact the poet does have something to say in the midst of chaos. The evolution of mankind is a continual process, remarkable for "la increíble potencia del hombre, de ese hombre cuya capacidad de abyección es sólo comparable a su capacidad más sublime" (the incredible power of man, of this man whose capacity for wretchedness is only comparable with his most sublime ability"). The seeds for these ideas can be traced back to those early articles of the twenties, and this gradual evolution of thought and ideology is reflected in the slow and careful creation of *Aire nuestro*. Guillén chooses first to exalt man and his relationship to the natural world, and *Cántico* is strictly limited to that. He has no doubt whatsoever that "Este mundo del hombre está mal hecho" (Man's world is badly made)[21] but refuses to consider it

[17] J. Guillén, "Anatole France", *España*, 303 (1922), 12.
[18] J. Guillén, *Language and Poetry*, p.205.
[19] Ibid., p.204.
[20] J. Guillén, "Poesía integral", *Revista Hispánica Moderna*, 31 (1965), 207-209.
[21] See the poem "Las cuatro calles" (The Four Streets), in *Cántico* (Barcelona: Barral, 1977), p.423.

fully until the first statement of affirmation is made in detail. *Fe de vida*, the subtitle of *Cántico*, first given in 1945, means both "faith in life" and "verification (or affirmation) of life".

Clamor's subtitle is *Tiempo de historia* (Time of History). The minor voices of *Cántico*, chaos, evil and death, come forward here. However, while *Clamor* gives full rein to negative influences, those created by man, it cannot be said to be Guillén's recantation. Such a view would negate absolutely the validity of *Cántico*'s affirmation of life. Instead, the same clear-sighted observation is directed at Society, the world created by man. If the vision of man in *Cántico* is ideal, but nevertheless ultimately real, so the vision of man in *Clamor* is realistic but positive in implication. Here chaos and disorder appear as integral parts of man's existence. We see how to come to terms with disharmony and the principal theme of the poems consists of an exhortation that we never forget our duty to be *human* – "ser hombre". The sense carried by the noun "el hombre" (man) is immense in Guillenian terms: it has ethical, moral and physical connotations that resound through *Aire nuestro*. And in being human, we find our salvation, as is implied by the initial dedication of *Clamor*: "A mis hijos, a la posible esperanza" (To my children, to possible hope).

The third volume, *Homenaje*, has as a subtitle *Reunión de vidas* (Reunion of lives) and is dedicated "A todas las musas" (To all the Muses). As the title and subtitle imply, this volume is a homage to the creative writers and philosophers who have contributed to the elaboration of man's existence by means of the written word. It is, then, a homage by Guillén and, by extension, the reader, to the greatness that man can achieve within the world he has made. The first section ends with a series of poems under the general title of "Al margen de un Cántico" (In the margin of a *Cántico*), and in this way Guillén has not only moved forward with the creation of this third volume of *Aire nuestro*, but has also reviewed poetically his first book of poems. Continuity thus becomes an important element in the work as a whole: if *Clamor* looks to the future and the possibility of continuity in succeeding generations, so *Homenaje* brings into contemporary focus the history of man's creative endeavour. The poems affirm the value of life and art and while disharmony is also present, so too is humour, indicating that this volume balances the various modes of presenting reality.

The idea of continuity mentioned above is particularly obvious in the last two volumes of Guillén's work, *Y otros poemas* and *Final*.

Both comprise poems which continue, clarify and complement those of the three earlier volumes. In *Y otros poemas* there is a section entitled "Al margen de *Aire nuestro*" where the idea, from *Homenaje*, of reviewing what was already published is repeated. Many of the poems in the volume as a whole are dedicated not only to fellow poets but also to critics of Guillén's work. Personal experiences are recorded, and many poems reflect Guillén's understanding of, and reaction to, old age. But there still remains the familiar theme of amazement and gratitude for life and what the world has to offer. This combination of age and vitality is summed up in the line "Vejez es ya victoria" (Old age is even so a victory). *Y otros poemas* is dedicated "En mi memoria, a mi padre, fuego del que soy chispa" (In my memory, to my father, fire of which I am a spark), suggesting not only the idea of generations and the debt of life each of us owes to our collective ancestors, but also the essential theme of continuity.

Final is dedicated "Al lector superviviente" (To the everlasting reader), thus projecting the whole cycle of *Aire nuestro* into the future. The five sections of the book reconsider many of the themes and ideas set out in the earlier works. Life and time are the main themes, and the eternal and historical are again considered. Man's greatest gift, his powers of expression, is celebrated in poems which highlight the importance of the written word, both for author and reader. In addition, man's tendency to inhumanity, in the form of aggression, dictatorship and tyranny, is seen in terms of the tension between order and disorder. This historical context is, of course, one aspect of the theme of time, whose eternal dimension is represented by poems which are, in the manner of both *Homenaje* and *Y otros poemas*, glosses on writers and philosophers and their sources of inspiration. The book begins with a section entitled "Dentro del mundo" (In the world) where earthly existence and mortality are simply accepted. The final section, "Fuera del mundo" (Beyond the world), sees life as a history sensibly concluded by death. Immortality is the purlieu only of "the gods", for the human being is nothing without the essential boundaries of reality: time and place.

Throughout Guillén's work there are constant reminders that the protagonist of the poems is each and every one of us. The "Yo" (I) of the poems is never exclusively Guillén, although clearly many of the poems are based on personal experiences. The mother, father, children, close friend and reader, to whom the volumes are variously dedicated, symbolize the relationships that unite all men. There is no sense of chronological development in the five volumes, for each represents moments in the life of man, not the gradual evolution of Guillén's views as a poet. The themes which are discussed are universal, they are ever-renewable and inexhaustible, and in precisely this does the value of *Aire nuestro* lie. The entire work reflects each man's life: the joy of living (*Cántico*), the effort to live courageously (*Clamor*), the ability to create (*Homenaje*), and to meditate and to come to certain conclusions which are open to constant re-evaluation and clarification (*Y otros poemas* and *Final*).

Guillén's hopes for the continuity of his work were characteristically humble. He believed the "immortality" of his work to be precarious, for it depends on willing readers. While he accepted, with some irony, that something of his work will remain, if only because he belonged to a group of writers whom the student of Spanish poetry cannot ignore, he also acknowledged fear for the future. Not because of the danger of nuclear war as such, but because of the possible breakdown in human integrity that could make potential annihilation a reality. Clearly, man's creative ability is tremendous, and this must enable us to guard against our destructive tendencies. It is so easy to label Guillén an "optimist", a word and attitude to which he was vehemently opposed. What he preferred, with eminent justification, is what he called "un acto vital de adhesión a la vida . . . una cierta esperanza. Una cierta esperanza de llegar al momento siguiente, de estar en la vida. Todo dirigido hacia la vida" (a vital, living act of adherence to life . . . a certain hope. A certain hope of arriving at the next moment, of participating in life. Everything is directed towards life).[22] In this way the problems and difficulties wilfully ignored by the optimist are acknowledged and the acknowledgement of them must make that "act of adherence to life" the broader and stronger in consequence.

---

[22] J. Guerrero Martín, *Jorge Guillén: sus raíces. Recuerdos al paso* (Valladolid: Miñón, 1982), p.91.

CHAPTER 2

THE EARLY EDITIONS OF *CANTICO*

The 1928 edition

The poems from the 1928, 1936 and 1945 editions of *Cántico* discussed here illustrate the thematic evolution of this first major volume of Guillén's poetry. The fact that Guillén retained the title of the 1928 publication for each subsequent edition shows that the main preoccupations of the poems remained the same, although there are clear distinctions to be discerned in the thematic content of each volume. The rich variety of verse forms in the 1928 publication reveals not only mastery but a concern for structure and symmetry that gradually intensified as each successive edition was organized. In fact, the poems of this first edition illustrate various ways of deducing form, shape and contour in the world. Guillén's observations of and reactions to the world about him conclude in a dynamic understanding of that world and his relationship to it. The most important affirmation that results from this is:

> El mundo está bien
> Hecho. $(C_1 \ 68)$
>
> (The world is well-
> Made.)

While it is dangerous to overemphasize these lines, isolating them from their context in one short though famous poem, they can be taken, together with the title of the volume, to indicate that Guillén is concerned above all with harmony: harmony in man, in nature, and between the two.

The occurrence of "form" in the world is seen, for example, in the straight and curved lines which form the horizon ("El horizonte" [The Horizon], C_1 35) or the dome of the sky ("Perfección del círculo" [Perfection of the Circle], C_1 13). The most important sense for Guillén is sight,[1] for through it he becomes aware of these lines and curves, aided by his own keen intelligence and the impulse to describe them. Sight in turn, affirms Guillén, is aided by such natural phenomena as a tree in autumn ("Otoño, pericia" [Autumn, expertise], C_1 46, and "El otoño: isla" [Autumn: island], C_1 50), the cold of winter ("Capital del invierno" [Winter's Capital], C_1 81) and the clarity of daylight ("Presencia del aire" [The Presence of Air], C_1 19). Perception of form alone brings with it an intoxicating happiness ("Desnudo" [Nude], C_1 79) or calm serenity ("Estatua ecuestre" [Equestrian Statue], C_1 65). The observer is thus able to affirm his joyous commitment to life.

In the poem "Desnudo" (Nude, C_1 79) we can see Guillén's particular preoccupation with form, for here he traces the gradual perception of a nude figure, beginning with the initially vague awareness of colour alone, which gradually becomes an awareness of shape, as a form emerges from the shadows. The slow appearance of the figure parallels the mental process of the observer as his sight enables him to distinguish between a solid object and the surrounding penumbra. Once the outlines of the figure have been distinguished from its surroundings, visual confusion ends:

> Claridad aguzada entre perfiles,
> De tan puros tranquilos,
> Que cortan y aniquilan con sus filos
> Las confusiones viles.   (3)

> (Clarity made acute amidst outlines
> Of such purity, such serenity,
> That cut away and destroy with their edges
> All hateful confusion.)

The physical presence of the sleeping figure has been brought into the foreground, and the mental effort by the observer in stanzas 1-2 to order a confused impression of colour, light and shade, and finally volume, has been resolved. His recognition of the sleeping figure and his consequential mental repose occur together and what results is an overwhelming awareness of presence:

> Desnuda está la carne. Su evidencia
> Se resuelve en reposo.
> Monotonía justa: prodigioso
> Colmo de la presencia.   (4)

[1] "El poder esencial lo ejerce la mirada" (The essential ability is that exercised by sight) (J. Guillén, "Aire-aura", *Revista de Occidente*, 2,4 [1923], 4).

> (The flesh is naked. Proof of it
> Is resolved in repose.
> Just monotony, the prodigious
> Extreme of presence.)

What is important in this carefully documented process of visual perception is the physical presence of the woman who, even without the accoutrements of consciousness and clothing, is consummately real. She is a supreme symbol of the reality of the present moment, understood completely through the observer's perception of the moment of presence that the poem celebrates:

> ¡Plenitud inmediata, sin ambiente
> Del cuerpo femenino!
> Ningún primor: ni voz ni flor. ¿Destino?
> ¡Oh absoluto Presente!   (5)

> (Without ambience, the striking plenitude
> Of the feminine body!
> Nothing exquisite: neither voice nor flower. Destiny?
> Oh absolute Present!)

The poem "Desnudo" demonstrates that perception of form can lead to a heightened awareness of the fullness and permanence of the present moment. "Tornasol" (Iridescence, C_1 15) also traces the awareness of concrete form in a physical way, but the poem has a metaphysical dimension too. "Tornasol" is remarkable for its gradual build-up of vague, intangible shapes and reflections; clarity is deduced through a confusion of gleams and glitters of light. The poem is a single sentence and the numerous subordinate clauses intensify the feeling of vagueness in much the same way as the complicated syntax of "El prólogo" (The Prologue, C_1 12) reflects the problems which obstruct the poet in his desire to create the poem.

On the physical level, a smooth calm sea is finally perceived through a profusion of glitters, reflections and sparkles of light coming initially through the blinds of a room and the foliage of an arbour. The calmness of the sea prompts the observer to think of a lake, and it is here that the perception of form is considered in metaphysical terms:

> los visos   (3)

> Informes de un mar
> Con *ansia* de lago
> Quieto   (my italics) (4)

> (the unformed sparkles

Of a sea
With the *desire* to be a
Calm lake)

The lake is a scaled-down version of the sea, but it is the sea which has more symbolic importance for us. It conjures up visions of danger and uncertainty which derive from our inability to conceive of such vast form. A lake is far easier to envisage:

claridad
En un solo plano   (4)

(clarity
In a single plane)

The subjunctive verbs of the final stanza indicate the metaphysical nature of the poem, coming as they do after the word "ansia" in stanza 4. Such clarity is desirable because its limits, like the shores of a lake, are more apt for comprehension. The reality of the complete shape is in itself affirmation:

claridad
En un solo plano,

Donde esté presente
Como un firme sí
Que responda siempre
Total, el confín.   (5)

(clarity
In a single plane,

Where the limits may be forever present
Like a resolute affirmation
Which always responds
In completeness.)

The poem "El horizonte" (The Horizon, C_1 35) describes the sense of security which can be derived from an awareness of clarity of form. The coming together of field and sky at the horizon is expressed in its purest, essential form – a straight line. The line is "perfection" because it makes clear the limits of air, invisible to us until defined by the horizon. However, the horizon is an artificial line, an optical illusion which paradoxically strengthens our sense of reality because we feel it defines the space within which we live. The fact that light goes beyond the horizon does not matter, hence the exclamation "¡Oh perfección abierta!" (Oh open perfection!). The poet asks us to consider that the unique quality of a horizon is that it is a line which, for us, gives form to the world and enables us to understand its vastness by providing us with a visible boundary. This is the "don inminente" (the imminent gift) of the horizon, referred to in "Sazón" (The Ripe Moment, C_1 22) as "tardanza / Del infinito espacio" (the delaying of infinite space). The future verb in stanza 6 is the result of certainty; the air will be complete and will find its expression in the horizon:

> ¡El aire estará en colmo,
> Dorado, duro, cierto:
> Trasparencia cuajada!   (6)

> (The air will be complete,
> Golden, hard, certain:
> Substantial transparency!)

The last phrase "substantial transparency" seems to be a paradox ("cuajar" means to thicken, to congeal) and yet the two words are complementary. The horizon is a line which delineates transparency; air has taken form, become established. This is important for the observer, for the feeling of certainty, evident in stanza 6, is transformed into an awareness of security. Having sought to clarify, delineate and put into perspective the vastness of the world, the observer feels that the reward for his effort lies in the validity of what he has seen. It is as though the world reciprocates, by being exactly what he had envisaged, in confirmation of his hopes:

> Ya el espacio se comba,
> Dócil, ágil, alegre,
> Sobre esa espera, mía.   (7)

> (Now space curves,
> Obedient, agile, cheerful,
> Upon this hope of mine.)

In "El horizonte" something invisible is given form. In "Elevación de la claridad" (Ascent of Clarity, C_1 14) the observer once again deduces form in the world around him. In stanzas 1-2 his equilibrium is threatened by the softness of a marsh. In fact that water which is such a menace to him is the hidden life-force of trees, which soar above. From his position beneath the branches he knows that the small patches of light visible form a far greater light, that of the unlimited sky, towards which the trees strive:

> Entre los follajes,
> Diminutos cielos
> Suman un ileso
> Término sin partes.   (4)

(Amongst the foliage,
Diminutive skies
Add up to an untouched
Undivided end.)

Guillén is careful not to end his poem in the mood expressed in stanza 4, that suggested by unlimited space. The final stanza sees the sky as the specific point on which all plant life is centred. To corroborate this image of the sky as a centralizing agent, it is described as the zenith to which everything aspires:[2]

Y se centra el vasto
Deseo en un punto.
¡Oh cenit: lo uno,
Lo claro, lo intacto!   (5)

(And that vast desire
Is centred on one point.
Oh Zenith: unique,
Clear, intact!)

The four poems discussed above all demonstrate an observer exerting his visual ability to the full. Something relatively insignificant is considered in detail and its implications for the observer are always discovered to be profound. Moreover, his ability to link physical vision with mental insight is also remarkable, yet there is nothing especially abstruse or esoteric in his conclusions. They are the result of paying attention to the phenomena about him, of willingness to observe and to speculate upon the reality of what he sees. In "Estatua ecuestre" (Equestrian Statue, C_1 65) the same combination of physical sight together with insight is found, but the poem stresses above all the importance of language, used to give linguistic form to the object it describes. What is important in the carefully controlled development of this poem is that the impulse to re-create an object in words exactly parallels the image of control that the object represents. As the hand of the rider controls the trot of the horse, so the hand of the sculptor controls the representational force of the statue, and so too does the poet control the development of the poem. In it we "see" the statue, with the horse's leg raised in permanent representation of movement. Clearly, there is no "trot", but it is made real both by the art of the sculptor and by the poet's

[2] Compare Juan Ramón Jiménez's "Su sitio fiel", *Pájinas escojidas: Verso* (Madrid: Gredos, 1968), p.197.

representation of it in words:

> Permanece el trote aquí,
> Entre su arranque y mi mano:
> Bien ceñida queda así
> Su intención de ser lejano.

> (The trot remains here,
> 'Twixt its own impulse and my hand:
> Thus is well curtailed
> Its desire to be far away.)

The statue is a clear representation of movement immobilized, given particular emphasis in the poem by Guillén's use of "ser lejano" which indicates that the intrinsic nature of the statue is one which implies movement. It creates a feeling of spirited immobility, exactly the impression given by the choice of words and syntax in the poem. Language, for the poet and reader, is like a "corcel" (charger), for it specifies precisely the emotion conjured up by the object; sight and intellect combine to rationalize that emotion. If the horse and rider of the statue are movement immobilized, so too the poem and its vocabulary represent intellectual activity refined and "stilled" to perceive and convey these details. The words represent in stasis the lightning activity of the combination of sight, thought and emotional response. Both statue and poem are thus accurate representations of the marvel of stilled vigour created by the sculptor and the poet in their respective media:

> Porque voy en un corcel
> A la maravilla fiel:
> Inmóvil con todo brío.

> (Because I race on a charger which is
> Faithful to the marvel:
> Immobile with all its vigour.)

The final three lines show the results of such activity. The words "fuerza" (force) and "calma" (calm) continue the ideas of tension and control. The soul, all the creative talent and intelligent judgement of the poet, understands the very essence of the statue. The object is now intellectually perceived; it has, as it were, come forward and stands out against a clear background. The final relationship of poem and statue is clarified at the end: the poem is "cast" on the white page by the hand of the poet:

> ¡Y a fuerza de cuánta calma
> Tengo en bronce toda el alma,

Clara en el cielo del frío!

(And by force of so much calm
I have my soul in bronze
Cast clear against a cold sky.)

Another poem which stresses the importance of language as a shaping, informing force, is "Los nombres" (Names, C_1 17). The poem's formal structure, from the opening eyes of the horizon (dawn, beginning) to their closing (dusk, end), provides a framework to express transience and permanence, both of which are symbolized by names. In stanza 1, the gift of sight, the dawn of a new day and the individual's awakening combine to facilitate knowledge of the reality of objects:[3]

Albor. El horizonte
Entreabre sus pestañas,
Y empieza a ver. ¿Qué?: nombres.
Están sobre la pátina   (1)

De las cosas.

(Dawn. The horizon
Opens up its eyelids
And begins to see. What?: names.
They are on the patina

Of things.)

For Guillén names are exemplified by the rose. The poet feels that its mutability, like the passage of time, should prompt us to live our life to the full:

¡A largo amor nos alce
Esa pujanza agraz
Del Instante, tan ágil   (3)

Que en llegando a su meta
Corre a imponer: Después!   (4)

(May it raise us to long love,
This premature impetus
Of the Instant, so quick that

When it arrives at its goal it
Hurries to impose: Afterwards!)

Vigour and vitality should be our impulse:

[3] Compare Jiménez's "A un poeta para un libro no escrito", *Segunda antolojía poética* (Madrid: Espasa-Calpe, 1952), p.142, and poem number 266 from *Pájinas escojidas: Verso*, p.179, which is glossed by Guillén in "La florida" (C_1 82 stanza 3).

¡Alerta, alerta, alerta!
¡Yo seré, yo seré!   (4)

(Look out, look out, look out!
I will be, I will be!)

Three symbols of transience or death, the rose, sleep and dusk,
are brought together in the final stanza:

¿Y las rosas? ... Pestañas
Cerradas: horizonte
Final. ¿Acaso nada?
Pero quedan los nombres.   (5)

(And the roses? Closed
Eyelids: the final
Horizon. Perhaps nothing?
But the names remain.)

The query "And the roses?" has already been answered in stanza 2:

La rosa
Se llama todavía
Hoy rosa, y la memoria
De su tránsito, prisa.   (2)

¡Prisa de vivir más!

(The rose
Is still called rose
Today, and the memory of
Its passage, haste.

Haste to live more!)

The rose is indeed a traditional symbol of transience but Guillén
suggests that in its mutability can be seen the epitome of the process
of living. The evocative power of the word is important and its
resonances are paralleled in the excited exclamations of stanzas 3-4.

By depicting the dawn as an opening eyelid, Guillén creates a
powerful visual image which also brings into play the idea of a
human being awakening. In the final stanza the same personification
takes place with the inference of sleep and night. But dawn and
awakening are what began the poem. Dawn will certainly occur
again and again. Man will awaken to a new day for as long as life and
its affirmation are his *raison d'être*: "I will be, I will be!" Over and
above this, immortality for all things is proclaimed because of the
triumphant existence of language and the "names" of poetry.

All the above poems can be said to depend primarily on

physical sight, to a greater or lesser extent. However, in the poem "Tránsito" (The Passing, C_1 27) physical sight is used in a more abstract way to envisage rather than "see" the world and its faultlessly smooth and sure movement as a symbol for life, to the point where the fear of imminent death is forgotten. In stanza 2, this secure movement is overwhelmed by swift, impetuous activity and the extended metaphor creates for us something that we cannot actually see but which expressively describes the disappearance of life into amorphous death. The poet asks if something so final can be accepted so easily, and lines 3-4 of stanza 3 represent the dead body, empty of life. It is nothing more than an outline, an unrepresentative sketch of no substance:

> ¿Tan fácil un fin
> De veras final?
> ¡Oh nulo perfil,
> Croquis del azar!   (3)

> (Is so easy an end
> Really the end?
> Oh useless profile,
> Sketch of chance!)

Stanza 3 can further be interpreted as asking whether the metaphor is convincing and the following exclamation suggests that it simply provides us with a rather perfunctory, superficial representation of mortality which, however expressive it may be, is in some ways inadequate. The ingenuity of the metaphor is difficult to accept at face value, as the knowledge of life ending in death can be:

> ¡Horror! Ningún astro
> Mantuvo solemne
> La espera del tránsito.   (4)

> (Horror! No star
> Ever kept its gravity
> While awaiting death.)

Guillén makes no attempt to resolve this problem. What he does suggest is that the individual's attitude should be one where the inevitability of death is accepted as precisely that: inevitable, and therefore "en sazón" (at the right time), whenever or whatever that may be. Neither does Guillén suggest any alternative reality in which life and death might have different perspectives: "*Sea* el universo" (*Let* the universe *be as it is*) (my italics). The important thing for Guillén, and for the individual, is that there should be a fully-drawn picture in place of the empty sketch. The reader should use his intellectual faculties to the full, understand the terms of the metaphor and be able to accept its linguistic perfection as an adequate parallel that gives form to our understanding of the cycle of life ånd death:

> Astros: concededme
>
> Final en sazón.
> Sea el universo.
> Pero que el adiós
> Lo deje perfecto ...   (5)

> (Stars: concede to me
>
> An end at the right time.
> Let the world be as it is.
> But may our every farewell
> Mar not its perfection ...)

Death is an integral part of life, and only by its occurrence is life made "perfect". As Guillén was to write later:

> ... la muerte es considerada como un final exigido por el orden
> mismo de la vida ... Vivir no es un ir muriendo ...   (*AO* 30)

> (... death is considered as an end required by the very order of life
> itself ... To live does not mean to be dying ...)

The poem which provides us with a key to Guillén's search for clarity of form in this 1928 edition of *Cántico* is "Perfección del círculo" (The Circle's Perfection, C_1 13). The first three stanzas carry the two basic ideas of the poem: clarity and mystery. The sense of mystery is conveyed in stanzas 1-2 by complex syntax, the verb coming in the first line and the subject of the main clause, preceded by two adjectives, occurring in line 6. The complexity of the statement being made in these lines is evident; however, the vocabulary used to describe this mystery and its qualities suggests concise delineation and concrete shape:

> Con misterio acaban
> En filos de cima,
> Sujeta a la línea
> Fiel a la mirada,   (1)

> Los claros, amables
> Muros de un misterio,
> Invisible dentro
> Del bloque del aire.   (2)

> (With mystery they end,

In summit's edges,
Dependent on line
Faithful to sight,

The clear, friendly
Walls of a mystery,
Invisible within
The block of air.)

Lines 7-8 heighten the complexity of the concept. We have a concrete form within a concrete medium, yet both are invisible. Stanza 3 shows us that this "mystery" is pure clarity. No evil can be connected with it. It is noteworthy that in this stanza clarity is equated with divinity, which is as difficult a concept to apprehend as the mystery of the perfect circle. In stanza 4 we understand that the circle is a perfect mystery because it seems to the observer to be a boundary over the earth, forming a dome, undoubtedly a "block of air," but just as certainly invisible. The mysterious activity of this circle is twofold – a shining forth and a concealing of itself at the same time:

Misteriosamente
Refulge y se cela.
—¿Quién? ¿Dios? ¿El Poema?
—Misteriosamente ...   (5)

(Mysteriously
It shines forth and conceals itself.
– Who? God? The Poem?
– Mysteriously ...)

No explanation is given for its identity, though the queries of the third line can be seen as macro- and microcosmic symbols respectively of a perfect circle. The final word of the poem, the reply to the queries of line 3, is "Mysteriously ..." Thus what is important for us *vis-à-vis* this circle, which we are at liberty to see represented by the ideas of either God or poem, is our *perception* of its perfect shape.

Clarity of form has been achieved in a variety of ways in these poems. The observer is able to understand his position in time and space, and the resulting heightened awareness is one of the harmony of Creation and of his own life within it. In his efforts to come to terms with the realities of the world about him, the observer senses that world reciprocating by offering its forms to his perception. Creation's essential unity is understood and the cyclical process, celebrated in "Elevación de la claridad", becomes a symbol of perfection repeated throughout *Cántico*.

The 1936 edition

After the obvious concern to find and define form and shape in the world about him in the poems of the 1928 volume, Guillén intensifies this process in the 1936 edition of *Cántico*. The predominant impression gained from the poems is that while simple objects or emotions continue to be discussed or investigated, the use of the senses in the process of perception is also stressed. Again sight is vital and a key phrase is to be found in the poem "Naturaleza viva" (Unstill Life, C_2 87). The poem's title is a variation on the Spanish phrase "naturaleza muerta" (still life). Guillén's use of the adjective "viva" (live or living) indicates that the poem, while recalling the phrase used for a particular kind of artistic perception and its presentation in plastic form, actually deals with the opposite process, moving from the sight of an inanimate object to the presentation of its living source in intellectual terms. The subject of the poem is a table whose flat wooden surface nevertheless contains within it the essence of the tree from which it came. The type of wood, walnut, also implies the living tree, evident in the knots and grain-lines that can be seen in the level plane of the inanimate table – referred to as "vigor inmóvil" (immobile vigour). The important phrase "Mental para los ojos / Mentales" (Mental for mental eyes) indicates that sight must be allied to thought. These, in conjunction with touch, enable the observer to perceive the reality of the table. This combination of the senses of sight and touch – and in many other poems, hearing – indicates that in this volume the fullness and completeness of the individual's perception is being investigated. The observer is seeing, understanding, grasping reality in all its multi-dimensional variety, and the affirmation which results is correspondingly stronger and surer.

The word "mano" (hand) occurs frequently in the new poems in this edition and indicates not merely the simple sense of touch but also the manipulation, mental and spiritual, of the various phenomena of reality with which the individual comes into contact. For example, in "Lo esperado" (The Awaited, C_2 90) the arrival of dawn signifies a cyclical activity whose dependable repetition is an invitation to the individual to participate. In the final stanza the combination of "soul" and "hand" indicates the process wherein the physical acquisition of experiences by means of the senses causes wonder and amazement. This is absorbed by the intuitive faculties (the soul) and transformed into absolute knowledge, something which, once acquired, is constantly available and forms a secure part of the individual's future relationship with reality:

> El alma, sin perder
> El cuerpo, va creando
> Su plenitud: nivel
> Pasmoso de la mano.   (5)

> (The soul, without losing
> The body, is creating its own
> Completeness: the wondrous
> Plane of the hand.)

The poem "Tiempo perdido en la orilla" (Time lost by the riverbank, C_2 91) shows a similar process of intuition, provoked by surrounding realities, which can be further used as a basis for forging links with the world and fellow human beings. The combination of "hand" and "soul" is used interestingly in "La nieve" (Snow, C_2 153) where the sense of touch tells the observer that snow is cold but the soul sees in it an example of natural vitality and animation. These qualities are expressed in antithetical terms – it is as though the snow "burns" with energy:

> ¿Nieve ligera, copo blando?
> ¡Cuánto ardor en masa!
> La nieve, la nieve en las manos
> Y el alma.   (3)

> (Light snow, soft snowflake?
> So much heat en masse!
> The snow, the snow in hands and
> Soul.)

A similar natural phenomenon to snow, frost, is described in "Temprano cristal" (Early crystal, C_2 154). Here the space and silence experienced early on a frosty morning are considered. The world is fresh and seemingly remote, partly because sight is still investigating it, partly because it appears in a new guise with its covering of frost:

> —¡Cuánta amplitud aborda las manos y los ojos!

> (– So much spaciousness is accessible to the hands and eyes!)

There is an overwhelming amount of spaciousness for sight to apprehend and for the senses to appreciate – it is accessible for the observer to come to terms with and the experience is another tiny facet of his investigation of reality. A further example of natural phenomena contributing to the acquisition of knowledge of the environment is to be found in "Redondez" (Roundness, C_2 233). Here neither the blue colour nor the roundness of the sky actually exists. By using these concrete terms to apprehend the vast space of the sky, the human mind can endow both with a dynamic activity in the form of energy which enables the observer to grasp a sense of the harmony of the world:

> El firmamento derrama,
> Ya invasor, una energía
> Que llega de puro azul
> Hasta las manos ariscas.
> ....
> ¡Azul que es poder, azul
> Abarcador de la vida,
> Sacro azul irresistible:
> Fatalidad de armonía!

> (The firmament pours down,
> Already an invader, an energy
> Which comes from pure blue
> To shy hands.
> ....
> Blue which is power, blue
> Embracer of life,
> Sacred irresistible blue:
> Ordained harmony!)

In contrast to the above poems which describe natural phenomena, "Callejeo" (Walking around, C_2 230) is a poem which considers the individual's attitudes to his own activity, in this particular case, aimlessly walking through streets. The quality of aimlessness is here implicitly positive, for the individual is simply strolling along, free from the need to accomplish something specific, free from having his activities controlled by time. Here he himself is in control of time for his own purposes and as a result time becomes "dúctil" (flexible). He is at liberty to experience whatever may occur during his walk, rather than being confined to some particular aim:

> No trascurre
> La hora. Permanece
> Con todo su volumen
> Bajo la mano aquel
> Tiempo sin norte, dúctil,
> Propicio a revelar
> Algo impar en el cruce
> De unas calles.

```
(              The hour
Does not pass by.  It remains
With all its mass
Beneath the hand, that
Time with no lodestar, flexible,
Favourable for revealing
Something unusual at the crossroads
Of some streets.)
```

In the 1928 volume several poems attribute shape or outline to invisible forces. This is found in the 1936 edition also but here there is the added dimension of space being filled with invisible forces. For example, in "Amplitud" (Spaciousness, C_2 188) it is the smell of pine trees which fills the air, but in the poem the phrase used to express this is "Aquel olor a espacio" (that aroma of space):

> Mientras cunde y se exalta por sus círculos
> Aquel olor a espacio siempre inmenso.

> (While there expands and moves upwards through its circles
> That aroma of always immense space.)

In "Viento saltado" (Leaping Wind, C_2 214) the violence and animation of the wind gives the individual a sense of the firmamental confines within which it blows, while in "Esos cerros" (Those hills, C_2 191) the empty sky against which the hills are set is called "Una Nada amparada" (a favoured Nothingness): the hills contribute, as it were, to the emptiness of the sky and help to demarcate it as a reality.

The first poem of the 1936 edition is "Advenimiento" (Dawn, C_2 73), as it was in 1928, but in the second volume this poem is placed before the first section, thus acquiring the status of a prologue to the edition as a whole. In the poem there is a constant interplay between dawn and the individual, and the poet skilfully uses the traditional symbols of nightingale, moon and dawn chorus to suggest the temporary nature of darkness. Awake during that pre-dawn period when night is almost over, though daylight has not yet begun to show, the individual assesses his situation. Stanzas 1 and 3 are clearly divided, the first two lines commenting upon the timelessness of the night, lines 3-4 being a statement of affirmation by him about his own position:

> ¡Oh luna! ¡Cuánto abril!
> ¡Qué vasto y dulce el aire!
> Todo lo que perdí
> Volverá con las aves.   (1)

> La luna está muy cerca,
> Quieta en el aire nuestro.
> El que yo fui me espera
> Bajo mis pensamientos.   (3)
>
> (Oh moon! So completely April!
> How vast and sweet the air!
> All that I lost
> Will return with the birds.
>
> The moon is very near,
> Quiet in our air.
> The man that I was awaits me
> Beneath my thoughts.)

In stanza 1 the exclamations of lines 1-2 indicate delighted amazement at the depth and beauty of a spring night – there is no sense of fear at the expanse of darkness. This is amplified by the assurance of lines 3-4. The birds of the dawn chorus in stanza 2 and the nightingale of stanza 4 show the individual's attitudes to two different aspects of night. In stanza 2 the dawn chorus is an instinctive song repeated each morning. Paralleling this is the individual's knowledge that the clarity of daylight on which he depends will also return:

> Sí, con las avecillas
> Que en coro de alborada
> Pían y pían, pían
> Sin designio de gracia.   (2)
>
> (Yes, with the little birds
> Who in their dawn chorus
> Sing and sing, sing
> Artlessly.)

In stanza 4 the nightingale, unlike the birds of stanza 2, will always sing at night:

> Cantará el ruiseñor
> En la cima del ansia.
> ¡Arrebol, arrebol
> Entre el cielo y las auras!   (4)
>
> (The nightingale will sing
> At the height of desire.
> Red flush and glow
> Between sky and dawn breezes!)

The positive exclamation of joy in lines 3-4 of the above stanza contrasts strongly with the nightingale's song, for it is the individual's own dawn song, prompted by exuberance at the prospect of a new day.

The structure of stanza 3 is similar to that of stanza 1, although the absence of exclamations gives lines 3-4 an aura of calm. The proximity of the moon and the illumination it affords are nocturnal versions of the sun and daylight. The same parallel occurs with the individual; the man, his sensitive awareness of the night, his intuitive knowledge that returning daylight grows out of the night – all are images or reflections of the man in full daylight, able to see clearly and completely the objects of everyday reality.

In stanzas 1, 3 and 5 the main theme of the poem is developed. First we have a statement of confidence in the return of daylight:

> Todo lo que perdí
> Volverá con las aves.

> (All that I lost
> Will return with the birds.)

This is followed by a further statement which implies a process similar to loss of daylight and its return, but this time carefully related to the individual's mental faculties, deprived of sight by darkness and subsequently "enlightened" by his own efforts to grasp intellectually the significance of a natural phenomenon in direct relationship to himself:

> El que yo fui me espera
> Bajo mis pensamientos.

> (The man that I was awaits me
> Beneath my thoughts.)

The resolution of this thematic development comes, paradoxically, in the form of a question. This is a device frequently used by Guillén where the inclusion of a question which restates an argument already made avoids dogmatic repetition and enables the reader to supply the answer, as though making a discovery for himself:

> ¿Y se perdió aquel tiempo
> Que yo perdí?

> (And was that time lost that
> I lost?)

The suggestion that night can be thought of as a time of loss is, of course, rejected. The whole of the poem has been a constant balancing of night versus day, of the individual deprived of his visual faculties versus the potential one of daylight, connected visually with reality. The final lines of the poem show that he is able to manipulate the accepted, linear process of time and transform it. The notion of constant change with implied loss is simply reduced by the strength of his intellectual conviction in the validity of renewal:

> ¿Y se perdió aquel tiempo
> Que yo perdí? La mano
> Dispone, dios ligero,
> De esta luna sin año.   (5)

> (And was that time lost that
> I lost? The hand, like a
> Gentle god, makes use of
> This timeless moon.)

The above poem clearly deals with the particular relationship of the individual to the passage of time as he experiences it. The fact that the poem is placed as a prologue to this 1936 edition indicates that the construction of relationships with the rest of reality is the main theme of the volume.

That dawn and its connotations of enlightenment are important is emphasized by the first poem of section I of the volume, "Más allá" (Beyond, C_2 79). This long poem of fifty quatrains describes in detail the process of awakening, from the moment of returning consciousness, imaged by the two vital faculties of man's metaphysical and physical make-up, the soul and sight respectively, to the final sense of sharing harmoniously with fellow men in the reality of the surrounding world. The poem documents the individual's wonder and amazement at the orderly way in which he fits into the extraordinary pattern of reality, from his awareness of nearby objects (the pillow and sheet over his body) to objects in a room, and further to a knowledge that these simple everyday things form part of the framework of harmony that spreads beyond his room, beyond his physical sight, to the point where he intuits the same harmony on a vast cosmic scale. What is important in this poem is that the individual is never diminished by his perception of cosmic harmony. He is the one whose ability to observe and understand is rewarded by what he observes being as he observes it. This is not to say that he imposes his own idea of reality upon what he sees. On the contrary, reality imposes itself on him, his sight is aided by the natural phenomena of light and air, and intellect and intuition combine to render reality in terms comprehensible to him as a human being:

Pero el día al fin logra
Rotundidad humana
De edificio y refiere
Su fuerza a mi morada.   (my italics) (41)

(But at last the day achieves
Human roundness of
Structure and brings its
Force to my dwelling.)

Thus waking initiates in the individual an intellectual process which extends from knowledge of external, physical reality to knowledge of self by means of sentient contact with what is beyond:

Un aroma presiento,
Que me regalará
Su calidad: lo ajeno,   (34)

Lo tan ajeno que es
Allá en sí mismo. ¡Dádiva
De un mundo irremplazable:
Voy por él a mi alma!   (35)

¡Oh perfección: dependo
Del total más allá,
Dependo de las cosas!
Sin mi son y ya están   (36)

Proponiendo un volumen
Que ni soñó la mano,
Feliz de resolver
Una sorpresa en acto.   (37)

(I sense an aroma
Which will present to me
Its quality of distance,

Such distance that is there
In its essential self. Oh gift
Of an irreplaceable world:
Through it I go to my soul!

Oh perfection: I depend
On the complete Beyond,
I depend on things!
Without me they exist and are already

Suggesting volume and mass
Never dreamt of by my hand,
Happy to resolve
A surprise in motion.)

"Más allá" is a key poem of *Cántico*, for it contains many

important themes which are reiterated in the rest of the work. The poem's main theme, that of awakening, the rebirth of experience, enables one to understand that the relationships between man and the world are not static and unchanging but rather are constantly renewed and developed. Further poems about dawn and the awakening of the senses are "Las ocho de la mañana" (Eight o'clock in the morning, C_2 174), "El viaje" (The journey, C_2 161) and "Ahora sí" (Now for sure, C_2 166). In the first, dawn is seen as "La Marcha Inmortal" (The Immortal Procession) and its light is personified as a young girl, whose marching advance proclaims another day. In the *décima* "El viaje" the first six lines contain statements of certainty about the early morning, all expressed by verbs in the future tense:

> Habrá un agua entre peñas,
> Habrá con hojas viento,
> Los mirlos buscarán alturas de álamos,
> Unos cerros sin nada
> Serán la pista buena de la luz,
> Hasta el fondo del coche tendrá aurora

> (There will be water amongst peaks,
> There will be wind in leaves,
> The blackbirds will seek high poplars,
> Some bare hills
> Will be the good track for light,
> Even the back of the car will have dawn)

Such statements of certainty contrast strongly with the weary, travel-worn individual, one whose faith in the renewal of day enables him nevertheless to overcome personal fatigue, both physical and mental. The imagery of his final comment, "Veré avanzar los inmortales / Himnos de amor" (I will see the immortal hymns of love advance), indicates his own attitudes: seeing daylight breaking in terms of hymns of love is a measure of his own love and faith in the dependability of the cycle of the transformation of night (weariness) into day (confident happiness).

This combination of love and joy is also to be found in "Ahora sí" (Now for sure, C_2 166). Here the horizon at dawn is seen as the bearer of gifts, a development from the pure line of "El horizonte" and the personification of "Los nombres". Its gifts are light and love, love being dependent on light for its own emergence. This is so in all spheres: the birds which nest in the trees; the fronds of foliage which respond to light, urged on by roots in the dark recesses of the earth;

the human lovers who love not only each other physically, but also existence and reality. Emergence from sleep is seen as rapture, not simply because the lovers once more become aware of each other, but also because reality about them is made visible by daylight – hence the double meaning of "forma tendida":

> ¡Forma tendida al lado, confiada!
> Desnudez que es feliz impulsa al día.
> La verdad embelesa a los albores.
>
> (Trusted form stretched out alongside!
> Nakedness which is joy impels day on.
> Truth enraptures the dawn light.)

"Nakedness" is not only human nakedness but also the light of dawn giving way to the clarity of day and objective reality. Rapture associated with emergence from sleep and awareness of surroundings is converted into its ultimate form, that of truth: the truth of love between the lovers, the fact of reality revealed by and to the dawn.

Common to all the poems which deal with dawn and enlightenment is a positive attitude which stems from the individual. This is possible because of the incontrovertible existence and presence of objective reality combined with the individual's discovery that his predisposition to wonder and joy is always rewarded.

An unusual poem in the 1936 volume is "El desterrado" (The Dispossessed, C_2 156), a free-verse poem which deals with the phenomenon of fog in a city and in relation to the individual. A similar subject is to be found in "Niebla" (Fog, C_1 41), the only poem in the first edition of *Cántico* where reality is not visible, for everything is made remote and abstract by the fog. The impersonal tone of "Niebla" becomes more discursive in "El desterrado" but it is not until the end of the poem that the word "fog" is actually used. What is discussed is a situation in which objects lose their clarity. The all-enveloping vagueness assumes a threatening aspect and an attempt is made to rationalize this confusion:

> La luna no puede estar ausente.
> Así, tan escondida,
> ¿Eres tú, luna, quien todo lo borra o lo tacha?
> ¡Torpe, quizá borracha,
> Mal te acuerdas de nuestra vida!
>
> (The moon cannot be absent.
> Thus, so hidden,
> Is it you, moon, who wipes out, who erases everything?

> Sluggish, befuddled perhaps,
> How badly you remember our life!)

The uneasy fear which pervades these lines culminates in dejection:

> El mundo cabe en un olvido.
>
> (The world fits easily into oblivion.)

Purposeful life is only possible with the power of light to illumine objects and their reality. If light is lacking, life is immediately in jeopardy. Moreover, there is always the possibility of nothingness, even in a city square, a symbol of activity:

> Cero hay siempre, central. ¡En esta plaza
> Tanta calle se anula y desenlaza![4]
>
> (There is always a blank, at the centre. In this square
> So much street is annulled and undone!)

The downward spiral of negativity in the poem thus far is halted by the sudden passing of a cyclist. This movement inevitably implies a destination, which in turn suggests some sort of existence. Movement of the blanket of obscurity immediately revives the attention, and the expression of dejection mentioned earlier now turns into a question: "¿El mundo cabe en un olvido?" (Does the world really fit into oblivion?). Activity brings about revitalization in the individual, and the obscurity into which the cyclist disappears is referred to as "an as yet unassuming chaos":

> La bicicleta
> Se escurre y se derrumba por un caos
> Todavía modesto.
> —¿Qué es esto?
> ¿Tal vez el Caos? —¡Oh,
> La niebla nada más, la boba niebla,
> El No
> Sin demonio, la tardía tiniebla
> Que jamás anonada!
> Es tarde ya para soñar la Nada.
>
> (The bicycle
> Slides and tumbles headlong through a chaos
> As yet unassuming.
> – What is this?
> Perhaps Chaos? Oh,

---

[4] Compare Antonio Machado's sonnet, "Al gran Cero", *Poesías completas*, 12th ed. (Madrid: Espasa-Calpe, 1969), p.247.

It's just fog, the stupid fog,
The undemonic
No, the tardy darkness
Which does not stupefy!
It's already late to be dreaming of Nothingness.)

In fact, Chaos and Nothingness do not exist in this world of *Cántico*: chaos, apparent negation and blankness do exist as temporary reactions to or rationalizations of things which are not perfectly understood, but they can be confronted by an individual who brings to bear the power of his own intellect fed by his senses. This is clear from the last two lines of the poem, which are separated from the main text. The force of the imperative verb contrasts with the depression and uncertainty suggested by the vocabulary, the questions and exclamations, and the hesitancy of long and short lines used earlier. The individual has rationalized the confusion created by the phenomenon of fog and its characteristic obscurity, and confidently demands the return of what is his by right and by light:

¡Devuélveme, tiniebla, devuélveme lo mío:
Las santas cosas, el volumen y su rocío!

(Give me back, darkness, give me back what is mine:
Sacred things, shapes and dawn-dew!)

The use of the word "dew" at the end of this poem is unusual, for dew is not necessarily the result of clearing fog. It functions as an image which, with its connotations of dawn and light, symbolizes the renewed clarity which is the result of both lifting fog and the individual's mental efforts to clear the confusion of his mind, temporarily separated from visible reality. A similar topic is to be found in the sonnet "El hondo sueño" (Profound sleep, C_2 212). Here dawn and Spring are used in much the same way as dew in "El desterrado", but the absolute values which they represent, light and renewal, are unnoticed by an individual who suffers a dislocation from reality, symbolized by solitude and darkness. His normal relationship with reality, temporarily lacking, is seen in terms of companionship, reality being personified as an individual:

Este soñar a solas ... ¡Si tu vida
De pronto amaneciese ante mi espera!
¿Por dónde voy cayendo? Primavera,
Mientras, en torno mío dilapida

Su olor y se me escapa en la caída.

(This solitary dreaming ... If only your life

Were suddenly to dawn before my expectation!
Where am I falling? Spring, meanwhile,
  All around me squanders
  Her aroma and escapes from me as I fall.)

His present experience is potentially dangerous because "dreaming" implies possible introversion, symbolized by the image of him falling into a world of his own imagining, without the vital companionship of his surroundings. As Guillén says, "No ha lugar el engreimiento del yo" (There is no place for the vanity of the Ego) (*AO* 11). The second stanza ends with an exclamation which indicates the individual's awareness that his solitude and tendency to introversion increase with his continued isolation in self. The tercets resolve this conflict and once again the future tenses indicate his confidence that confusion will end if his efforts to overcome it are in conjunction with external reality:

Pero tanto sofoco en el vacío
Cesará. Gozaré de apariciones
Que atajarán el vergonzante empeño

De henchir tu ausencia con mi desvarío.
¡Realidad, realidad, no me abandones
Para soñar mejor el hondo sueño!

(But so much suffocation in isolation
Will cease. I will have pleasure in apparitions
Which will short-cut my shameful undertaking

To fill your absence with my wild ravings.
Reality, reality, do not abandon me
To dream better the profound dream!)

The above lines begin with the word "Pero" (but), a simple conjunction which Guillén invests with great strength and meaning on many occasions [for example, "Elevación de la claridad" (C_2 105), "Los amantes" (C_2 94), "Los nombres" (C_2 118), "Tránsito" (C_2 111)]. In all these cases, the word effectively stops one line of reasoning and shows the individual's efforts to arrive at the essential value of his experiences. In "El hondo sueño" he knows that darkness and solitude, the external circumstances contributing to his malaise, will end. He also knows it lies within himself to convert external circumstance into personal gain. He resolves to enjoy "apparitions", not those of a dream-world, but those of reality which will obviate the need or desire to sink into an auto-created world. The verb "soñar" is obviously used figuratively in the last line. There is no sense of retiring into a dream-world, which is equated with "shameful undertaking" and "wild ravings". "Soñar" is best understood if one takes into account its two very different qualifiers and their significant positions, the first at the beginning of the poem, "a solas" (alone), and the second at the very end, "hondo" (profound). Solitary thoughts or imaginings are rejected in favour of shared and therefore substantiated thought.

The benefits that are to be gained from this dynamic relationship with reality are shown in poems like "Perfección" (Perfection, C_2 184) and "Las doce en el reloj" (Twelve of the clock, C_2 227). The *décima* "Perfección" is a remarkable example of control of imagery and tempo which respectively enhance one's appreciation that enjoyment of momentary beauty can, with the willing involvement of the individual, be transformed into an experience that has lasting value:

> Queda curvo el firmamento,
> Compacto azul, sobre el día.
> Es el redondeamiento
> Del esplendor: mediodía.
> Todo es cúpula. Reposa,
> Central sin querer, la rosa,
> A un sol en cenit sujeta.
> Y tanto se da el presente
> Que el pie caminante siente
> La integridad del planeta.

> (The firmament is a curve
> Of compact blue, over the day.
> It is the rounding-out
> Of splendour: midday.
> Everything is a dome. In repose,
> Effortlessly central, is the rose,
> Subject to a sun at its zenith.
> And so much does the present give of itself
> That man travelling in time feels
> The absolute integrity of the planet.)

The title of the poem is its theme, suggesting not only perfection of the moment emphasized in lines 1-7, but also the individual's apprehension of that perfection beyond the limits of the time in which it is perceived. The nouns and adjectives of the first seven lines constantly remind one of circular shape, already seen in the 1928 volume as symbolic of perfection. The verbal components of these same lines give an impression of absolute stillness, while other elements of the poem, "azul" (blue), "esplendor" (splendour) and "rosa" (rose), intensify the cumulative effect of singling out the components of universal perfection, starting with the most extensive, the firmament, and gradually closing in on a specific symbol of beauty, the rose. This flower, "effortlessly central", sums up the ordered beauty of the natural world.

The final three lines of the poem continue the impression of stilled perfection in the words "planeta" (planet) and "presente" (present), although the two lines of enjambment and a smoothly articulated single sentence give a sense of movement in sharp contrast to the previous seven lines. In these first lines there are no "danger signs" of the poem "running itself to a standstill" as Havard suggests.[5] The division of stasis / tempo is deliberate and is made clear once the significance of "el pie caminante" is understood. This refers not to an "unknown protagonist" but to *the* protagonist, the generic individual who is the I of the poems of *Cántico*. The literal translation of this phrase is "the travelling foot", though this does not accurately reflect the Spanish: "caminante" has a substantive function, but the English translation lays undue stress on a part of the body, an emphasis which is lacking in the Spanish. The phrase implies man in contact with the earth and also moving, or travelling, through time, and hence, together with the sentence structure and syntax, contrasts strongly with the image of the universe created in lines 1-7, whose symbols of rose, midday, sun, firmament, and blue sky are not mere ciphers for stillness, but represent the eternal aspects of beauty in the world. The impression of perfection that the individual feels makes him aware of the immense spatial and chronological harmony of Creation, "the integrity of the planet". His appreciation of the beauty of a moment is something which will accompany him always.

"Perfección" is a serious, well-modulated expression of joy at the perfection of Creation, and is successful partly because the *décima* form demands extreme concision of imagery and syntax. "Las doce en el reloj" (Twelve of the clock, C_2 227) is a *romance* whose more discursive form accords well with the exclamatory and less cerebral nature of the emotion expressed. The poem creates a similar impression to "Perfección", for it uses further elements like sunshine, bird-song, cornfields, to symbolize the "perfect day":

Un álamo vibró.
Las hojas plateadas

---

[5] See R.G. Havard, "The early *décimas* of Jorge Guillén", *Bulletin of Hispanic Studies*, 48 (1971), 120.

Sonaron con amor.
Los verdes eran grises,
El amor era sol.
Entonces, mediodía,
Un pájaro sumió
Su cantar en el viento
Con tal adoración
Que se sintió cantada
Bajo el viento la flor
Crecida entre las mieses,
Más altas.

(A poplar trembled.
The silvered leaves
Rustled with love.
Greens were greys,
Love was sunshine.
Then, midday,
A bird plunged
His song into the wind
With such devotion
That the flower growing between
The taller grain felt itself
Serenaded beneath the wind.)

The individual's perspective is different here. His act of attentiveness to the scene about him places him at the centre of the perfect circle of Creation. The poem begins with an exclamation: "Dije: ¡Todo ya pleno!" (I said: All now full!), and the subsequent lines are an expression of this harmony, where time and space complement each other. The sun, at its zenith at midday, is identified as love, just as the poplar leaves moving together are a visible expression of that love. The spatial dimension is given by Guillén's use of the verb "sumió" (plunged), which creates a picture of the bird, high in the sky, whose symbolic harmony is paralleled by the suggestion that the wild flowers, outstripped by the height of the corn, are even so part of the total harmony. Everything in the landscape is motivated by love, a word whose human connotations nevertheless accurately express the harmony of the natural world. At this point the individual is aware of his own position, both physical and spiritual:

Era yo,
Centro en aquel instante
De tanto alrededor,
Quien lo veía todo
Completo para un dios.

(It was I,

The centre at that moment
Of so much around me,
Who saw everything
Complete for a god.)

His attentiveness has enabled him to perceive the wholeness of Creation, almost as if he has created all things anew merely by being fully aware of them. Herein lies the significance of the final lines. The individual is like a "god" and says, "Dije: Todo completo" (I said: All complete), with the serenity of having achieved an understanding of natural perfection and his intimate relationship with it. Midday is the starting point of the poem and thus becomes a symbol which characterizes plenitude. The final exclamation, "¡Las doce en el reloj!" (Twelve of the clock!), together with the title, gives the poem a circular shape which symbolizes the links, both physical (sight and senses) and metaphysical (perception and intuition), which unite the individual with the world.

In the fifty new poems of the 1936 volume there are many references to specific times: eight o'clock in the morning, midday, the past, the present and the future, all closely linked with the life of the individual. Since the I of these poems refers to the generic individual, time should be seen in a similarly broad dimension. Eight in the morning refers to the general time of renewed activity in man's day, twelve noon is a symbol of completeness, as is midday in "Perfección". The present is the most significant time in *Cántico*, for it bears witness to the actual experiences of the individual and, as was seen in "Perfección", the present moment is one of intensity and impact which continues to have bearing on and for the individual. Guillén is aware of the passage of time but his poems are designed to maximize the absolute value of the present. The shorter poems consider an object, emotion or thought that is essentially limited in time and yet the lasting or permanent value of each is secured by careful juxtaposition of the external reality, the individual's perception of it, and his subsequent understanding of the links that bind them both together. Critics frequently refer to the atemporal or timeless quality of *Cántico*, a description which Guillén, in conversation with the present author, as well as in published interviews, energetically refutes. His response to such views takes the form of a question: how can poetry which deals with human life be outside the sphere of time? Human life is temporal and as such is constantly following its inevitable trajectory from birth to death. As Guillén says, "Temporalidad es mortalidad" (Temporality is mortality) (*AO*

29) and "Mortalidad no es muerte" (Mortality is not death) (*AO* 30). These sentiments are repeated in *Guillén on Guillén*:

> ... mortality which is not the act of death, as the Stoics, and some Christians – Quevedo – would have it ... Is life, then, a dying by degrees? A sophism – an inadmissable "venerable sophism".[6]

Clearly mortality means that one lives subject to the passing of time, but the idea of life being "a dying by degrees", though a possible interpretation of mortality, is one which Guillén rejects as unacceptable. The individual is never overwhelmed by the grandeur of the world in which he lives because his relationship with it enables him to contextualize it (symbolized in the poetry by the perception of shape and form). Time is treated in a similar way: it is kept within certain dimensions and seen as an accompaniment to life, but never allowed to overwhelm that life. This was seen in "Tránsito" and is also discussed briefly in "De paso por la tristeza" (Passing through Sadness, C_2 171):

> Lenta la hora, ya es todo
> Breve ... ¡Bah! Por más que el codo
> Cavile, no, no hay lamento.

> (Slow hour, now all is
> Brief ... Bah! However much one may
> Brood, no, there is no lament.)

A more ample treatment of the theme of "Tránsito" is to be found in the sonnet "Muerte a lo lejos" (Death at a distance, C_2 210), a particularly good example of Guillén's control of the sonnet form and a frequent anthology piece:

> Alguna vez me angustia una certeza,
> Y ante mí se estremece mi futuro.
> Acechándole está de pronto un muro
> Del arrabal final en que tropieza

> La luz del campo. ¿Mas habrá tristeza
> Si la desnuda el sol? No, no hay apuro
> Todavía. Lo urgente es el maduro
> Fruto. La mano ya le descorteza.

> ... Y un día entre los días el más triste
> Será. Tenderse deberá la mano
> Sin afán. Y acatando el inminente

---

[6] Geist and Gibbons, *Guillén on Guillén*, p.161.

Poder, diré con lágrimas: embiste,
Justa fatalidad. El muro cano
Va a imponerme su ley, no su accidente.

(Sometimes a certainty gives me anguish,
And before me my future trembles.
Suddenly stalking it is a wall of
The final suburb against which the

Light of the countryside stumbles. But will there be sadness
If sunlight strips it bare? No, there is no need to worry
Yet. What is important is the ripe
Fruit. The hand already peels it.

... And one day amongst all days will be the
Saddest. The hand will have to stretch out
Without desire. And respecting the imminent

Power, in tears I will say: charge on,
Just destiny. The white wall is going to
Impose on me its law, not its accident.)

The poem begins with a statement which is already an admission, an apparently *de facto* acceptance that life is "a dying by degrees". The fear of death is such that future life itself is uncertain. A symbol of death, the white wall of the cemetery, is personified by the power of fear, as a creature stalking its living prey. The man-made structure, the cemetery, visibly encapsulates death, and it should be remembered that the cemetery in Spain is most often to be found on the outskirts of a town, at the "end" of the sphere in which man has his life. In a similar way the "venerable sophism" alluded to earlier is a man-made concept which can, if allowed to, encapsulate life and limit its scope and energy. However, the cemetery is illumined by sunlight, the life-giver of the natural world. The parallel for man's ability to create intellectual conceits to rationalize his experiences, is to be found in the question of stanza 2. If the life-giving sun illuminates all, so too can man's intellectual powers further illumine accepted notions and diminish their negative aspects. The sadness of inevitable death can be reduced to its essence – death at the end of life –, but life comes first and the living of it is a more urgent duty, both intellectually and emotionally. Life and the living of it are symbolized by the image of a ripe fruit and a hand peeling it: life is accepted as complete in itself and the individual is dedicated to experiencing its plenitude by constant involvement and participation in its multidimensional richness. Thus the fear of stanza 1 is mitigated by intellectual contemplation of its cause. Unusually in the sonnet form, these two quatrains contain an argument and its resolution, though the latter normally comes in the tercets. In Guillén's poem, the first tercet returns to a consideration of death. The anguish caused by the inevitability of death, at the beginning of the poem, is lessened. The future, uncertain in stanza 1, is clear, signified by the future tense and the statement of the first tercet. Death, now seen in terms of sadness, will come, but the individual, true to the dictates of life, will accept it, albeit with reluctance. The latter indicates his emotional stance, balanced by an intellectual respect for death as the last dictate of life itself. In the final stanza he is able to confront death as something just, because it is part of the order of life. The final line and a half return to the image of the cemetery wall whose power is now limited and static; it no longer stalks an individual who is haplessly prey to uncertainty and fear. Death can only impose its power upon man once; that power is strictly limited by life and by man's intellectual ability, which, as this poem has shown, is able to strip death of the incidental and capricious qualities it formerly had.[7]

Arthur Terry, in his commentary on "Muerte a lo lejos", mentions the attitude of resignation evident in the poem.[8] This is true of the text quoted above, but Guillén constantly revised his poems and in the 1945 edition of *Cántico* a small but significant change occurs in lines 11-12:

> Y acatando el inminente
> Poder, diré *sin* lágrimas: embiste,
> Justa fatalidad.   (my italics)
>
> (And respecting the imminent
> Power, I will say *without* tears: charge on,
> Just destiny.)

The attitude of resignation of the original is removed in the 1945 version and the balance of intellect and emotion is changed in favour of the strength of the intellect. There is no need for resignation, which gives the impression that the individual has battled with the problem of death and finally conceded its superiority. "Con lágrimas" (with tears) implies that death retains the power to subject the individual to an emotion which he cannot control: sadness which wells up and breaks through. "Sin lágrimas" (without tears) shows that sorrow is

---

[7] Compare "La 'muerte' con minúscula" (*H* 561).

[8] Arthur Terry, *Two Views of Poetry* (Belfast: Queen's Univ. Press, 1964), p.22.

admitted but kept within limits. Sunlight, the natural giver of life, is eternal; man's intellectual powers can be developed to the point where they are sufficient to illumine and sustain his perception even of his life's end.

Once it can be understood that time has limits, that its passage does not invalidate life, but is an opportunity for infinite exploration and fulfilment, then the individual is at liberty to make time more flexible, fuller and more meaningful. And the present is the time which is most apt for this. The present comes from a past and goes into a future, but is apprehended as a continuum of fulfilment, rather than a linear process of gradual vitiation. This is exemplified in the poem "Los tres tiempos" (The three tempos, C_2 104) where the passage of time is given a richer perspective. A similar theme is treated in the first volume of *Cántico*, in "Los amantes" (The lovers, C_1 23), whose final stanza contrasts with the previous four which celebrate the act of love between the lovers. Love itself is shown to be as transient as the mortal lovers by the stark, uncompromising words which end the poem:

> Sólo, Amor, tú mismo,
> Tumba. Nada, nadie,
> Tumba. Nada, nadie.
> Pero ... —¿Tú conmigo?   (5)
>
> (Only, Love, you yourself,
> Tomb. Nothing, nobody,
> Tomb. Nothing, nobody.
> But ... You with me?)

The short-lived rhythms of these lines, combined with an absence of verbs (the life-giving or active elements of syntax), encourage a negative interpretation. Once again, the word "Pero" (but) prevents this happening and in fact the absence of verbs is a virtue, for what results is a statement of unchanging and unchangeable truth – love, like the lovers, is finite; nothing remains of the individuals' experience or of the experience itself. The phenomenon of love does remain, signified by the capital letter of "Amor". It is given life by lovers and the rhetorical question expresses this with extreme concision. Companionship, sharing, the experience of being together, provide a complete perspective against which to balance what is finite.

"Los tres tiempos" considers love and time from the point of view of the lovers themselves. In stanzas 1-2 something occurs to spark off the memory of an occasion enjoyed in the past by the lovers:

De pronto, la tarde
Vibró como aquellas
De entonces, ¿te acuerdas?,
Íntimas y grandes.

Era aquel aroma
De Mayo y de Junio
Con favores juntos
De flor y de fronda.

(Suddenly, the afternoon
Trembled like those
Intimate and vast afternoons
Of the past, do you remember?

It was that perfume
Of May and June
With conjoined pleasures
Of flower and foliage.)

From his position in the present – for recollection is essentially in the present – the individual understands what it is that has the power to enrich the passage of time. The heart, symbol of love, though distanced from the perfumed days of a past summer, provides the emotional stimulus to the mind which prompts memory into recall:

Fijo en el recuerdo,
Vi cómo defiendes,
Corazón ausente
Del sol, tiempo eterno.   (3)

Las rosas gozadas
Elevan tu encanto,
Sin cesar en alto
Rapto hacia mañana.   (4)

(Fixed in recollection,
I saw how you,
Heart absent from the sun,
Buttress eternal time.

The enjoyed roses of the past
Raise your rapture
Ceaselessly in sublime
Ecstasy towards the morrow.)

The mental process of memory, stimulated by emotion, creates out of the past an eternal enchantment which is not only a revitalization of the lovers' feelings but which also constitutes a lasting foundation for further experience:

¡De nuevo impacientes,

> Los goces de ayer
> En labios con sed
> Van por Hoy a Siempre!   (5)
>
> (Newly impatient,
> The joys of yesterday
> On thirsting lips
> Go through Today to Always.)

The fact that the poem ends with the word "Always" rather than, for example, "the future", illustrates the ample perspective given to time. The experience of love is understood as a source of joy and companionship which pervades the whole of the individual's life. "Always" effectively avoids the rather barren linear trajectory that "the future" would imply.[9]

Guillén's greatest poem of human love is included in the 1936 edition of *Cántico*. "Salvación de la primavera" (Salvation of Spring, C_2 120) is comparable to "Más allá" in length and thematic importance. From the title we see that love is associated with the natural world and the theme of human love in Guillén's poetry usually finds its expressive force in images of and allusions to the world of nature.[10] The word "love", as has been said, is used to symbolize the harmony of the natural world and is, of course, the quintessential symbol of human harmony, both between man and woman and in the more general but no less fervent relationship of man with his fellow human beings. In "Salvación de la primavera" the beloved is as pure and vital an element to the lover as are light and air. Through her he is able to perceive the world which, because of their relationship, becomes a "fábula irresistible" (an irresistible marvel). The harmony implied by physical union is, like the appreciation of momentary beauty, the key to lasting harmony, both in terms of fulfilled personal perspectives and from the point of view of the individual in relation to reality. Love renders time comprehensible; the future, though unknown, is a source of infinite richness:

> ¡Nuestro mañana apenas
> Futuro y siempre incógnito:
> Un calor de misterio
> Resguardado en tesoro!   (45)

---

[9] Compare Antonio Machado, "Hoy es siempre todavía", *Poesías completas*, p.198.

[10] For example, "Sol en la boda" (*C* 158) and "Anillo" (*C* 178).

(Our future, which is hardly
Distant, yet always unknown:
A warmth of mystery
Kept safe in treasures!)

The individual's faith in love protects it from destruction and love as a life-force is personified by the beloved:

Un ver hondo a través
De la fe y un latir
A ciegas y un velar
Fatalmente —por ti—   (49)

Para que en ese júbilo
De suprema altitud,
Allí donde no hay muerte,
Seas la vida tú.   (50)

(A seeing in depth through
Faith and a sightless
Heartbeat and an instinctive
Vigil – over you –

So that in this joy
Of supreme greatness,
There where there is no death,
You are life itself.)

The final section of the poem is one long exclamation of joy and reverence for the beloved and all the symbols of universal perfection, so familiar from other poems of *Cántico*, are gathered together as rapturous descriptions of her. The poem has been compared in greatness with "Cántico espiritual" by Saint John of the Cross. Guillén's poem is indeed a canticle, but it is concerned with more than spiritual dimensions. Spiritual vigilance ("un velar / Fatalmente") is there, but so too are emotional impulse ("un latir / A ciegas") and intellectual clarity ("Un ver hondo"). Love is celebrated in its profoundest human form and Spring and the natural world provide a setting commensurate with the fervour which delights in the terrestrial realities of our world: "... henos ante la presencia terrestre. A su exaltación se limita *Cántico*" (... we stand before earthly presences. *Cántico* is limited to the exaltation of them) (*AO* 20).

Love is an expression to equate natural and human harmony. Man without the objective reality of Creation would have few resources with which to approach, assess and respond to what and who he is. The impulse to do this is symbolized by blood in "Siempre aguarda mi sangre" (My blood always awaits, C_2 192):

Siempre aguarda mi sangre. Es ella quien da cita.
A oscuras, a sabiendas quiere más, quiere amor.
No soy nada sin ti, mundo. Te necesita
La cumbre de la cumbre en silencio: mi estupor.

(My blood always awaits. She it is who makes the rendez-vous.
In darkness, knowingly she wants more, wants love.
I am nothing without you, world. The pinnacle
Of pinnacles in silence, my amazement, needs you.)

The juxtaposition of "A oscuras" (in darkness) and "a sabiendas" (knowingly) emphasizes that this impulse to be involved with Creation is both intuitive and conscious. When the individual confesses, simply and with humility, his need of the world about him, then the relationships between him and that world and between him and his fellows can both be affirmed. This is clarified in "Afirmación" (Affirmation, C_2 193). Again instinct and extreme perception are joined and the final line briefly and effectively summarizes the multiplicity of relationships that have been discovered in this second edition of *Cántico*:

¡Afirmación, que es hambre: mi instinto siempre diestro!
La tierra me arrebata sin cesar este sí
Del pulso, que hacia el ser me inclina, zahorí.
No hay soledad. Hay luz entre todos. Soy vuestro.

(Affirmation, which is hunger: my always dexterous instinct!
The earth ceaselessly moves me to this throbbing
Assent, which impels me, clairvoyant, towards being.
There is no solitude. There is light amongst all. I am yours.)

The 1945 edition

The process of defining the particular thematic developments of the 1945 edition of *Cántico* is fairly straightforward, thanks to an addition of great significance. For the first time *Cántico* is given a subtitle, *Fe de vida*. As A.L. Geist writes:

> More than just an expression of "faith in life", Guillén's poetry stands as a document of certification, a "verification of life".[11]

The general impression conveyed by the one hundred and forty-five new poems in this volume is that Guillén gives the "faith" of the subtitle a tangible form or dimension of its own. Faith acquires

[11] *Guillén on Guillén*, p.6.

reality and objectivity and the individual gains security from his understanding of external realities:

> Los ojos del espíritu se complacen en registrar objetos compactos de su propio ser, acordes a su definición, fieles a su esencia.   (*AO* 13)

> (The eyes of the spirit take pleasure in registering objects, compact with their own being, in accord with their meaning, faithful to their essence.)

The phrase "the eyes of the spirit" is important, for it embraces both physical and spiritual perception. Hence the word "objects" must be considered as including the less tangible realities of life and Creation. Examples of these can be found in a variety of poems, but in the ones quoted here it is noteworthy that Guillén is still concerned with the perception of form. By endowing a variety of experienced phenomena or concepts with shape, he is able to show their relevance to the individual's understanding of his role in the "dialogue with Creation". In each case the giving of form to intangibles results in reassurance. In "Las horas" (The Hours, C_3 58 / C 70) the isolation and fear of the insomniac give way (with the reassuring moonlight to shed clarity) to an acceptance of the immensity of time and space. These realities are given dimension and substance in the final section of the poem:

> La luna da claridad
> Humana ya al horizonte,
> Y la claridad reúne
> Torres, sierras, nubarrones.   (16)

> Se abandona el desvelado.
>   ¡Firme el borde
> Nocturno! *La inmensidad*
>   *Es un bloque.*   (my italics) (17)

> (The moon gives clarity,
> Now human, to the horizon,
> And the clarity unites
> Towers, hills, storm clouds.

> The insomniac abandons insomnia.
>   Firm the nocturnal
> Boundary! *The immenseness*
>   *Is solid.*)

Similar usage of the notion of solidity, by means of the word "bloque" (block), is to be found in "Descanso en jardín" (Rest in a garden, C_3 57 / C 75) and "Lectura" (Reading, C_3 144 / C 196). In the former, death is seen as "Calma en bloque" (Calm en bloc) and the phrase serves as an image not only for the individual grave and the communal cemetery, but also to encapsulate death, to reduce it in order to minimize its influence on the living. Emotional stance and visual perception are both linked with serenity. In "Lectura" even the act of reading and subsequent enlightenment are brought into focus by the key word, here an obvious image of a page of typescript. Coupled with the adjective "potencial" (potential) it implies the infinite capacity of the written word to illumine the mind of the reader:

> En la página el verso, de contorno
> Resueltamente neto,
> Se confía a la luz como un objeto
> Con aire blanco en torno.   (8)
>
> ¡Oh bloque potencial! Así emergente
> De blancura, de gracia,
> Lleva los signos más humanos hacia
> Los cielos de la mente.   (9)

> (On the page the poem, with a resolutely
> Clear outline,
> Trusts to the light like an object
> With clear air around it.
>
> Oh potential block! Thus immanent
> With clarity, with grace,
> It carries the most human of ciphers to
> The heavens of the mind.)

Where it is difficult to attribute outline or profile to a phenomenon or concept, for example, love, Guillén resorts to terms which imply mass, weight or volume. In "Pleno amor" (Complete love, C_3 371 / C 509) love is likened to a force which weighs on the lovers and is in exact proportion to the love they feel for each other:

> este clarísimo
> Destino: nuestra ventura.
> Y la ventura despacio
> Va confiándose —nunca
> Más estrellas en el cielo—
> A una pesadumbre suya.

> (this supremely clear
> Destiny: our fortune.
> And good fortune gradually
> Entrusts itself – never
> More stars in the sky –
> To a force of its own.)

Similarly, in "Salvación de la primavera" (C_2 120), referred to earlier, spiritual perception of love and the unity it provides fill the soul with awareness which is expressed by vocabulary connoting physical qualities of volume and weight:

> Pesa, pesa en mis brazos,
> Alma, fiel a un volumen.
> Dobla con abandono,
> Alma, tu pesadumbre.   (15)

> (Weigh upon my arms,
> Soul, true to your mass.
> Increase without constraint,
> Soul, your force.)

Seen in the light of giving form to concepts, it is not, therefore, "curious", as González Muela suggests, to find such adjectives as "visible" qualifying the noun "soul".[12]

The subtitle, combined with the kind of imagery outlined above, indicates that in this third volume of *Cántico* it is the depth and intensity of the relationships between the individual and his surroundings which are of especial importance. The new poems continue the themes discussed already in this chapter. Dawn and renewal are further investigated and, like "Más allá", the poem "Buenos días" (Good morning, C_3 226 / C 296) links light and emotion. The first three lines sum up this individual's attitude to Creation, the first word being perhaps the most important. It signals his acceptance of the world, linked with gratitude for the gifts of light and reality:

> ¡Sí!
>   Luz. Renazco.
>   ¡Gracias!
> . . . .
> Despertar es ganar.

> (Yes!
>   Light. I am reborn.
>   My thanks!
> . . . .
> To wake is to gain.)

In the final line quoted above we see a further dimension to the allied ideas of dawn / awakening / renewal. Instead of simply participating

---

[12] J. González Muela, *La realidad y Jorge Guillén* (Madrid: Insula, 1962), p.61.

in the renewal of the day, the individual now sees his awakening in terms of gain for himself. It is as though he himself is reborn, has another opportunity to experience the intensity of both the return of light to the external world and of sentient power within himself. In the last lines of the poem, reality, newly perceived, offers the individual the opportunity to dream ("La realidad propone siempre un sueño" [Reality always proposes a dream]). Here the use of "sueño" is similar to the concept explained in "El hondo sueño", discussed earlier, where "sueño" is used figuratively to imply thought or meditation. The poem ends with a familiar figure of a dawn scene, a crowing cockerel, and the bird's instinctive cry is a parallel for the individual's faith in what he gains from awakening – a faith which has been arrived at by means of reason:

> Canta, gallo jovial,
> Canta con fe. Te creo.

> (Sing, jolly cockerel,
> Sing with faith. I believe you.)

In the poem "Luz diferida" (Deferred light, C_3 77 / C 79) the protagonist wills dawn to be slow in coming so that he may experience second by second the joy of gradual then total perception of reality. And in "Despertar" (Waking up, C_3 286 / C 343) he wakes up to gain not only external reality but also complete being:

> Yo. Yo ahora. Yo aquí.
> Despertar, ser, estar:
> Otra vez el ajuste prodigioso.   (5)

> (Me. Me now. Me here.
> To awaken, to be, to exist:
> Once again the incredible adjustment.)

Just as dawn and renewal are important in *Cántico*, so their opposites, darkness and loss, are carefully considered. Night and its consequential obscurity constitute a potential threat to one who so openly declares his dependence on light, and ways of approaching those phenomena have been described in the commentary on the two earlier editions of *Cántico*. The theme is further investigated in the new poems of the 1945 volume. "A la intemperie" (At the mercy of the elements, C_3 309 / C 426) reveals that the title has a double implication. Its negative connotations appear first and we see an individual, held in thrall by his fear of darkness, described as ". . . sin defensa, / Oculto y expuesto a la vez / Bajo tanta noche" (. . .

defenceless, at the same time hidden and exposed beneath so much night). Though he may be hidden from sight he is nevertheless exposed to his natural fear of the obscurity which hides reality from his gaze. In addition to fear, he suffers solitude and alienation from his surroundings. With so much awry in his emotional state, the individual's rational faculty also deterioriates, and it is only with the appearance of stars and their faint light that balance begins to be restored. The individual recognizes that night, though a time of obscurity, has inherent within it a defence against that very darkness. Night "levels out" all details, so that one is left with the phenomenon of darkness, never the harbinger of evil once its essence is understood:

> La noche imponía su inmensa
> Nivelación de pormenores,
> Todos oscuros. ¡Qué defensa
> Tan ajustada a mis temores!   (15)
>
> La oscuridad ya no era extraña.
> El mundo se ceñía al grito.
> Soñaba el astro con la hazaña.
> Cobijaba el mismo infinito.   (16)

> (Night imposed its tremendous
> Flattening-out of details,
> All obscure. What a well-adjusted
> Defence against my fears!
>
> Darkness was no longer strange.
> The world encircled the cry.
> The planet dreamed of exploits.
> The very infinitude offered shelter.)

A similar theme is to be found in the poem "Anulación de lo peor" (Removal of the worst, C_3 256 / C 333) where the imagination of the individual, deprived of light and its human counterpart, reason, is influenced by emotion. Darkness is personified as a wild creature rearing up with an entourage of howling beasts. Confrontation with it is necessary, but takes the form of an acknowledgement of fear – for that is the emotion which distorts the individual's understanding of the essence of darkness. Once fear is acknowledged then the fictitious beasts of night melt away and fuse with the darkness. The individual's perception of darkness is readjusted and the phenomenon of night is understood for what it is: "La noche toda es fondo" (All night is background). The cyclical progress of night into day has a parallel in human terms, already seen in "Advenimiento". In "Anulación de lo peor" the progression from the

darkness of fear to equilibrium through mental effort is confirmed
and rewarded by the renewal phase of the natural world. Equilibrium
can be maintained because of faith in the arrival of dawn whose light
will reveal to the observer the reassuring simplicity of reality:

>Espera, pues.
>
>El sol descubrirá,
>Bellísima inocente, la simple superficie.

>(Wait, then.
>
>The sun will uncover
>The simple surface, exquisitely innocent.)

By using night as a metaphorical context for insecurity and
fear, Guillén is able to emphasize the links between the individual
and the natural world, as has been seen in the poems commented on
above. A similar device is used to contextualize death, whose hold on
our imagination is powerful precisely because we have no opportunity to test ourselves against it in any personal, immediate way.
Light is precious because it provides us with the possibility of
achieving physical and spiritual enlightenment. Darkness threatens
and limits our perceptive faculties. Death can menace life in a much
more profound way, for the redeeming features of the cyclical
process exemplified by night and day have no role to play. In
"Descanso en jardín" (C_3 57 / C 75) the cemetery is referred to as "el
último jardín" (the last garden) and while this description cannot
change the fact of death ("Los muertos están más muertos / Cada
noche" [The dead are more dead every night]), it nevertheless creates
a picture and mood of order and serenity. The gravestones and
marble ornaments are offset by elements from the natural, living
world of flowers, trees and stars. Death itself is described as "el gran
cansancio" (the great weariness), a term which brings it into the
context of ordinary life. Another poem in which death is con-
textualized is "Vida urbana" (Urban life, C_3 82 / C 94) where the
urban setting emphasizes the idea that it is only the fact of death that
separates the living from the dead:

>Hervor de ciudad
>En torno a las tumbas:
>Una misma paz
>Se cierne difusa.   (4)

>Juntos, a través
>Ya de un solo olvido,
>Quedan en tropel
>Los muertos, los vivos.   (5)

(Bustle of the city
Around the tombs:
A similar widespread
Peace hovers.

Together, by means of
A single oblivion,
The dead and the living
Are thronging.)

The poem "Una sola vez" (Once only, C_3 244 / C 334) continues the theme of the individual confronting death seen in "Muerte a lo lejos", but in a more triumphant and boldly assertive manner. The individual scorns the passive existence that merely awaits death, and exults in the active pursuit of life and love. The success of the poem lies in the uncompromising directness of the following lines, the sentiment of which is possible with faith in the validity of life:

Muerte: para ti no vivo.
. . . .
Espera.
          ¡Sólo una vez,
De una vez!
          Espera tú.
. . . .
Vivo: busco ese tesoro.

(Death: I do not live for you.
. . . .
Wait.
          Only once,
All at once!
          Wait, you.
. . . .
I live: I seek that treasure.)

A rather different perspective, however, is given in "Camposanto" (Cemetery, C_3 202 / C 266):

Yacente a solas, no está afligido, no está preso,
Pacificado al fin entre tierra y más tierra,
El esqueleto sin angustia, a solas hueso.
¡Descanse en paz, sin nosotros, bajo nuestra guerra!

(Lying alone, neither anguished nor imprisoned,
At peace at last between earth and more earth,
The skeleton unafflicted, only bones.
Rest in peace, without us, beneath our war!)

The afflictions of life have been shed together with life itself, in exchange for the peace and solitude of death. What is unusual in this poem is the suggestion that peace and solitude are impossible in life. The emphasis in line 3, "unafflicted, only bones", implies that it is out of the very essence of our life, our flesh and blood or physical and emotional responses, that we make of life a battleground. This is true in so far as life can be seen as a struggle against death. But in this struggle we are aided by such allies as only the flesh can give: life itself and love. In "Nivel del río" (The level of the river, C_3 236 / C 202) we are urged to continue the struggle, not to give in to the pleasures of peace and repose held out by the release from life. The final line is an inspired variation on the theme expressed by Manrique:

> Nuestras vidas son los ríos
> que van a dar en la mar,
> que es el morir [13]

> (Our lives are rivers
> which go down to the sea
> which is death)

Guillén's statement shows his belief that though the essence of each individual life (symbolized by water) ends with death, the possibility for life (symbolized by the river) remains:

> El agua corre al mar y queda el río.

> (The water runs to the sea and the river remains.)

What is important, then, to each individual is the quality of his life, surely the significance of the title of this poem.

This idea of the quality of life is shown particularly well in "Sabor a vida" (Taste of life, C_3 55 / C 61) and is demonstrated once again by the harmonious links between man's physical life-source, breathing, and the air around him:

> Hay ya cielo por el aire
>   Que se respira.
> Respiro, floto en venturas,
>   Por alegrías.   (1)

> (Already there is sky through the air
>   Which is breathed.
> I breathe, I float in good fortune,
>   Through joy.)

---

[13] See *Floresta de lírica española*, ed. J.M. Blecua (Madrid: Gredos, 1963), I, 61.

In stanza 1 the relationships linking man and world are concisely expressed. The immediacy of physical coordination is emphasized by the juxtaposition of a passive verb (the air / which is breathed) with the same verb in the present indicative, to express the individual's participation (I breathe). As has already been seen elsewhere in *Cántico*, the formlessness of air is given shape by defining it as sky, visible through or by means of air ("*por* el aire"). Again, intellectual perception of form fills the individual with a sense of well-being, which stems from his joy ("*por* alegrías") in perceiving himself as an intimate part of Creation. That joy intensifies in contact with the natural world. Stanzas 3 and 4 each begin with a single word which effectively delineates the preoccupations of this individual during a country walk:

¿Aventuras? No las caza
   Mi cacería.
Tengo con el mismo sol
   La eterna cita.   (3)

¡Actualidad! Tan fugaz
En su cogollo y su miga,
Regala a mi lentitud
El sumo sabor a vida.   (4)

(Adventures? My hunt does not
   Pursue them.
With the sun itself I have
   The eternal rendez-vous.

The present! So fleeting
In its heart, in its essence,[14]
It regales my slow pace with
The supreme taste of life.)

He is not aggressively in search of stimulating events, but rather remains actively receptive during his loitering walk to the delights that immediate experiences have to offer. These are then understood as ciphers of something absolute. In the final stanza, the individual is not alone, but rather accompanied by his surroundings, and the last two lines demonstrate the dynamic tension that exists between individual and reality:

¡Lenta el alma, lentos pasos
   En compañía!

---

[14] The literal meanings of "cogollo" and "miga" respectively are heart (e.g. heart of lettuce or cabbage) and crumb (e.g. soft part of bread); their figurative meanings are respectively the best part, centre and core, substance. Each meaning contributes to the metaphorical idea of the "sustenance" that life offers.

> ¡La gloria posible nunca,
> Nunca abolida!   (5)

> (Leisurely soul, leisurely footsteps
>   In company!
> Possible glory never,
>   Never revoked!)

The spiritual overtones supplied by "soul" and "glory" are fitting adjuncts to the relationships celebrated in *Cántico*. The glory of reality is always available but its potential can only be realized by a receptive individual prepared to use responsibly his own gifts of senses and intellect in order to arrive at the essences of his existence. In "La hierba entre las tejas" (Grass amongst roof tiles, C_3 197 / C 261) the individual's attention is caught by the sight of grass growing on roof tiles and sees it as the epitome of growth, vigour and joy in being: "Es alegre la hierba entre las tejas" (Grass amongst roof tiles is joyous). The elements of human existence, symbolized by windows and their blinds and house walls, are less important when one is confronted by the vitality of the natural world. The final line of this discursive *décima* is a repetition of the first, quoted above, from the point of view of structure, but broader in scope as regards meaning and context:

> Es tenaz la esperanza con paisaje.

> (Hope with landscape is tenacious.)

The immediate response of the individual – to see joy in nature's vitality – is transformed into a philosophical observation as to the implications of this reaction in relation to his own psyche. Landscape is a constant source of joy and has a counterpart in human joy or expectation which, in allegiance with such a constant, is aptly described as tenacious.

The two poems above effectively show the intimacy of the bonds between the world and the individual, always stressing the sentient and intellectual involvement of the latter. Moreover, the individual constantly strives to increase his awareness of reality, as we see in "Más verdad" (More truth, C_3 272 / C 364):

> Sí, más verdad:
> Objeto de mi gana.

> (Yes, more truth:
> The aim of my desire.)

Reality itself becomes an object, and it is reality in all its aspects that he strives to possess. It is not simply that he responds only to that which is good or pleasant. On the contrary, the individual tries to make everything around him meaningful by expressing the truth of that vision in words. The process of stimulus and response, discussed in relation to the 1936 edition, is given further scope here with the addition of articulation. The individual not only responds but seeks to verbalize his responses, for which he needs acute intellectual perception – hence his demand for more "light":

> ¡Más sol!
> Venga ese mundo soleado,
> Superior al deseo
> Del fuerte,
> Venga más sol feroz.
>
> ¡Más, más verdad!
>
> (More sun!
> Let this sun-drenched world come on,
> Superior to the wishes
> Of the strong,
> Let more fierce sun come on.
>
> More, more truth!)

The dramatic tone of the first part of this poem, created from the use of many exclamatory and short lines, changes markedly in the second part to one of calmness and conviction. While the sun illumines many people and nations, the reality it reveals has an absolute value. He is able to recreate reality by confronting it, not in an aggressive way, but simply by being aware:

> Intacta bajo el sol de tantos hombres,
> Esencial realidad,
> Te sueño frente a frente,
> De día,
> Fuera de burladeros.
>
> (Essential reality,
> Intact beneath the sun of so many men,
> I dream you face to face,
> By day,
> Out in the open.)

At this point in the poem Guillén added seven further lines in the 1950 edition.[15] These lines reinforce the individual's awareness of

---

[15] "Eres tú quien alumbra / Mi predisposición de enamorado, / Mis tesoros de

his physical and spiritual involvement with reality, and they also refer to his reverence for reality which leads him to consider the earth he touches as holy ground. Contact with it imparts to him a sense of sanctity, but a sanctity stripped of conventional religious connotations:

> El santo suelo piso.
>
> Así, pisando, gozo
> De ser mejor,
> De sentir que voy siendo en plenitud,
> A plomo gravitando humildemente
> Sobre las realidades poseídas,
> Soñadas por mis ojos y mis manos,
> Por mi piel y mi sangre,
> Entre mi amor y el horizonte cierto.
>
> (I tread the sacred ground.
>
> And thus, by touching, I enjoy
> Improved being,
> Feeling that I am complete,
> Bearing true and humbly
> Upon possessed realities,
> Envisaged by my eyes and my hands,
> By my skin and my blood,
> Between my love and the sure horizon.)

It comes from consciously making an effort to be, and the complexity of such effort is expressed by the combination of instinctive, sentient and intellectual activity, all interacting within the parameters of his will to participate, symbolized by love, and the known and therefore secure world, symbolized by the horizon.

It is obvious that the attitude of the individual is most important in all the poems considered so far. Equally obvious is the fact that he is predisposed to be positive and joyous. In his quest to understand the "extraordinary phenomenon of normality" (*AO* 12) he seeks to investigate every aspect of reality, while not imposing in any deliberate way his personal or subjective view of it. A further example of acceptance rather than selection is to be found in "Más verdad". In lines 3-6 we find the following:

> ¡Jamás, jamás engaños escogidos!
>
> ¿Yo escojo? Yo recojo
> La verdad impaciente

---

imágenes, / Esta mi claridad / O júbilo / De ser en la cadena de los seres, / De estar aquí." (You it is who illumines / My lover's predisposition, / My treasury of images, / This my clarity / Or joy / In being in the chain of beings, / Of existing here.)

(Never, never selected delusions!
Do I select? I gather up
Impatient truth)

The Spanish verbs used above describe precisely the fine line that distinguishes the individual's attitudes. The basic verb common to each is "coger" (to tàke) and "escojo" implies taking out or selecting, while "recojo" emphasizes the fact that all that is available is taken or gathered up by the individual's perceptive faculties. All that surrounds him represents an absolute truth and his role is that of clarifying and defining its relevance to himself and his role as participator in reality. Thus an all-embracing acceptance of everything that surrounds him and affects him is the true reflection of the individual's attitude. This, of course, includes negative or unpleasant experiences or phenomena which are themselves as much a part of "impatient truth" as pleasure and good, and therefore they have a place in *Cántico*. As Guillén himself points out:

> *Cántico* nunca ha sido un *Cántico* rigurosamente puro, en el sentido de que no todo es *Cántico*. Ha sido siempre un poco mordido, un poco rebajado. Desde el primer momento, el *Cántico* rigurosamente *Cántico* está acompañado de otros poemas en que hay elementos negativos, fuerzas de oposición: el tiempo, la muerte, el azar, el desorden, el mal. Yo, desde el primer momento he querido que eso estuviese.[16]

> (*Cántico* has never been a rigorously pure *Cántico*, in the sense that all is not joy. It has always been a bit corroded, a bit diminished. From the first moment, the rigorously joyous *Cántico* is accompanied by other poems in which there are negative elements, forces of opposition: time, death, chance, disorder, evil. From the beginning I wanted it to be this way.)

Some of these "forces of opposition", time and death, have been considered already. In the commentary on the 1936 edition many poems were found to emphasize that an important facet of the individual's response to his existence lies in the union or harmony of "hand" and "soul" working in conjunction. This symbolizes a fully integrated, perfect human being. Such a state of perfection is not permanent, as is obvious when one considers the implications of "perfect" and "human" when used together. In fact, it is the existence of the imperfect in the sphere of human life which enables

---

[16] Cited by R.J. Weber, in "De *Cántico* a *Clamor*", *Revista Hispánica Moderna*, 29 (1963), 109.

Guillén to create so complete and profound a vision of our world, not only in *Cántico* but in the following volume, *Clamor.*

In the 1945 edition "Aguardando" (Waiting, C_3 152 / C 208) describes the experience of pain or grief which conspires to divide and cripple the harmonious conjunction of spirit and body. The advent of disorder of this kind is described through the experience of an individual who, engulfed in depression, finds his being diminished and himself isolated from the world. He is "minúsculo en su pena" (minuscule in his trouble). The setting of the poem is dusk, a time which can be interpreted in two different ways: either as the glorious moment of the setting sun, or as the dreary ending of the day. What the poem makes clear is that the individual's state of mind prevents him from choosing to see the positive aspects of dusk, even though he knows they are there:

> Él no ignora que allí con su mirada
> Se alzaría maestro de verdades
> A nivel de las fábulas que impulsa
> La manifestación de aquel Poniente.

> (He is not unaware that there with his sight
> He could rise to become master of truths
> On a par with the wonders which the
> Presence of that dusk gives rise to.)

Soul and mind are no longer joined and, locked in his own personal torment, he is unresponsive to the glory of sunset. By not exercising the power of sight he is automatically cut off from appreciating anything at all. Thus the wedge driven between mind and soul remains:

> No existe nada
> —En torno al corazón acongojado.

> (Nothing exists
> – Around the anguished heart.)

It is almost as if he had ceased to exist, for sight is to the intellect as air is to respiration. The next five lines are a metaphorical exposition of what could happen were the individual able to see unencumbered by his misery:

> Cristal hay que recoge el centelleo
> De los rayos finales y, feliz,
> Se ciega en la explosión paradisíaca,
> Delira bajo el súbito amarillo,
> Es sol también: amor, y todo es uno.

(There is glass which gathers up the sparkle
Of the final rays of sun and, happy,
Is blinded by the celestial explosion,
Is delirious beneath the sudden gold,
Is sun also: love, and all is one.)

The window, catching the last rays of the sun, becomes a blazing reflection of yellow light, a loving sublimation of itself in the object it reflects. This is a possibility for the individual too, for his eyes, the "windows" of the soul, could also reflect the essential beauty of the scene were they not isolated by the barrier of depression. The individual is one of the many to whom the "incessant gifts" of Creation are offered, but he remains oppressed and bestows but a cursory glance on the beauty around him. This amounts to voluntary blindness, and because of it, the phenomenon of sunset no longer possesses beauty of any meaningful kind. Thus the individual is the one who, by his positive reaction to the world, can bring about the only true sense of beauty, that which it is within himself to express. For equilibrium to be re-established, for mind and soul to be united, he must wait, resigned but impatient:

Aguarda el turno de su fase libre:
De su poder de vibración acorde.

(He awaits the turn of his phase of freedom:
His ability to react harmoniously.)

By making clear that the individual is subject to moments of disorder and disunity, Guillén acknowledges that the perfect equilibrium of mental and emotional states is not constant, but the use of "turno" (turn) and "fase" (phase) indicates that balance and imbalance occur in cycles. Furthermore, the word "poder" has two meanings: power and ability; and the latter shows that the individual can exercise some control in both reducing the impact of negative experiences and holding fast to those that are positive. One way in which this may be achieved is by sharing the negative experiences – another facet of the relationships between individuals to which *Cántico* bears witness. By sharing, neither past happiness nor future life are seriously threatened. Disorder, symbolized in "Así" (Thus, C_3 237 / *C* 308) by "dolor" (pain), is seen as an integral part of the fervent attitude to life and though one may experience pain or sorrow the important thing is that it is shared:

¿Te esconde tu dolor? Te busca el mío.
Ni ahora tanta dicha gozada se oscurece

> Ni se vela jamás el gran destino:
> Sentirse juntos ser, y ser contra la muerte.
> ¿Dolor? Furor de ser. Así sufrimos.
> (Does your pain confine you? Mine searches for you.
> Now neither so much enjoyed pleasure is obscured
>   Nor is the great future hidden:
> To experience life together, to live opposed to death.
> Pain? Frenzy of life. Only thus do we suffer.)

Just as the individual feels reborn with each new day, so too can he gain from the experience of disorder. The poem "Ser" (Being, C_3 242 / *C* 314) is an exposition of the individual's potential to recover personal harmony, and the spiritual strength he gains from such experience is expressed in terms of the soul being "doubled" or achieving greater sensitivity to the world which had been lost to him. The words "juvenil" (youthful), "matinal" (morning fresh) and "dispuesta a concretarse" (ready to become more definite), as descriptions of the soul, indicate the familiar themes of renewal and fully defined form. In this recovered state of completeness even reality seems to respond to his eagerness, coming in search of him and approving his new-forged integrity:

> El contorno dispone su forma, su favor,
> Y no espera, me busca, se inclina a mi avidez,
> Sonríe a mi salud de nuevo ilusionada.
> El intruso dolor —soy ya quien soy— partió.

> (All around me offers its form and favour,
> And doesn't wait, it seeks me, inclines to my eagerness,
> Smiles at my newly-hopeful heartiness.
> Now I am what I am – pain the intruder departed.)

What is important in the above poems is the individual's disposition, the extent to which he is prepared to overcome the forces of opposition which threaten his integrity and equilibrium. Moreover, he is not alone in his efforts; such experiences can be shared and even so, they always occur within the constancy of the external world. Man's integrity is subject to attack and weakness, but that of Creation remains as an example which he can emulate. In fact, he has only to consider that fundamental link between himself and the world, respiration, and he finds immediately a further link, sight and objects, all brought into being by air. The miracle of air, its insubstantiality, has a parallel in the human soul, whose sensitivity is similarly miraculous for being indefinable. He is thus irresistibly drawn to reality with an ever-increasing capacity to marvel. These ideas are to be found in "Equilibrio" (Equilibrium, C_3 245 / C 318) and the calm and tranquillity evoked by the unhurried pace of the fourteen-syllable metre are an invitation to have faith in man's potential for harmony. Under his serene gaze the white wall becomes whiter, the view through the window is of beautiful normality. This awareness in tranquillity extends even to an appreciation of the invisible: the wind rippling over cornfields, silence becoming an audible reality. The final line "Todo me obliga a ser centro del equilibrio" (All requires me to be the centre of equilibrium) provides evidence that there are infinite opportunities to remain in harmony with self and surroundings.

As can be seen from the above poem, the elements which contribute to man's understanding of harmony are all of the utmost simplicity, and yet they are always the source of profound joy. Just as the experience of momentary beauty provides knowledge of lasting value, so the simple phenomena of normality offer the possibility of discovering dynamic complexities that actively encourage one's faith in their validity. As Guillén says in *El argumento de la obra*:

> El hombre surge así, copartícipe de un valor universal, y su parte será
> siempre más pequeña que la del Otro.   (*AO* 11)

> (Man appears thus, sharer in a universal value, and his role will always
> be smaller than that of the Other.)

Such an attitude is found at the end of "Más verdad" (C_3 272 / C 364) whose final line "Son prodigios de tierra" (They are the wonders of earth) indicates that all experiences have positive or "fabulous" implications. A poem which illustrates this particularly well is "Además" (Besides, C_3 116 / C 136). An all-pervading sense of joy erupts at the beginning of the poem. It does not matter by whom this joy is felt: the emotion stands in its own right. The vocabulary of the first seven lines gives an impression of unhurried ease and an early sunlit morning in May, with cars moving smoothly along, is described as "Un sonreír ya general" (An already widespread smile). An idea of everyday normality is conveyed, and it is this that is the cause of joy. Normality finds its expression in a variety of sensations, ranging from the heady aroma of fresh-cut grass and of pine trees to the gentle warmth of the spring sun. This is the phenomenon that *Cántico* portrays:

> *Cántico* atiende a esos instantes en que no sucede sino el fenómeno
> extraordinario de la normalidad ... En estas ocasiones prorrumpe de
> las entrañas mismas de la vitalidad, y con toda su fuerza de surtidor,

un júbilo físico y metafísico, ya fundamento de una convicción entusiasta, de una fe: la fe en la realidad, esta realidad terrestre.

(*AO* 12-13)

(*Cántico* is about those moments in which nothing occurs but the extraordinary phenomenon of normality ... On such occasions there bursts forth from the very centre of vitality, with all its surging force, a joy both physical and metaphysical, already the basis of an enthusiastic conviction, of a faith: faith in reality, this earthly reality.)

The faith that the individual feels in "Además" is innocent and fresh, qualified as it is by the adjectives "clara" (clear) and "primaveral" (spring-like). By linking human faith with the pristine constancy of the natural world, Guillén is able to emphasize its validity. In addition, such faith confirms the destiny of the individual, which is to participate in Creation. While it is his fervour which is essential for reciprocation between man and the world to be appreciated, the final words of the poem continue to show wonder and amazement on his part:

Todo es prodigio por añadidura.

(On top of all that, everything is marvellous.)

The objects of a seascape in "Una ventana" (A window, C_3 276 / *C* 155) are symbols of the same "normality" as the May morning evoked in "Además". Normality always causes wonder in Guillén's protagonist, reminiscent of the emotion expressed in lines from Thomas Traherne's "The Salutation":

... that they mine should be, who nothing was,
That strangest is of all, yet brought to pass.[17]

The reality of such objects as sky, cloud, sea, dunes and spray is incontrovertible:

Están ahí de bulto con una irresistible
Realidad sonriente.

(They are there in mass with an irresistible
Smiling realness.)

It is the window that enables the seascape to be seen and for this

---

[17] Thomas Traherne, *Centuries, Poems and Thanksgivings*, ed. H.M. Margoliouth (Oxford: Clarendon Press, 1958), II, 46. See also Willis Barnstone, "Two Poets of Felicity: Thomas Traherne and Jorge Guillén", *Books Abroad*, 42 (Winter 1968), 14-19.

reason the window becomes as important to him as air and light, the two external media which make vision possible. The statement "Yo resido en las márgenes . . . " (I live on the margins . . .) would appear to contradict the view of such poems as "Equilibrio" and "Las doce en el reloj", which have shown the individual to be at the very centre of reality. However, these margins are the physical limits – the metaphorical window-frame – of the space and light of Creation. These, though intangible, are made substantial by the window itself:

> Yo resido en las márgenes
> De una profundidad de trasparencia en bloque.
>
> (I live on the margins
> Of a depth of solid transparency.)

Objects bathed in light contribute to the peace which fills the afternoon and by looking at this scene, and thereby being part of it, the individual is also imbued with serenity:

> El aire está ciñendo, mostrando, realzando
> Las hojas en la rama, las ramas en el tronco,
> Los muros, los aleros, las esquinas, los postes:
> Serenidad en evidencia de la tarde,
> Que exige una visión tranquila de ventana.
>
> (The air is encircling, showing, enhancing
> Leaves on the branch, branches on the tree,
> Walls, eaves, corners, posts:
> Obvious serenity of the afternoon
> Which demands vision in tranquillity from the window.)

The individual is not carried away by his own vision of the world. What he sees is what is there, uncontaminated by any romantic flights of fancy. As Guillén says:

> Importa la plenitud de esas realidades, no su hermosura. (Claro que la hermosura muestra el objeto en su cumplido esplendor.) "Guijarros", "valla", "alambre" evocan un trozo modesto de planeta. Pero son exactamente lo que son. Ahí está el quid.   (*AO* 13)
>
> (What is important is the abundance of those realities, not their beauty. [Obviously beauty shows the object in its fulfilled splendour.] "Pebble", "fence", "wire" evoke a modest bit of the planet. But they are exactly what they are. That is the whole point.)

Just as the light of the sun emphasizes the reality of objects, so the light of the individual's intelligence is like a window which makes visible that same reality. Moreover, the intelligence provides him with the ability to articulate his responses to reality:

> Soy como mi ventana. Me maravilla el aire.
> ¡Hermosura tan límpida ya de tan entendida,
> Entre el sol y la mente! Hay palabras muy tersas,
> Y yo quiero saber como el aire de Junio.

> (I am like my window. The air fills me with wonder.
> Such limpid beauty now so understood,
> Between the sun and the mind! There are very smooth words,
> And I want knowledge like the air of June.)

Having made the links between sight and intellect with almost geometrical accuracy (beauty is literally perceived between the combined forces of external light and human intelligence), Guillén ends the poem with an allusion to the relationship between world and individual:

> En círculo de paz se me cierra la tarde,
> Y un cielo bien alzado se ajusta a mi horizonte.

> (In a circle of peace the afternoon closes round me,
> And the high sky adjusts to my horizon.)

In this instance the protagonist becomes the final link in the circle of perfection. The afternoon closes round him and, because of his efforts to clarify for himself the realities of the world, it seems that reality and his perception of it are in absolute harmony.

Many of the new poems of the 1945 edition consider the riches to be gained from involvement with reality, continuing a topic already discovered in the earlier editions. An interesting example of this theme is to be found in "Rosa olida" (A Rose Savoured, C_3 200 / C 263), where the individual's awareness of his relationship with the beloved is intensified by what *she* gains from contact with the natural world. Thus the intensity of his feelings is brought about indirectly; he gains vicarious pleasure from her experiences. In the poem the woman leans forward to smell a rose, a metaphor for her own fervent participation in life:

> Te inclinaste hacia una rosa,
> Tu avidez
> Gozó el olor, fue la tez
> Más hermosa.
> Te erguiste con más brío,
> Más ceñida de tu estío
> Personal,
> Para mí —sin más ayuda

Que una flor— casi desnuda:
Tú, fatal.

(You leaned towards a rose,
Your eagerness
Enjoyed the fragrance, your complexion became
More beautiful.
You straightened up again with more energy,
More encircled by your personal
Summer,
For me – with no more help
Than a flower – almost naked:
You, destiny.)

It is the aim of *Cántico* to record the phenomenal quality inherent in everyday events. For this reason, as a result of her contact with the flower, the woman gains more beauty and energy and is more profoundly integrated with her love of life, "summer" being an image of plenitude and fulfilment. Here in this poem we have a circle – individual, beloved and Creation – of perhaps the most harmonious kind.

Reciprocal responses between individuals and the world are an essential aspect of these poems, and are expressed concisely by Guillén's frequent use of the "se me + verb" construction. A recent example was seen in the line "se me cierra la tarde" (the afternoon closes round me) from "Además". Others are to be found in "Una ventana", "Hacia el poema" (Towards the poem, C_3 207 / C 273) and "Las horas". Such a construction emphasizes the action or influence of the world upon the individual and stresses the force which external reality exerts on the perception of the human being. This is particularly evident in "Mayo nuestro" (Our May, C_3 72 / C 98) where, in the first four stanzas, Guillén uses verbs connoting energy and activity on the part of Creation which heighten the individual's awareness not only of spring but also of the supreme companionship offered by the beloved:

Mayo, con verdor
Que todo lo puede,
Se entrega asaltando,
Verde, verde, verde.   (1)

¡Hojas! Y la rama
Prorrumpe hacia el sol.
Más sombra en la sombra
Se ciñe al amor.   (2)

    ¡Balcones abiertos!
    Por el aire viene
    Dicha aparecida.
    ¡Hay tierra presente!   (3)

    Follaje oreando,
    La suma sazón
    Se levanta. Cumbre:
    Mayo con tu voz.   (4)

(May, with greenness
All powerful,
Offers itself in a rush of
Green, green, green.

Leaves! And the branch
Bursts forth towards the sun.
More shade in shadows
Encircles love.

Open balconies!
Through the air comes
Fortune personified.
The earth is here!

Rustling the foliage,
The supreme moment
Rises up. Summit:
May, with your voice.)

The interidentification of May – a symbol of spring through its linked connotations of renewal, hope and love – with the beloved brings about a vital change in life itself:

    Encumbrada así,
    La vida convierte
    Su arranque fugaz
    En alma de siempre.   (5)

(Thus elevated,
Life converts
Its fleeting impulse
Into everlasting spirit.)

Life, seen in terms of an abrupt and fleeting impulse, becomes the very essence of permanence when love of woman and of Creation is acknowledged. Moreover, the unity that love brings has the power to make of life an exciting adventure and also provides a defence against the forces of opposition, time (symbolized by "hours") and disorder (symbolized by "masks"), which are acknowledged in stanzas 7 and 10:

Cierto, ¡cuántas horas
Más graves que leves!
Somos uno entonces,
Uno. ¿Quién le vence?　　　　　　　　　　　　(7)

Sonríes. Contigo
Todo es realidad.
¿Quedan, lejos, máscaras?
Tu faz es tu afán.　　　　　　　　　　　　　(10)

(Certainly, so many hours to come
More of seriousness than levity!
We are one even then,
One. Who can overcome it?

You smile. With you
All is real.
Are there masks in the future?
Your face is your desire.)

Unity and fervour of and for life are spiritual qualities, possessed by the lovers, which link them with the constancy and sanctity of the natural world. In fact, the beloved is, for the lover, a kind of godhead and is referred to in the central stanza as having grace. He himself has faith in the grace she imparts and these two qualities, together with their joint perception of the spirit of Creation, make up a secular trinity of profound but *human* significance.[18]

Time is perhaps the most imposing and threatening negative force with which man has to contend. But his greatest defence against it is love, of woman, of life, of Creation. "Más amor que tiempo" (More love than time, C_3 250 / C 324) makes it clear that it is not only time as an external factor that is a threat. It is also the individual's awareness of time's effect on life that causes anxiety. In this poem time is stilled by the intimacy of the lovers, but the individual is suddenly assailed by the prospect of marching time as "una sola masa de precipitación" (a single mass of hurrying haste). It is almost as though the future years of loving have been telescoped into "un terrible porvenir fugacísimo" (a terribly fleeting future). He regains his equilibrium by reminding himself that the present moment or experience of love has an absolute value, that of fulfilment which is never contingent upon nor conditioned by the passage of time:

> ¡Si el presente nos colma de tal dominación,
> De un ímpetu absoluto sin encaje en el tiempo!

[18] See C. Pinet, "The Sacramental View of Poetry and the Religion of Love in Jorge Guillén's *Cántico*", *Hispania*, 62 (1979), 47-55.

(For the present crowns us with such dominion,
With an absolute impulse that is not dependent on time!)

The theme of time and its effect on the lovers is explored in greater depth in "Tarde mayor" (Greater afternoon, C_3 294 / C 380). The poem was written in the early forties, the decade which saw the commencement of poems which are heralds of *Clamor*.[19] The principal antagonist in the poem is time, and its pervasive force is expressed by words like "tyrant", "enemy" and "destroyer" whose human connotations reinforce the idea that the task of the lovers is to struggle against their concept of the passage of time. Their ally is the natural world. The negative aspects of temporality are personified in "tyrant", "enemy" and "destroyer", all representatives of the desire to truncate any potential fulfilment. Their opponents in the natural world are chestnut trees, whose renewed growth in spring symbolizes victory over the passage of time.

In stanza 1 the golden light of afternoon provides a background against which the vitality and permanence of the beloved is revealed. She has, for the lover, qualities of stillness and reassuring clarity, which contrast with the movement of time, symbolized by the gradual changes of light and its intensity during the passage of a day:

> Así te yergues tú, para mis ojos
> Forma en sosiego de ese resplandor,
> Trasluz seguro de la luz versátil.   (2)

> (So you appear, for my eyes
> A figure of calm in all the splendour,
> A sure gleam in the changeable light.)

This does not prevent their lives being affected by hostile forces, but what does remain is the spirit or essence of their love:

> Oscurecidos y desordenados
> Penaremos también. Y no habrá alud
> Que nos alcance en la ternura nuestra.   (4)

> (Diminished and disordered
> We too will suffer. And there will be no avalanche
> That can reach us in our tenderness.)

Stanzas 5-7 provide a point of comparison within the natural world. The chestnut trees are dedicated to the sun in their will to survive. They may occasionally be threatened by the passage of time,

---

[19] See Weber, "De *Cántico* a *Clamor*", 109-19.

but rise above this simply by reaffirming themselves through the vigour of Nature's cycle. They are thus able to transcend time's destructive force:

> Si tal fronda perece fulminada,
> Rumoroso otra vez igual verdor
> Se alzará en el olvido del tirano. (6)

> Y pasará el camión de los feroces.
> Castaños sin Historia arrojarán
> Su florecilla al suelo —blanquecino. (7)

> (If such fronds are struck and perish,
> Rustlingly the same greenness once again
> Will arise in the oblivion of the tyrant.

> And the vehicle of the fierce ones will pass away.
> Chestnut trees without History will throw to the
> Ground their tiny flowers – and make it pure.)

The violence suggested in the vocabulary above is indicative of the power of time, a power which can be mitigated by confronting it intellectually. Though part of a chaotic world, the lovers are protected by the essential vitality of love, just as the trees are by their natural life cycle. The harmony implied by the parallels between the human and the natural world lends an air of perfection to the afternoon. It becomes a "greater afternoon" because the anguish that the passage of time causes is seen to be superable:

> Un ámbito de tarde en perfección
> Tan desarmada humildemente opone,
> Por fin venciendo, su fragilidad (8)

> A ese desbarajuste sólo humano
> Que a golpes lucha contra el mismo azul
> Impasible, feroz también, profundo. (9)

> (An atmosphere of afternoon in such disarmed
> Perfection humbly, and finally overcoming,
> Opposes its fragility

> Against that solely human disorder
> Which by blows fights the sky itself
> Impassive, fierce as well, profound.)

Regeneration is the natural world's innate defence against the ravages of time's destruction. Man has no such defence in physical terms and at times even his intellectual control fails, creating "that solely human disorder". But it is the mind's power which enables man to rationalize. By personifying the destructive force of time it

becomes clear that this particular aspect of temporality is limited
when put into perspective. Destruction is not time's only attribute. It
is also full and vital, as has been seen in those poems which equate
love with the present, the continuum of fulfilment. Moreover,
throughout *Cántico* love is equated with the natural world, shown
here to be a powerful adversary for time's destructive potential:

> Fugaz la Historia, vano el destructor.
> Resplandece la tarde. Yo contigo.
> Eterna al sol la brisa juvenil.   (10)

> (History is fleeting, vain the destroyer.
> The afternoon shines forth. Me with you.
> Eternal in the sun the youthful breeze.)

Liberty to put time's devastation into perspective is the theme
of "Tarde mayor", hence its superscription, "Libre nací, y en
libertad me fundo" (I was born free, and am founded in liberty), from
Cervantes. The freedom which intellectual contemplation brings is
the keynote of the poem "Sin embargo" (However, C_3 203 / C 269).
It is divided into three parts, sections I and III being in the form of a
dialogue where the individual who is the protagonist of the poems of
Cántico skilfully turns the negative comments of another potential
protagonist into a positive defence of life. In section I, life is
symbolized by the day, where dawn and dusk represent birth and
death. The intervening time, some would claim, witnesses an obscure
and gloomy struggle. The protagonist points out that the value of life
lies in the fact that it can be understood, just as day is illumined by the
sun. In section III love is accepted as symbolic of a life lived to the
full. Others see it only as a bitter-sweet experience which must be
suffered. The protagonist's view is that companionship, the essence
of love, becomes part of one's very existence, and it is this that
remains as proof of the value of life and love. Section II is a summary
of sections I and III in so far as the conclusion inherent within it
justifies the protagonist's affirmation:

> Hoy huele el día a gozo recordado. Disfruta
> Del camino: ya es ruta.

> (Today the day's fragrance is of remembered joy. Enjoy
> The road: it is already a route.)

If we approach life with our senses, these will tell us that life is linked
with pleasure: it is remembered joy. Intellectual acceptance of this
gives us confidence positively and actively to participate in life, for a

pleasant memory is a stimulus to become further involved. Thus the road of life, because it is familiar, becomes a known route to absolute existence.

The thematic evolution of the early editions of *Cántico* is very clearly and intimately connected with the process of time and natural life within Creation. Beginning with the seventy-five poems which emphasize the individual's efforts to perceive form and meaning in both his surroundings and his own life, Guillén goes on to elaborate that perception until it becomes not only a means to secure knowledge of the individual's position with regard to time and space, but also a vigorous, resounding affirmation of his faith in the validity of human life within the confines of Creation. Harmony is established by means of subjective and objective experiences of involvement with other people and with reality. Time is confronted in many poems, and sorrow at the transience of life is mitigated by the ability to perceive its absolute value. Creation is the sphere in which man has his existence; its form is a symbol of perfection through which he is able to arrive at a knowledge of his own essential being. The development of *Cántico* over the years parallels the road which Guillén's protagonist follows. That "road", initiated in 1928, and established in 1936, becomes the "route" of 1945, achieved by having faith in Creation and in the validity of life. This faith is expressed by means of poetry, and is acknowledged in the appropriate and definitive subtitle added to *Cántico* in 1945:

Fe de vida

(Faith in life)

CHAPTER 3

CANTICO (1950): SIX MAJOR POEMS

Introduction

The second chapter of this book dealt with a variety of poems from
the first three editions of *Cántico*, and ways of interpreting the mood
of each were suggested. The sense of affirmation which is already
present in the 1928 edition is consolidated in the 1936 and 1945
volumes and is symbolized in particular by the appearance of the
subtitle *Fe de vida* in 1945.

    The definitive edition of *Cántico*, published by Sudamericana
in 1950, appeared with both initial and final dedications in new and
extended forms.[1] The first dedication, to Guillén's mother, celebrates
the initial gifts of mother to child: "ser" (being), "vivir" (life) and
"lenguaje" (language). Of these, language is the gift which takes
longest to mature, in speech and in creative writing, but it is this gift
which is the primary and most important instrument for Guillén,
since with it he is able to express his response to "life" and "being".
With language he is able not only to say but to show:

> con qué voluntad placentera
> consiento en mi vivir,
> con qué fidelidad de criatura
> humildemente acorde
> me siento ser   (*C* 21)

> (with what pleased goodwill
> I consent to my life,
> with what faith as a humble
> and harmonious creature
> I am aware of my being)

The second dedication is to his friend and fellow poet, Pedro Salinas,

---

[1] The initial and final dedications in the editions previous to 1950 are simply, "A mi
madre / En su cielo", and "Para / Mi amigo / Pedro Salinas". All the references to
poems in *Cántico* are from the 1977 Barral edition, Barcelona.

whose interest in the gradual evolution of *Cántico* epitomized for Guillén perfect friendship, not only personal but professional. Together the dedications show how one individual life, that of Jorge Guillén, is extended through language and companionship, to all who, by reading *Cántico*, become aware of the value for themselves of those three initial gifts of the first dedication:

> Hombre como nosotros
> ávido
> De compartir la vida como fuente,
> De consumar la plenitud del ser
> En la fiel plenitud de las palabras.   (*C* 537)

> (A man like us
> eager
> To share life as a fountain,
> To consummate the fullness of being
> In the faithful plenitude of words.)

An interesting departure from the format of the three previous editions of *Cántico* is to be found in the index of this 1950 edition only, where certain poem titles are printed in capital letters. Throughout sections I, II, IV and V, these "major poems" are placed regularly and symmetrically. Moreover, the overall structure of the four sections is perfectly balanced. Sections I and V are divided into three subsections with two major poems in each. The undivided sections II and IV contain eleven major poems whose distribution is almost exactly the same in both cases.

Guillén selects compositions from all the editions of *Cántico* as major poems. Thus, for example, the free-verse poem "Hacia el sueño, hasta el sueño" from 1928 was elaborated and extended to become "La rendición al sueño" in the 1936 edition and eventually a major poem in 1950. Over the years of the creation of *Cántico* Guillén was concerned to establish the breadth and profundity of the initial statement of belief made in 1928. Significantly enough the final 1950 edition of *Cántico* is made definitive by Guillén's decision to identify long poems from all the editions as major elements, together with the eleven new major compositions. These works, in fact, can be seen as a key to *Cántico*, though it should not be assumed that a complete knowledge of it can be gained without reference to the other poems. The major poems are all long compositions in a variety of verse forms and are of considerable complexity. They are extended and elaborated versions of the themes contained in the majority of the other poems.

A diagram of the placing of major poems within *Cántico* shows a gradual concern for symmetry and balance, not only in the number of sections (reduced from seven in 1928 to five in 1936), but also in the number and placing of the poems within each subsection.[2] The diagram also shows the even concentration of major poems, apparent in 1945 in sections II, IV and V.

DISTRIBUTION OF MAJOR POEMS IN *CÁNTICO*

I	**Al aire de tu vuelo**				
	Más allá		1936		
	Todo en la tarde		1936		
	Jardín en medio			1945	
	Las horas			1945	
	Muchas gracias, adiós			1945	
	Salvación de la primavera		1936		
II	**Las horas situadas**				
	Paso a la aurora			1945	
	Esperanza de todos			1945	
	*El diálogo				1950
	†La rendición al sueño	1928			
	Sol en la boda				1950
	Tiempo libre				1950
	Anillo			1945	
	*El concierto				1950
	El distraído		1936		
	Caballos en el aire			1945	
	*A vista de hombre				1950
IV	**Aquí mismo**				
	Los balcones del Oriente			1945	
	*Luz natal				1950
	Vario mundo				1950
	Santo suelo			1945	
	El infante				1950
	Más vida			1945	
	*Vida extrema				1950
	Más esplendor			1945	
	*Las cuatro calles				1950
	Noche del caballero				1950
	Amistad de la noche			1945	
V	**Pleno ser**				
	Mundo en claro			1945	
	Caminante de puerto, noche sin luna			1945	
	La vida real			1945	
	Su persona			1945	
	El aire			1945	
	Cara a cara			1945	

* Poems analysed in this chapter.
† Originally "Hacia el sueño, hasta el sueño".

[2] See Ignacio Prat, *"Aire nuestro" de Jorge Guillén* (Barcelona: Planeta, 1974), for a comprehensive study of the structural symmetry of Guillén's first three volumes of poetry.

The length of these poems is such that only general comments could be made about them all in an overall study such as the present one. However, detailed analysis of the long poems of *Cántico* is not frequent, most critics preferring, justifiably, to examine the poetry in thematic terms, using parts of several poems in support of their arguments. Analysis of the long poems is a rewarding exercise, for while the major preoccupation of each is easy to discern, it is elaborated in ways which are always far-reaching.

Broadly categorized, the major themes of *Cántico* are Life, Harmony, Time and Creation. The latter term implies both Creation, meaning the natural world, and creation in the sense of creative ability. However, it is difficult to point to major poems from *Cántico* as examples of only one of the particular themes mentioned above. Each area of existence, or theme of *Cántico*, functions in terms of others, and the complexity and greatness of *Cántico* is visible only in an awareness of its many aspects:

> Esos cuatro temas – vida, tiempo, armonía, Creación/creación – son, efectivamente esenciales, a través de variaciones, aclaraciones y complementos.[3]

> (These four themes, life, time, harmony and Creation/creation, are, in fact, essential, through variations, clarifications and comparisons.)

Balance and ordered vision are the hallmarks of *Cántico* and the various editions from 1928 onwards are dedicated to demonstrating this. However, the result is not monotonous. For amazement and delight in reality are to be found, though knowledge of the accidental or negative aspects within it, usually stemming directly from man's sphere of existence, is also revealed.

The titles of the sections containing new major poems are significant. "Las horas situadas" (The Appointed Hours) and "Aquí mismo" (Right Here) both imply concern with time and space and the position of the individual in relation to them. Time, of course, implies both mortal, human time and natural, eternal time (space for its part implies position and place, though the qualifying adjectives in each title indicate that it is reality which is at the heart of the poems.

"Las horas situadas" and "Aquí mismo", then, are concerned with man's position in time and space, elaborating the duration of man's life and his place in the world. Each individual must come to terms with these concepts, as Guillén clearly states elsewhere. His exhortation that we should enjoy our progress through life is made in the full knowledge that that progress, though mortal, will reveal its own intrinsic worth:

> Zumba el reto
> Público. ¿Quién, hostil? Sumiso el hado.
>
> ¿Sumiso? No se engañan. Saben todo
> Lo muy terrestre que será su ruta,
> Rica de recta simple y de recodo
> Quizá a merced de una intemperie bruta.
> ("Sol en la boda" [Sun at the Wedding], *C* 163)

> (The public challenge
> Buzzes. Who is hostile? Fate is docile.
>
> Docile? They are not deceived. They know
> How very earthly their pathway will be,
> Rich in straight lines and in twists
> Perhaps at the mercy of harsh elements.)

Of the five new major poems in "Las horas situadas" and the six of "Aquí mismo", I propose to study three from each section: "El diálogo" (Dialogue, *C* 139), "El concierto" (Concert, *C* 189), "A vista de hombre" (In Sight of Man, *C* 222), "Luz natal" (Native Light, *C* 348), "Vida extrema" (Extreme Life, *C* 398) and "Las cuatro calles" (The Four Streets, *C* 419). All six poems were written between 1945 and 1949.

"El diálogo" is concerned with dialogues between man and man, and man and Creation. The poem gradually reveals a greater sense of unity on both human and cosmic levels. The very obvious fluctuations in tenses from the imperfect to the present, with only the occasional preterite, indicate a sense of the importance of past friendship and its influence on the present attitudes of the individual.

"El concierto" is an extended musical metaphor about the potential "concertedness" or oneness of humans symbolized by the interaction of the listener with the music. The listener is raised to an extreme level of awareness and the music (the work of a human composer) is raised to an absolute level, that of the divine. Macrí finds reminiscences of both Fray Luis de León and San Juan de la Cruz in this poem.[4]

The whole of "A vista de hombre", begun in a hotel room in New York in August 1946, is based on a series of paradoxes. The

---

[4] Oreste Macrí, *La obra poética de Jorge Guillén* (Barcelona: Ariel, 1976), pp.145-47.

most obvious is that which exists between the title and the subject, a solitary depressed individual suffering from insomnia in the darkness of night, an individual, furthermore, who strives for mental acuity. A further paradox is to be found in the contrast between the essence of the city, a visible symbol and external manifestation of man's creative ability, and the accidental aspects of the city – crime, violence – which are not easily visible:

> ¿Quién la hizo
> Terrible, quién tan bella?   (*C* 224)

> (Who made it
> Terrible, who made it so beautiful?)

The protagonist of the poem can also be seen to be paradoxical – a solitary man, yet intensely and remorsefully aware of the "solitude of brotherhood". The protagonist's own attitudes and mental struggle resolve these paradoxes and make of them a more confident philosophy whose strength lies in himself, in his own efforts to overcome the drama of insomnia, loneliness and spiritual darkness:

> . . . este ser profundo a quien me debo   (*C* 227)

> (. . . this profound being to whom I owe what I am)

"Luz natal" has as its setting the hills outside Valladolid, specifically the Hill of Saint Christopher. The fact that the poem was written in America, and has as a starting-point the memory of this hill during the poet's childhood, dictates the vital tension throughout the poem between "the light of the universe" and "the light of this Castile". The light and air of Spain and of America give the poem its national and universal significance, but both are subsumed in a "native light", which symbolizes the existence of the protagonist as an individual and as one of the human race:

> Y el aire se me ensancha en luz natal,
> En eso que yo soy.   (*C* 360)

> (And the air swells about me into native light,
> Into this which makes me what I am.)

"Vida extrema" is the third of the central trio of poems of "Aquí mismo", which deals broadly with aspects of personal importance in Guillén's life – the grandson Antó ("El infante" [The Infant], *C* 384), the son Claudio ("Más vida" [More Life], *C* 392) and poetry ("Vida extrema"). As always with Guillén, the personal sources of these poems do not impose limitations on the significance of the content for the reader. "El infante" considers the child who as yet has no linguistic ability, and the poem stresses the integrity of being that even a child possesses (this is to be seen in the frequent use of the verb "to be" in relation to the child). "Más vida" traces the relationship between father and his son and the value of an extended life through son for father:

> A través de tus horas, sin descanso
> Más allá de la muerte,
> Hasta el año 2000 he de llegar
> Calladamente.   (*C* 394)

> (Through your hours, without rest
> Beyond death,
> I shall reach the year 2000
> Silently.)

"Vida extrema" is the most unusual of the three poems in its implications for all men. The last line, "Gracia de vida extrema, poesía" (Grace of extreme life, poetry), is easily understood in relation to Guillén himself. Indeed the life of this man, Jorge Guillén, is a symbol of dedication to the three gifts from his mother, "ser", "vivir" and "lenguaje", and one might easily be led to believe that the following lines refer specifically to him:

> —Se salvará mi luz en mi futuro.
> Y si a nadie la muerte le perdona,
> Mis términos me valgan de conjuro.
> No morirá del todo la persona.

> En la palpitación, en el acento
> De esa cadencia para siempre dicha
> Quedará sin morir mi terco intento
> De siempre ser. Allí estará mi dicha.   (*C* 404)

> (My knowledge will be salvaged in my future.
> And if death pardons nobody,
> May my words have value as a magic spell.
> The individual will not die completely.

> In the vibrations, in the sound
> Of that cadence for ever spoken
> My stubborn attempt to exist always will
> Remain alive. Therein will be my happiness.)

However, belief in his own immortality on the strength of his published life's work is neither easy nor automatic for Guillén, as he reveals in a letter to the present author:

Tema de la inmortalidad. Tema complejo, delicado y según sus varios
sentidos. La duración de la obra literaria es una cosa insegura,
precaria, frágil.[5]

(The theme of immortality. A complex theme, delicate and with
various meanings. The durability of the literary work is something
uncertain, precarious, fragile.)

In fact, "Vida extrema" is not dedicated to the poet as an artistic
creator and its significance lies rather in the fact that all men have the
gift of being, life and language. What is it, then, in the word "poetry"
which signifies an extreme, supreme life for non-poets? The "extreme
life" for each individual is that which is found in man's ability to put
into words what he sees:

> Nombres.
> Están sobre la pátina
>
> De las cosas.   ("Los nombres", *C* 36)
>
> (Names.
> They are on the patina
>
> Of things.)

All men must, if they live actively in the world, put their emotions
and attitudes into words. They must articulate, not only in the sense
of "saying in words" but also in the sense of "joining up" the
emotions and receptivity of the individual with the reality of the
world around him. The additional gift for all men is thus the supreme
life of verbalized emotions and responses, which is, as this poem
shows, poetry. Reality itself is harmony (the whole of *Cántico* is an
effort to prove this) and poetry imitates this in its combination of
speech, words, rhyme, rhythm and verbal harmony. Poetry is words
structured to reflect reality's structure, a bringing together of words
in harmonious format to mirror the harmonious ordering of the
universe.

"Las cuatro calles", like "Luz natal", has a real physical setting
– the streets which lead into the Plaza de Canalejas in Madrid:
Carrera de San Jerónimo, calle de Sevilla, del Príncipe and de la
Cruz.[6] As in "A vista de hombre" the essential and the circumstantial
are considered in this poem. The essential aspect of "Las cuatro
calles", however, is the world, while the circumstantial is the city:

[5] Letter dated 30 May 1980.
[6] Macrí, p.203, note 45.

> Mundo en esencia late, fabuloso,
> Mientras ¡Ay! la ciudad
> Y sus torres mantienen contra el tiempo su acoso.

(C 420)

> (A world in essence beats, fabulous,
> While, ay!, the city
> And its towers keep up their relentless pursuit against time.)

Sunset and its effects on the city are seen simultaneously with the darker side of man. The line "the world of mankind is badly made" should be seen as the complement to the famous "the world is well-made" of "Beato sillón" (1928). By analogy, it explains precisely and simply the meaning of that early claim. In "Las cuatro calles" there is an exhortation to man to accept the negative and disagreeable aspects of his own nature and of his fellow men, similar to the mood which pervades the end of "A vista de hombre" in its awareness of brotherhood and individual self-knowledge, achieved once the paradox "solitude of brotherhood" has been resolved.

The major poems of the 1950 edition have varied structures and metres but can be loosely divided into those of varying line and stanza length and those of quatrains, using four-, seven-, eight- and eleven-syllable lines. The verse forms are always symmetrically ordered but quatrains and free verse are not mixed within individual sections. Sections II and IV are identically structured from the point of verse forms, the central trio of poems and the four flanking poems having the same format, with minor variations in "Esperanza de todos" (Everybody's Hope, *C* 128), "Las cuatro calles" and "Amistad de la noche" (Friendship of the Night, *C* 448). Once again the often remarked care for symmetry of structure is evident.

"El diálogo"

Though the title of "El diálogo" (Dialogue, *C* 139-43) is in the singular, Guillén says it refers to "los diálogos" between himself and his youthful friends.[7] The numerous instances of conversation and the variety of types of dialogue – for example, spoken and unspoken – must, therefore, be borne in mind by the reader.

The poem starts with a personification of the day. It is a companion and, rather than being taken for granted, it is acknowledged as an "Esfera de existencia" (sphere of existence) by "la

---

[7] In particular Blas Ramos Sobrino. See José Guerrero Martín, *Jorge Guillén: sus raíces. Recuerdos al paso* (Valladolid: Miñón, 1982), p.41.

atención latente" (latent attentiveness). The protagonist's act of attention is now permanently active and aware, though, as in this case, it is not at a primary level. The things which indicate his awareness of day are shafts of light and shade which impress themselves on his consciousness. Light and warmth and colours combine to make a pleasant ambience. Moreover, the well-known highway which the companions walk is conducive to enjoyable dialogue, human communication. In the metaphorical sense, the familiar situation of a pleasant day ("Acompañaba el día" [The day was a companion]) and the awareness of the individual ("latent attentiveness") combine to make a well-known set of situations ("la carretera / Tan usual" [the highway, / so normal]), which then becomes a direct route to harmonious communication. The parallel set up between day and dialogue is clearly shown by the structure of this first stanza, where day and the protagonist's awareness are mutually dependent for recognition:

> Buen tiempo.
> . . . .
> Ruta para el buen diálogo.   (139/7-10)

The imperfect tenses of this stanza and the next signify not only something remembered from the past, but something which continued, which happened frequently and habitually in the past. So memory and familiarity are the emotions which guide the descriptions in these first two stanzas, as does also a sense of unity between landscape and person. The dialogue which is the subject of the poem is that between people, and also that between people and Creation. There is a clear narrowing down of perspective from the vastness of "el día" (the day), through "rastros" (tracks), "penumbras" (shadows), "Buen tiempo" (good weather), "la carretera" (the highway), to an awareness of the real and metaphorical sense of "Ruta" (route), all via "latent attentiveness".

In stanza 2 the description continues and broadens to show the physical, topographical limits of the setting:

> Se levantaban cerros
> Con sus blancos y grises
> Tan puros
> Que eran sólo horizonte.   (139/11-14)

In between are farmlands and woods, so that a distinction is set up between natural features and areas of Nature controlled by man:

> Se interponían zonas de una práctica:
> Pinar, viñedo, tierra poseída.   (139/15-16)

This contrasts specifically with the people who are present:

> ¡Oh, nada poseíamos!
> El diálogo,
> Tan libre así, marchaba a pleno impulso.   (139/17-19)

They have no connection with the countryside other than knowledge of the road and involvement with and awareness of the surroundings. There is also a reference to the freedom of youth from adult concerns, such as making a living from the land. However, youth enjoys that collective "ownership" of landscape conferred on the viewer by his visual senses. This freedom allows easy and active dialogue or communication, the sense of which is clarified by stanza 3. The landscape provides the surroundings to that dialogue which is the protagonist's real aim, though not the physical objective which the direction of their walking implies:

> Andar y hablar, hablar ... Ninguna meta.   (139/20)

Walking and speech are symbols of the two kinds of communication that the poem celebrates, that between man and Creation and that between man and man.

Stanza 3 is written in the present tense and deals in more general terms with the nature of dialogue:

> Sólo este cruzamiento de dos voces
> En aire
> Que no cesa de abrirse
> Frente a nosotros con diafanidad.   (139-40/21-24)

Voices are made manifest by sound waves which carry words through the air, air which is the medium of light, breath and now, in this poem, verbal communication, and which has an almost physical presence. Just as Guillén has carefully described the relationship between speakers, speech and air in the lines quoted (where it is noteworthy that air is the subject of an active verb), so he takes care to clarify the significance of the word "us":

> ¿Nosotros? Ni se dice ni se piensa.
> Amigos:
> Dos voces a nivel.   (140/25-27)

The reality of these people lies not in themselves as individuals but in what they mean to each other. Friendship can be seen as a dialogue between people of like minds, experience, and emotional and intellectual make-up. The equality of each individual within the friendship is also emphasized.

Stanza 4 begins with the recollection of some unspecified phrase uttered in the past, but a clear contrast is drawn between that phrase and the emphasis, now lost, which characterized it, the timeless quality of the world around them and the contribution of Nature to the dialogue:

> Se abalanzó una frase apresurada
> Dominando, montando,
> Aunque flotaban tiempo,
> Deleite,
> Y una anchura de atmósfera dispuesta
> Para la voz entonces tan central.   (140/29-35)

The world around them is characterized by three things: "tiempo", signifying both time and weather; "deleite", the delight of the people at pleasant surroundings and companionship; and "anchura", the vast proportions of the atmosphere that provides the ambit for the spoken words, which are thus the focus of attention. All these are controlled by the verb "flotaban" (were floating) and are described as being disposed and receptive to making the spoken words audible and comprehensible. Memory of those past circumstances makes it possible for the words of a phrase now forgotten to be elevated to a higher level, that of the phenomenon of dialogue. Clearly what is important is the birth of dialogue and communication made possible by the free, untrammelled existence of people within a familiar landscape:

> Salía al sol aquello tan informe
> Por entre los murmullos de los muchos.   (140/36-37)

What otherwise and elsewhere would have been "shapeless" is turned into "the voice, so central at that moment" by the relationship which exists between communicating people and receptive Creation. The key factor in all this is "air" which in respiration makes vocalizing possible, as sound waves make hearing possible and as light makes surrounding reality visible. Air makes possible the communication of thought, which is shared by people:

> Era nuestro en el aire el pensamiento.
> De ti,
> De ti nacía, diálogo de dos.   (140/38-40)

They are no longer isolated, muttering people ("the mutterings of the many") but communicating entities.

Stanza 5 returns to a consideration of the landscape as in stanza 2. Here, however, the hills are separated from the individuals by their distance and magnitude. They provide physical limits to the landscape and in addition facilitate man's comprehension of the sky – a symbol of vastness which could lead to disorientation and uncertainty. This stanza could be seen as the putting into practice of the implications of line 9 in stanza 4:

> Era nuestro en el aire el pensamiento.

The thought initiated by looking at distant hills – "—¿Quién los pisa o los vuela?—" (Who treads them or flies over them?) – leads to a conclusion: "Esa aspereza de horizonte es nítida" (This ruggedness of the horizon is pure). This is arrived at via an appreciation of the hills, whose foothills act as an intermediary and as a helpful boundary, making the unknown known:

> Se extienden, y muy próximos, en combas
> Que facilitan cielo
> Terrestre.   (140/44-46)

This stanza is in the present tense and seems to point up the deliberate distortion of time and distance in the poem. Conversations in the past provide the stimulus or starting point of this poem and lead to a consideration in general and philosophical terms of the nature and importance of communication, to be seen in stanzas 6-10. The tenses, predominantly imperfect and present, illustrate the fact that what happened in the past and what happens in the present, as registered in the poem, are all part of this poem's appreciation of the value of communication.

The conversation that now appears echoes the thoughts contained in stanza 5, as the initial questions indicate. Conversation is one of the most important aspects of friendship, as Guillén makes clear in the following excellent definition of this gift:

> Conversamos, entiendo.
> Vive tan nivelado hacia mi vida
> Que acierta a ser quien es:
> Amigo.   (141/53-56)

It is important because a sense of unity, companionship and perception stem from it:

Y *una común inclinación* escruta
Los varios espectáculos,
Doble luz esclarece algún atisbo
Mientras relampaguea,
Hay lenguaje en la pausa
Que lo recoge silenciosamente,
A una intención denuncia
Su presentida sombra.   (141/57-64; my italics)

These aspects, unity, companionship and perception, are the product of an adult mind's deliberate attempt to define the nature of friendship, and yet they are based on the instinctive youthful love of one for another from years before, and are even to a certain extent made vulnerable (and paradoxically more binding) by that love.

If friendship of an absolute kind is celebrated through dialogue, then the exclamation at the beginning of stanza 8, which expresses the wish for everything in the universe to be in a communicative and communicable state, is entirely fitting. We have already seen that surroundings are an active participator in communication, and the hope expressed by these lines is that dialogue, on this broadly interpreted scale, may continue as long as life continues. It cannot be otherwise, Guillén seems to imply, for as long as there is breath there will be verbal communication:

¿Cómo concluir?
Hartura no es posible entre los labios.
¿No casan las respuestas
O sin vacilación
Se precipitan a su justo encaje?   (142/82-86)

Stanza 8 ends with "Andar, andar y hablar . . . " (Walking, walking and talking . . .), a deliberate reminder of line 1 of stanza 3, "Andar y hablar, hablar . . . ". These two lines control the two major themes of the poem, for stanza 3 initiates a discussion of the nature of dialogue between people, which extends to the end of stanza 8. The latter also introduced the idea of mortal life and hence the purpose of it within Creation:

Diálogo con tropel
Que se improvise, dúctil,
Hacia la lejanía de un final
Interrumpido.   (142/79-82)

The rest of the poem considers this aspect and can be said to deal with the second major theme, that of dialogue between man and Creation.

The same images are used in these final stanzas as were used earlier (with the exception of stanza 12, to be discussed later). The highway, landscape and dialogue are again to be interpreted metaphorically. In stanza 9 the highway is still the sunlit path used by people, yet it is also the way towards illumination of a more spiritual kind – that of unspoken communication between man and Creation:

> Carretera hacia sol.
> Día y más día sobre la palabra,
> Que cede,
> Rumbo a cierto silencio.
> A los ojos complace
> Reconocer, ahondar en lo vivido.   (142/88-93)

This idea of "delving into experience" leads Guillén on, in stanza 10, to state that what is important about the many experiences of life is not that they are moments of novelty but that they have their place within the constancy of Creation – the natural landscape, illuminated always by light and air, which have the unique ability to reinvigorate our perception and thus enhance the quality of life. Thus the sense of stanza 11 lies in an awareness of the wholeness of man's existence within Creation. It is made possible by man's constant and active involvement in life by means of his permanent act of attention:

> Sin voces todavía,
> No deja de avanzar,
> De prosperar el diálogo
> Por la clara llanura
> Donde nuestros destinos
> Profundizan su propia libertad,
> A sus anchas en nuestro infatigable
> Convivir, trabajado
> Siempre por la atención.   (142-43/101-109)

The vocabulary of this stanza implies vast proportions and breadth, a kind of limitless freedom to enjoy and participate in life: "Profundizan" (deepen), "A sus anchas" (at ease), "libres las horas" (the free hours). Time and space are thoroughly grasped and understood because of a willingness to communicate and participate, to pay attention to surroundings and promote understanding with other people:

> Una atención que llega a ser ternura,
> Sólo dicha viviendo,
> Conviviendo. Nuestras, libres las horas.   (143/110-12)

The last phrase of this stanza seems to imply freedom to enjoy the passing hours. Yet Guillén is careful to show that he has not overly romanticized the experience. Spiritual and mental awareness of freedom from time for each individual is what has been achieved, though man will always live according to established patterns and time limits. He must live in a world controlled by the clock and subject to the technological innovations of his time. The meditative and philosophical quietness of the poem is suddenly interrupted by a very ordinary and normal event. A train, running according to its timetable, rushes through the landscape and hoots a warning to advertise its presence:

> El tren.
> Y pasó con su cálculo de cólera.   (143/113-14)

It is a controlled, limited action, a phenomenon which is known and understood, with no *Clamor*-like overtones. The train symbolizes a temporal and finite aspect of the vista considered in the poem. The humming telegraph wires upon which birds sit are a seemingly strange addition to this poem. So too is the sudden use of broken lines of description in a poem which has flowed smoothly up to this point. However, they all have their part – telegraph wires carry conversation across distances greater than the human voice can bridge. All the sounds of this stanza, the train, the birds, the humming wires, are part of the cosmic dialogue which goes on between attentive man and Creation, aided by man's technological achievements. The disruptive effect of these aspects of stanza 12 contrasts strongly with the serene mood created by the repetition of "flowed" in the final stanza. There is a sense of security and peace brought about by communication between friends and constant attentiveness to Creation (which can be described as a cosmic dialogue of unspoken involvement):

> Andábamos, hablábamos: amigos
> En amistad, sin meta.
>
> Fluía la atención. Tenía cauce.   (143/125-27)

Just as the highway provides a direction for the walkers and a metaphorical route to effective communication, so Creation provides a "channel", another pathway along which man may direct his attention. Morning is apprehended by people through cosmic dialogue, and illumination or mental clarity (the metaphorical sense of "morning") is provided for them through their own spoken communication:

> Fluía la mañana por el diálogo.   (143/130)

"El concierto"

"El concierto" (Concert, *C* 189-93) is made up of three-, seven- and eleven-syllable lines, with eleven stanzas of 7, 9, 10, 12 and 16 lines, though there is no clear or symmetrical pattern to be discerned. The poem, as the title indicates, celebrates the unity which can exist in the human world when men and music interact. A fundamental premise of the poem is that which sees music as a symbol of universal harmony. It provides a circle of perfect order which admits no discordant intrusion or disturbance and in which man, as listener, strives to be included. The purpose of music is to entice man into its circle of perfection and to bring about the same order and harmony in man's perception of his own existence. Music is seen as a kind of godhead towards which man strives – in much the same way as the mystic strives for union with God. This aspect is clear in the vocabulary and emotional undercurrents of the poem, which has reminiscences of Fray Luis de León and San Juan de la Cruz in both language and content.

Part of the power of music as a communicating and ordering force lies in its use as a means of communication before the advent of language. Music was used to convey the simplest emotions and as an accompaniment to the tasks of daily life. If such comparisons can be drawn with phenomena far in the past, so too can they be drawn with a poet much nearer our own time. Stéphane Mallarmé longed for a poetry as precise and communicatively accurate as music. Clearly this is impossible, for words and musical notes are distinct technical devices, and the ear and brain respond differently to them. What Guillén succeeds in doing, however, is to employ words and phrases which can be used for both musical and verbal interpretation.

Because of this, there are certain words in the poem which have double meanings. "Tiempo" means both time and tempo, "alma" (soul) implies both the rhythm of the music and the attentiveness of the listener, and the circle of harmony is the one provided by the music itself and also by the listeners responding to it. The memory of the listener enables him to recognize from earlier sections a repeated phrase or musical leitmotif which is itself a reminder of the unifying purpose it serves within the piece of music. The human composer and listener, who between them have made music a reality, are a parallel to the music itself, significantly described as a *"superhuman exemplum"* (my italics).

The first three stanzas of the poem trace the relationship of listener and music. Music is seen as a force which divides time resonantly to create a world of sounds and rhythms which communicate a coherent unity. The listener breathes the same air that carries the music. His silent cerebral and emotional response includes him totally in the world of music:

> Un mundo
> Donde yo llego a respirar con todos
> Mis silencios acordes. (189/8-10)

The verbs of stanzas 1-2 indicate the control of music and composer over listener and, as frequently happens with Guillén, they occur in threes, thereby clarifying and emphasizing the strength of the action taking place:

> Se levanta un mundo
> Que vale, se me impone, me subjuga (189/2-3)

> ¿Qué dice, qué propone?
> Se propone, se muestra,
> Se identifica a su absoluto ser. (189/17-19)

Having set the scene, where music is the controlling force, and having clearly indicated that the listener's role is that of submission, listening and participating in the music ("Sumiso ... Escucho ... Convivo" [Submissive ... I listen ... I coexist]), Guillén goes on to show, in stanza 3, that this domination is brought about by a series of sounds which one would not normally associate with concepts of power and control:

> Todo el ser en fluencia,
> De sonido a intervalo situado.
> Y todo se desliza,
> Coexiste seguro, deleitable,
> —¡Qué espera, qué tensión, qué altura ya! (189-90/22-26)

The protagonist's role gradually increases from that of attentive listener to one who through his memory actually participates in the creation of a harmonious structure:

> Mientras en la memoria permanece,

> Confín de mi placer,
> Una totalidad de monumento.[8]   (190/27-29)

"Memory", "soul" and "perception" can be seen as steadfast definers for the protagonist. What is brought into play now is the listener's "spirit", the inner, participating psyche which was preceded by "perception" and "soul" and which is now stronger and more acute. The listener experiences a feeling of renewal because he has entered into the circle of harmony proffered to him by the earlier sounds:

> Escucha un hombre sin querer ya nuevo,
> Ya interior a ese coto de armonía
> Que envuelve como el aire:
> Con mi vivir se funde.   (190/35-38)

Music has regenerative powers in the same way as air: it surrounds his spirit and reveals harmony, just as air surrounds man and reveals physiological harmony, and, of course, air is the carrier of music. Thus it fuses with the listener's existence in a threefold sense. The implications of this tripartite activity prompt the protagonist to question the very grandeur of what has happened:

> ¿Ahora seré yo,
> Yo mismo a mi nivel,
> Quien vive con el puro firmamento?   (190/40-42)

We can still understand the concepts which led early philosophers to believe that music represented the harmony of the spheres of the universe, but the question seems to indicate a sense of amazement that man can actually share in such harmony. In this case, no answer is given, neither is a particularly emphatic one implied. The next three lines, however, indicate the position taken up by the protagonist:

> Me perteneces, música,
> Dechado sobrehumano
> Que un hombre entrega al hombre.   (190/43-45)

The force of the phrase "Me perteneces" (You belong to me) is an indication of the seriousness of this claim, given that the music here is being listened to and is unlikely to be perceived in a form sufficiently concrete to be really possessed. Music belongs to this protagonist not

---

[8] The line "Mientras en la memoria permanece," is missing from the Barral edition of *Cántico*.

simply because a human composer has offered it, through players, to a human listener. Music is an example of something superhuman, in its perfection of form and harmony. If man is capable of creating perfection in music, is he not also capable of making harmony in other aspects of his life? The optimism implied by this question is to be found expressed in stanza 10:

> ¡Oh música del hombre y más que el hombre,
> Último desenlace
> De la audaz esperanza!   (193/119-21)

There is still, however, the significance of the phrase "Me perteneces" to be considered and Guillén leaves this until stanza 8. In between he considers in greater detail the inviolate perfection of the music's harmony in philosophical terms (stanza 5). In stanza 6 we have the actual setting where the protagonist's perception is mellowed, because of music, to the point where everything – the afternoon, fellow listeners and room – seem to provide an additional and more physical harmony.

The last line of stanza 4, "Que un hombre entrega al hombre" (which a man offers up to man), implies the creation of a circle of giving and receiving, or composing/performing and listening. Stanza 5 goes on to define this as

> Orbe en manos y en mente
> De hacedor que del todo lo realiza.   (190-91/49-50)

Composer, performer and listener all become the "maker", bringing about a supreme reality which is music, unfolding both aurally and visually a complete world into which all participators are gathered:

> Es el despliegue mismo
> —Oíd— de un firmamento
> —Lo veis— que nos recoge.   (191/53-55)

The order of the verbs is important here. Man's voluntary act of listening is nevertheless vital for the music's message to be successful, hence the imperative. Once attention is given it leads inevitably to a vision of harmony, both mental and physical, expressed by the indicative verb "Lo veis" (You see it) – an affirmative statement which has an element of the imperative within it.

Stanza 5 ends with the question "Ya ¿dónde estamos?" (Now, where are we?), a question answered directly by stanza 6, which deals with the physical setting that gives rise to the considerations of the whole poem. Stanza 7 begins with a slight variation of the same question:

> ¿Dónde, por dónde estamos?   (191/74)

The appreciation prompted by the imperatives "Oíd" (Hear) and "Lo veis" (You see it) is now moving to a higher plane of awareness, where the emphatic, repetitive nature of the musical figures demands and elicits a response from the listener:

> ¿Qué pide el ritmo?
> No responde su anhelo, no se basta
> Con toda su belleza ineludible,
> Y torna con retorno que suplica,
> Tal vez a mí buscándome.   (191-92/76-80)

In mystic terms, which seem appropriate throughout this poem, the disciple has made himself receptive to the call of the music, and music or godhead replies in kind by gradually revealing itself. This is symbolized by the use of the same word to signify both the emotional receiver and the prompter – listener and music respectively:

> El alma se abalanza a ese compás,
> Que es alma.   (192/81-82)

This mingling of souls leads to the ecstatic exclamation of stanza 8, with its strong overtones of mystical poetry:

> ¡Oh Bien! Y se desnuda.
> Le siento sin ideas, sin visiones,
> Reveladoramente   (192/83-85)

The protagonist's physical senses have ceased to function, and all is revealed through his soul, as is indicated by the sharp contrast between adverb and nouns.

It is this section of the poem which clarifies the sense of the earlier phrase "Me perteneces, música":

> Nada más por contacto
> Con mi naturaleza,
> Que acompasada ahonda en su vivir,
> En su dominio o su melancolía,
> En este ser ahora tan entero,
> Tan firme que es de todos.
> ¡Ninguna confidencia!   (192/86-92)

Communication of listener and music leads to illumination of a metaphysical and spiritual kind, but emphasis is put on the fact that it is through the involvement of the protagonist's own persona. Once in harmony with music he is able to delve into the complete being which the music has revealed itself to be. I believe that the third person possessive pronouns can be interpreted for both protagonist and music at the same time. The listener feels himself to be completed, fulfilled by the music's integrity. The music communicates to all listeners via composer and player so that all men become one in a collective integrity. The listener trusts in the fidelity of the music. The music is fulfilment and offers itself in perfection of harmony, sound and meaning but without being directed towards one specific listener.

The very nature of music is sound which exists as a coherent whole ("Jamás en soledad" [never in solitude]) and which is generated by a series of repeated notes, phrases, themes ("Sin ruptura de olvido" [without the break of oblivion]). This envelops the listener and makes him aware of a greater totality in which his individuality is minimal. His is a passive but alert involvement with the greater force. This passivity is clarified by stanza 9, where music is described as power. The subjugation of the listener to it calls forth an impassioned and ecstatic cataloguing of its effects, the response of the listener and the resulting benefits of the shared experience. These are all positive and, significantly, can be related to the protagonist's existence within the world: faith, certainty and joy.

The same depth of passion and ecstasy is maintained in the final two stanzas. The implications of the union of listener and music are succinctly presented in the first line of stanza 10:

> En una gloria aliento. (193/115)

Once again the physical and metaphorical meaning is clear. Man is able to surpass himself in this instance, because it represents human creation raised to the level of the divine.

Music, apprehended as "supreme reality", becomes the "culmination of reality" because of the absolute commitment to it by man, in the guises of composer and listener. Music, though the creation of man, is greater than man because of the power latent within it to bring him to an increased awareness of the harmony possible in life. Thus the final stanza begins with imperatives to music to take man to the edge of awareness and on beyond into the sure knowledge of the order of Life ("ventura" [happiness]), as exemplified by one individual's life ("el día mío" [my daily life]):

> Suena, música, suena,
> Exáltame a la orilla,

> Ráptame al interior
> De la ventura que en el día mío
> Levantas.   (193/122-26)

Man is then able to take a meaningful part in the greater harmony of reality:

> Remontado al concierto
> De esta culminación de realidad,
> Participo también de tu victoria:
> Absoluta armonía en aire humano.   (193/127-30)

As often occurs in the poems of Guillén with an uneven number of stanzas, the central stanza (6) has particular importance both structurally and thematically. Structurally it is the pivotal stanza and thus controls what goes before and after it. Thematically it occurs between the question as to physical setting ("Ya ¿dónde estamos?") and the question as to spiritual awareness ("¿Dónde, por dónde estamos?"). The original point of departure for the poem is the room, the music and the time (an afternoon). But each of these is given further significance:

> Música y suerte: cámara
> De amigos.
> La tarde es el gran ámbito.   (191/58-60)

Immediately a series of harmonies can be deduced – the hearing of music implies good fortune, a room of friends implies the emotional closeness of human beings, and the afternoon holds them all in an invisible circle which forms the outer limits of the whole experience. From these initial harmonies the music is able to take over and control the listener/protagonist who symbolizes all the people there. Music's power is made clear by the constant references to the personality or essence of the music in stanzas 1-3:

> Es así.
> . . . .
> Ha de ser en el aire   (189/5-7)

> Se propone, se muestra,
> Se identifica a su absoluto ser.   (189/18-19)

> Todo el ser en fluencia   (189/22-23)

This contrasts strongly with the repeated use, in stanza 6, of "estar" in relation to the afternoon:[9]

---

[9] "Estar" means "to be" in the sense of temporary state or presence. I have translated it as "to participate" to contrast with the essential or permanent nature of the music's harmony.

> Aliada a través de las vidrieras,
> Profunda,
> Consagrándose a estar,
> Estando,
> Sin oír nos atiende. (191/61-65)

Allied to the fact that the afternoon is not directly involved with the people or music ("Sin oír nos atiende" [without hearing it heeds us]), Guillén seems to be pointing to the fact that the rest of the poem deals with the essence of the experience between human beings listening to something of human creation. Moreover, man's music, which, from the evidence of the poem, is "supreme reality", "glory", "culmination of reality", "absolute harmony", can be seen as something as great as the natural glories of Creation, even though its divine qualities of order and perfection have been wrought by human hands and intellect. The presence of natural things in this stanza provides a secure basis from which the philosophical and spiritual considerations can depart. For this reason, several references are made to the place and the moment in time which were the starting point of the poem. Emphasis is given to the interrelatedness of the room and the external natural world:

> Muy diáfana la atmósfera,
> Arboleda en un fondo de balcones,
> Las ondas del nogal en la penumbra
> De ese mueble, tarima sin crujido,
> Un tono general, acompañante.
> Seguro este presente. (191/68-73)

A microcosm of harmony is created, giving a sense of security in time and place. The stanza appears in brackets, isolated from the rest of the poem yet constituting its very centre. Out of the impermanent and temporal setting where physical and mental sensibility is emphasized grows the everlasting experience of having listened to music where metaphysical and spiritual awareness are used to the full. The implications of this experience in terms of universality are suggested by the question which occurs in the central stanza 6, "¿Tal vez culmina aquí / La final amistad del universo?" (Perhaps ultimate universal brotherhood culminates here?), and the exclamation of stanza 10, "¡Oh música del hombre y más que el hombre, / Último desenlace / De la audaz esperanza!" (Oh music of man, and more than man, the final dénouement of audacious hope!). Stanza 6 could be described as the calm state preceding the musical experience and the question thus stems from an intellectual curiosity aroused by anticipation, heightened by amenable surroundings. The joyous exclamation of stanza 10 is an intellectual conclusion forced from the listener by his ecstatic communion with the essence of the music. That this is a conclusion of lasting significance is implied by the absence of exclamation marks in the final stanza. Momentary ecstasy has been and always will be replaced by the serene knowledge that man can produce and participate in the creation of absolute harmony.

"A vista de hombre"

"A vista de hombre" (In Sight of Man, *C* 222-27) is very similar to "Cara a cara" (Face to Face, *C* 524), begun in Montreal in 1939 and finished in 1943. Though the latter has a gloomy city setting, this is not of primary importance, since the negative aspects described there are referred to collectively as "the general aggressor." In "A vista de hombre" we again have a city setting, again in darkness, but the negative forces here are those of insomnia, as suffered by the protagonist, and the profound sense of isolation which it gives rise to. "Cara a cara", *Cántico*'s last poem, is in the section "Pleno ser" (Complete Being), and therefore lays stress on a protagonist who is confronting and accepting reality in its entirety. "A vista de hombre", the last poem of "Las horas situadas", traces the protagonist's efforts to "see" clearly in mental darkness, to find enlightenment in the night which may then serve as a bulwark against the pressures of the next day, overcoming wintry depression with the spring of illumination.

There are various constants throughout "A vista de hombre" which give the poem structural unity. Solitude characterizes the protagonist at the start of the poem and contrasts sharply with his situation in a hotel room in New York. A hotel is a building dedicated to the housing of many people yet each room can become a barrier to communication with others. The occasional illuminated windows in the huge skyscraper hotel puncture the idea of solid, collective existence which it symbolizes. Solitude here is also that caused by insomnia which leads the protagonist to an awareness both of his loneliness at this particular time, and of that of individuals within the greater concept of mankind, symbolized by the city. It is a solitude which at first causes remorse:

> Ésta es mi soledad. Y me remuerde:
> Soledad de hermano.
> (226/99-100)

This remorse is dwelt upon intellectually until solitude is seen as "restoring", because it has given the protagonist time to come to terms with the world in which he lives:

> Oh mundo, llena mi atención, que alargo
> Sin cesar hacia ti desde esta altura
> Que en noche se encastilla,
> Así jamás oscura.
> (226/114-17)

From this point the protagonist is able to understand that the only real solitude is that provided by sleep, a natural phenomenon necessary for man to replenish his physical and mental strength:

> ¡Única soledad, oh sueño, firme
> Transformación!
> (227/129-30)

Human solitude is an essential part of the state of mankind, seen as both an inclusive and an exclusive crowd:

> ¿Compañía
> Constante,
> Soledad? No se agota
> Cierta presencia, nunca fría.
> ¡Oh muchedumbre, que también es mía,
> Que también yo soy! No, no seré quien se espante,
> Uno entre tantos.
> (225/84-90)

All men experience moments of belonging and moments of alienation, and the latter should never be seen to be stronger or more lasting than the former. Both exist, at one time or another, in every man's experience. This aspect of duality or paradox is repeated throughout this poem, most obviously in the phrase "Soledad de hermano" (Solitude of brotherhood). The winter/spring, black/green, darkness/light, and sleep as "olvido/firme transformación" (forgetfulness/sure transformation) progressions are also clearly articulated and used as images which parallel the experiences of the protagonist. Duality is also to be seen in the latter's awareness of the essential and accidental aspects of the city.

The grandeur or essence of the city is what most impresses the consciousness of the protagonist in section I of the poem. From his vantage point high above the city, he can see the limits of the suburbs, tiny human beings, and vehicles whose headlights illuminate and clash in long cones of light. The city's immense sprawl does not diminish its impact:

> Prometiendo su esencia,
> Simple ya inmensamente,
> Por su tumulto no se desparrama,
> A pormenor reduce su accidente,
> Se ahinca en su destino. ¿Quién no le reverencia?
>
> (222/2-6)

As a physical manifestation of man's ability to create for himself a monument within which to live, the city calls forth admiration. However, Guillén shows this response to be equivocal, by phrasing it in the form of a question and by the inclusion of "su accidente" (the incidental) in the lines quoted. The accidental aspects of city life are also of man's making and are seen to be generally negative or alienating. Passers-by are described as "silent", pavements as "harassed", car lights clashing are referred to as "disputes of lights". Even street lights in distant suburbs paradoxically have the effect of emphasizing darkness at street level, in contrast to the natural darkness of the night sky above them:

> En un fondo de rutas
> Que van lejos, tinieblas hay de bruces.   (222/14-15)

The pavement is the only thing which serves to show up the natural phenomenon of rain by its changing colours and to prove to the protagonist that this is not a blurred vision caused by semi-somnolence. The following lines are an example of the remarkable clarity and succinctness that Guillén achieves so frequently in his poetry:

> ¿Llueve? No se percibe el agua,
> Que sólo se adivina en los morados
> Y los rojos que fragua
> De veras, sin soñar, el pavimento.   (222/16-19)

Once again beams of light are a source of illumination, though described in vocabulary of ominous implications:

> Lo alumbran esos haces enviados
> A templar en la noche su rigor de elemento,
> Las suertes peligrosas de sus dados.   (222/20-22)

Thus, while the essence of the city's grandeur is emphasized in this first section, so too are the "accidental" aspects of it.

These are referred to immediately and in more detail in the second section as "Contradicción, desorden, batahola: / Gentío" (Contradiction, disorder, rumpus: / People), a phrase echoed in section IV, "La confusión, el crimen, el litigio" (Confusion, crime, lawsuits). The idea of masses of human beings thronging the city is contrasted with that of the river, whose connotations of life, clarity and energy are diminished because of the protagonist's distance from it and the darkness of the night, though the essential aspect of the river, its movement, is intuitively sensed. The skyscraper building is described as "audacious", and a sarcastic reference to man's ugly ornamentation of his cities is suggested in the following lines, which clearly evoke in the reader's mind an image of neon-light advertisements set on the top of buildings to announce the latest product:

> Infatigable pulsación aclama
> —Plenitud y perfil
> De luminosa letra—
> La fama
> Del último portento. (223/30-34)

The "latest marvel" is nothing more significant than the latest creation of a consumer-product orientated society, and the strong rhyme of "aclama" and "fama" serves not only to imitate the flashing of the neon sign but also the more sinister aspect of consumer hypnosis by clever marketing techniques. It would even seem that the whole construction of the city is designed to attract the attention not only of humans but also of Nature, for the high buldings tend to funnel wind upwards from the streets and outwards into the night sky.

The effect of darkness on skyscrapers is to lessen their size, clearly visible by day. Nevertheless, illuminated windows also convey the illusion of bulk, though Guillén seems to imply that lights are put on in a pathetic attempt to combat the fears of darkness. The building is described in a striking image which emphasizes the bold thrust upwards of the skyscraper, riddled with pockets of light:

> Y late el muro
> Sólido en su espesura acribillada
> Por claros
> De energía que fuese ya una espada
> Puesta sólo a brillar. (224/51-55)

Words such as "pulsación" (pulses), "late" (beats), "claros de energía" (clear pockets of energy) suggest yet another aspect of the city: its vast consumption of electricity which battles against the natural phenomenon of darkness, in the same way as neon advertisements urge people, even during the night, to buy consumer products.

It becomes clear at the end of this section that the protagonist is at one of these lighted windows. The sense of awe and fear which produced the vocabulary mentioned in these sections describing the city and the implied feebleness of the light's challenge to darkness ("Esa luz de interior / Más escondido bajo su temblor!" [That interior light / more hidden beneath its tremor!]) must be associated with his state of mind:

> ¿Quién la hizo
> Terrible, quién tan bella?   (224/61-62)

"Terrible" and "beautiful" describe the "accidental" and the "essential" aspects of the city. It is the existence of these two concepts together in man's creation, the city, which provides the basis of the poem, just as reality with all its negative and positive aspects is the basis of "Cara a cara". Thus in these two sections Guillén has elaborated the first premise of his poem, that man's creations, epitomized by the city, include both good and bad. One cannot hope to exclude the one by exaltation of the other. Indeed, if one were to do this, imbalance would result and it would be in that most sensitive area of man's being – his intellectual appreciation of what constitutes existence.[10] As in "Cara a cara", so in "A vista de hombre" man must be aware of the dual nature not only of everything he creates, but also of his own self.

Section III begins with the initial effort to confront what the protagonist has become aware of:

> Sálveme la ventana: mi retiro.   (224/64)

The reminders of similar lines in "Cara a cara" and "Una ventana" are clear,[11] but in "A vista de hombre" the window provides a retreat and to some extent a refuge. Initially the window onto the world is a retreat, a secluded place from which to observe, rather than withdraw:

> Bien oteada, junta,
> La población consuela con su impulso de mar.
> (224/65-66)

---

[10] See Guillén's essay "Poesía integral", *Revista Hispánica Moderna*, 31 (1965), 209.

[11] J. Ruiz de Conde mentions the similar lines in the last stanza of section V of "Cara a cara" (*C* 531); see *El cántico americano de Jorge Guillén* (Madrid: Turner, 1973), p.199. It is also necessary to remember the line "Soy como mi ventana. Me maravilla el aire" (I am like my window. The air thrills me.) from "Una ventana" (Window, *C* 155) – significantly not "Soy mi ventana" (I am my window).

The people who exist within the city, for all that they were described as "silent" earlier on, are a consolation because they symbolize an active life-force to which the protagonist belongs, in spite of his present isolation. There are no sombre implications in the use of the phrase "impulso de mar" (sea-like impulse). The sea here has connotations of ceaseless activity; waves constantly moving signify the repeated actions of people in the context of urban life. The point of the protagonist's observation is that he is able to deduce some kind of answer or meaning from what he sees:

> Atónito de nuevo, más admiro
> Cómo todo responde a quien pregunta,
> Cómo entre los azares un azar
> A tientas oportuno sirve a los excelentes.   (224/67-70)

This contrasts strongly with his own situation. Weariness controls his perception of self and surroundings so that the city, "la trama / De tanta esquina y calle" (the configuration of so many corners and streets), is seen as a disorienting force and his being is felt to be "Laborioso, menudo, cotidiano" (laborious, insignificant, ordinary). Life within the city, with its effects of disorientation and mediocrity, has none of the strength attributed earlier to the buildings and makes him feel lost and useless:

> Tan ajeno a mi afán, en lo inútil perdido   (225/75)

The depth of this depression is made clear by the following lines, where, paradoxically, this life is earned for himself by the protagonist:

> Esta vida que gano
> Sin apenas quejido.   (225/76-77)

Yet there is hardly any complaint uttered and a vicious circle of depression – apathy – depression becomes evident.

The protagonist's admiration for the city as a whole in stanza 1 of section III contrasts strongly with the way in which he sees himself within it in stanza 2. However, the window can provide the salvation from insomnia and depression which he asked for at the beginning of stanza 1 if he uses it as his window on and to the world, as is made clear in the last sentence of section III:

> ¿Solución? Me refugio
> *Sin huir* aquí mismo, dentro de este artilugio
> Que me rodea de su olvido.   (225/78-80; my italics)

It is a retreat which paradoxically keeps him in the thick of the life and life-style which distress him. The city and the hotel room are and should be given over to sleep, "forgetfulness". The protagonist's sense of isolation, though great, is thus accepted both on the temporary level, this night's insomnia, and on the more permanent level, the negative aspects of his life which are an essential part of his existence as an urban dweller.

A kind of peace has been achieved, through a steadfast contemplation of the inimical surroundings implied by "artilugio" (contraption) and "olvido" (forgetfulness). The time and place of this nocturnal observation begin section IV, and are symbolized by the vast darkness of night:

> Espacio, noche grande, más espacio.   (225/81)

The place is one of emptiness, shown by the anonymity of his existence in a large hotel and also by the inclusive and exclusive nature of the "crowd", mentioned earlier. Moreover, the protagonist, in this state of mental imbalance, feels distant from that integral being which is of central importance in Guillén's concept of the individual.[12]

The duality which lies at the heart of the poem is then articulated:

> No hay nada accidental que ya me asombre.
> (La esencia siempre me será prodigio.)   (225/91-92)

However, here it is not linked specifically with the city as in sections I and II. The protagonist's faith in "essence" is clear, but this has already been proved by the position taken up in section III, where he "takes refuge without flight right here". The noise and confusion of city life, the momentary depression caused by unsatisfactory personal situations, are not in themselves things to cause surprise or fear. It is the dual existence of both, "terrible" and "beautiful" together, which constitutes an "essence" in which the protagonist can have faith because both aspects together are a source of vitality.

Up to this point in the poem, however, the negative aspect of the protagonist's situation is the one which has received most emphasis, with what might be called a transitional point to be found in the words "Me refugio / Sin huir". The positive aspects of his life are gradually revealed in the rest of the poem and are to be found in the solitude which is one of its major themes.

---

[12] See "Aguardando", "Ser" and "Equilibrio" (*C* 208, 314, and 318 respectively).

The poem is set in darkness and there is rain. The season of Nature is clarified at this point for the specific purpose of providing a parallel with the gradual emergence of the positive to signify not merely the protagonist's life but that of the whole of mankind:

> Es invierno. Desnudos bajo mantos:
> El hombre. (225/93-94)

The shock of finding a singular collective noun after plural qualifiers makes the reader aware of the hermetic structure of the poem. The anonymous and exclusive crowd in the city is a symbol of every individual who, like the protagonist, is subject to the same depression, insecurity and fear, but who, on the evidence of this poem, also has the potential to make of momentary insomnia a time of positive solitude in order to come to terms with himself. However, this is only slowly achieved in the following stanzas, for the nature of the plurality of "man" has first to be clarified. It is, of course, symbolized by the protagonist of the poem. To the imperfections of man's created world are added by man further problems, indicated symbolically by the image of Nature where the mud of winter is made even more foul by further rain:

> ¿Tú? Yo también. Y todos.
> La confusión, el crimen, el litigio.
> ¡Oh lluvias sobre lodos!
> Gentes, más gentes, gentes. (Y los santos.)
> (225/95-98)

The whole of mankind suffers in the degradation of society, and that suffering is brought about principally by alienation, a tragic but well-known concomitant of our collective existence:

> Ésta es mi soledad. Y me remuerde:
> Soledad de hermano. (226/99-100)

Once more Guillén brings the protagonist to the fore as a symbol of mankind. The solitude of insomnia has been developed into a sense of alienation (one wakeful person, surrounded by sleeping, unaware fellow beings), in the very midst of the populace, the city and the hotel. It is interesting to consider here the implications of the description of man as "Naked beneath blankets". Simply interpreted, this is a reference to the sleeping city dwellers, here a symbol of mankind. But Guillén uses "naked", rather than, say, "sleeping". This serves to emphasize the contrast between protagonist and others in a fairly complex way. The protagonist's inability to find sleep prompts his nocturnal observation and musing. Those who have found sleep are not, however, necessarily more fortunate, and their nakedness implies metaphorically that they have no defence against the kind of problems experienced by him. They are covered by blankets, but their sleep is not necessarily that "sure transformation" which the protection of a serene mind can give.

Paradoxically, it is the realization that solitude is an essential part of the human condition which initiates the lightening of the poem's sombre considerations. This is brought about by a reference to the blackness of the night sky gradually giving way to pre-dawn greenness:

> El negror de la noche ahora es verde
> Cerca del cielo, siempre muy cercano.   (226/101-102)

However, Guillén is careful not to move glibly into more positive channels. The coming of dawn means less opportunity for necessary sleep, which can only be achieved when the worries that initially caused insomnia are overcome. A kind of panic ensues. The next day is near, and so too are all the problems of everyday life which will only serve to deepen the protagonist's sense of disorientation and division of self:

> ¡Cuánto cielo, de día, se me pierde
> Si a la ciudad me entrego,
> Y en miles de premuras me divido y trastorno,
> Junto al desasosiego
> De los cables en torno!   (226/103-107)

Obviously, illumination or enlightenment is what is desired and this night's solitude is an opportunity to find it. Considerations of a matter of this importance, the nature of man's loneliness, cannot be rushed. The process of self-enlightenment must take its natural course.

The next stage is characterized by the beginning of the third stanza:

> Soledad, soledad reparadora.   (226/108)

This observation is a direct continuation of the realization reached at the beginning of the previous stanza. The solitary contemplation by the protagonist is rewarded by his awareness that man's loneliness is unavoidable. To that extent, therefore, it has been a profitable time. Even so, the very things which brought about the sense of alienation, not merely insomnia but also the more permanent aspects of inimical human society, are strongly desirable as part of the necessary duality of life. Once again there is no attempt to imply that once certain existential obstacles are overcome they should be consigned to oblivion as though they did not exist and need no longer be confronted:

> Y, sin embargo,
> Hasta en los más tardíos repliegues, a deshora,
> No me descuides, mundo tan amargo
> —Y tan torpe que ignora
> Su maravilla.
>
> (226/109-13)

It is our own world which can provide the wherewithal for both confusion and enlightenment. The protagonist has used his perception and has been able to rise to a spiritual height which carries with it its own fortification and illumination. Therefore his continuing hope is that the world with its positive and negative qualities should continue to prompt that attentiveness into life. The imperatives of the last seven lines, "llena mi atención" (fill my attention) and "Vive en mí" (Live in me), are addressed to the world and city respectively. The city, with its "essence" and "accident", has a living counterpart in the protagonist, who in addition has a wish to respond to its greatness:

> Vive en mí, gran ciudad. ¡Lo eres! Pesa
> Con tus dones ilustres. El alma crece ilesa,
> En sí misma perdura.
>
> (226/118-20)

The essence, "soul", of both protagonist and city remains basically inviolate and provides its own permanence.

The realizations of stanzas 2-3 of section IV mark a move out of the protagonist's sombre and depressed state of mind. The solace of sleep is now possible, for he has discovered that this time of solitude and alienation has served a beneficial purpose. The drama of life will continue but the knowledge that there are times for contemplation and spiritual renewal is sure:

> Vencido está el invierno.
> La fatiga, por fin, ¿no es algo tierno
> Que espera, que reclama
> Sosiego en soledad?
>   Y el drama ...
> Siga en lo oscuro todo.
> Básteme ya lo oscuro de un recodo,
> Repose mi cabeza.
>
> (226-27/121-28)

The parallel with Nature is most fitting. Winter takes over from the weariness of autumn, but life forces, though dormant, are nevertheless still alive, waiting for the light and warmth of spring. The protagonist, too, is now able to achieve his own spring of enlightenment and solace. There is no sense that he is feebly letting go of unsolved problems. The strength of the phrase "Siga . . . todo" (Let all continue) implies knowledge that problems will always exist but that the protagonist has found sufficient peace of mind to let them continue, knowing that they are superable. As the controller of his own peace of mind, he is able to say "Repose mi cabeza" (May my head find repose). Sleep is seen as a benefit granted by a benign angel, rather than withheld by the devil of uncertainty and alienation. Moreover, in lines reminiscent of "Advenimiento", the advent of sleep will serve as a protection against the trials of the next day. "Forgetfulness", instead of symbolizing distant fellow human beings, is now seen as sleep:

> ¿Es fortuna interina,
> Perderé?
>   Ganaré. Creciente olvido
> Negará toda ruina.
> Gran pausa.
>   ¡Cuánto, nuevo!
> Y yo despertaré. No será lo que ha sido.   (227/133-39)

The musical metaphor implied by the words "Gran pausa" (Long pause) shows that sleep is in fact the harbinger of a new day which is about to begin, just as a new phase of music follows after an extended pause in a score.

The importance of a night of contemplation for the protagonist is clarified by the last five lines of the poem:

> (¿Padecerá en su ayer el malherido?)
> Mi existencia habrá hincado sus raíces
> En este ser profundo a quien me debo:
> El que tan confiado, gran dormir, tú bendices.
> Todo, mañana, todo me tenderá su cebo.
>
>   (225/140-44)

The question here carries with it a strongly implied negative which is made clear in the next lines. The effect of the protagonist's contemplation is to strengthen his own being. His existence, in this poem so full of negative attitudes and situations, will be more surely founded because of the spiritual strength which has been tried and has triumphed. His negative characteristics have been balanced by his "essence" and the power of this united self is called "this profound being". The new person thus established has earned his rest, given as a gift and as a blessing by the angel of sleep. The future verbs of this section strengthen the claims being made, which are that the protagonist will be offered in future life all the various incentives, both positive and negative, of existence:

<blockquote>Todo, mañana, todo me tenderá su cebo.</blockquote>

"Luz natal"

"Luz natal" (Native Light, *C* 348-60) is one of the longest poems in *Cántico*, written in seven- and eleven-syllable lines and six sections, with a varying number of stanzas within each section. Like "El diálogo", it has as its setting the hills outside Valladolid.

The setting of section I is clearly Spain. References to the Hill of St. Christopher and Castile demonstrate this, of course, but various lines and phrases establish a more complex series of relationships. Firstly, one could assume that Spain and Jorge Guillén are the main protagonists, but as so often there are universal implications. The poem begins by establishing the vastness of the landscape. The clarity of light is so great that the horizon seems distant and the plain endless. This breadth of vision in the physical setting so far established becomes the hallmark of the whole poem. The grandeur of the landscape, with the Hill of St. Christopher rising out of it, is emphasized. So, too, the absence of human beings is implied by the "Never ploughed peaks", and the landscape is seen as "A piece of universe". Nevertheless, its durability is described in terms of human attributes, and an immediate comparison is thus invited between the eternal durability of the natural landscape and some aspect, as yet unspecified, of human durability.[13] This comparison is continued in the next stanza, for the hill, symbolized by the word "planet", is referred to for the first time by name, a name which has been bestowed by human beings. The perspective has narrowed from the vastness of the landscape to the single hill, and from the presence of unpopulated hills to that of a single protagonist whose first

---

[13] One can note here an echo of the anthropomorphized landscape in Antonio Machado's "A orillas del Duero" and other poems of *Campos de Castilla*, in *Poesías completas*, 12th ed. (Madrid: Espasa-Calpe, 1969), pp.76-166.

appearance in the poem is as an insignificant human being, his perception enhanced by the natural elements of stone and light around him.

The universality of the landscape has been catalogued, and out of the awareness of a specific hill and a single protagonist comes a more universal perception of that person's existence:

> ¡Oh luz del universo,
> Para mí tan natal
> En alegría de revelación
> Henchidamente!   (348-49/21-24)

Amazement at this discovery, implied by the exclamation marks, is replaced by a calm appraisal of what this means for him. While the light and air of the world are the sources of his existence, the light of Castile makes him Spanish. This is his "destiny", though one which is described in general terms common to all human beings:

> Luz de esta Castilla
> Me impone mi destino:
> Ser ahora y vivir
> Dentro de este retorno del minuto
> Que a respirar me fuerza
> Frente a un mundo que tanto me define.   (349/25-30)

Just as waking up in "Más allá" is described as finding oneself in the centre of objects which are boundaries for one's own self-appraisal,[14] so existence here is seen as controlled by laws. These are not laws which the protagonist is abjectly forced to obey but which he submits to with joy because he himself carries them out actively by living. They are laws that imply a finite existence, a "limit", which nevertheless has an element of grandeur:

> Persistiendo en mi ley
> Gozo determinándome,
> Preciso ante un confín
> De criatura alzada
> Sobre su propia cima: criatura
> De las generaciones.   (349/31-36)

In the same way as the vastness of space is reduced to a single hill, so the vastness of time is exemplified in the single individual's own minute-by-minute existence through respiration. Two "peaks" have

---

[14] "Mientras van presentándose / Todas las consistencias / Que al disponerse en cosas / Me limitan, me centran!" (*C* 26) (While I am presented with / All the realities which, / On becoming objects, / Limit me, centralize me!)

been established: a topographical one whose immortality is described with human attributes, and a human one, a protagonist who is the present representative of his family line and who stands in a similar relationship to mankind as a whole. The aspect of human durability mentioned earlier can now be seen to be the existence of generations of human beings represented by this single protagonist.

Section II is a historical perspective in broadly universal terms and continues the idea of generations with which section I concluded. They are described in an image of Nature, and the components which make up the image, river and woods, both give an impression of teeming life and vitality. There are no Manriquean overtones in Guillén's use of rivers to symbolize many lives, as is made clear by "Corren hasta perderse, / Nuevas" ([They] run till they are lost, / Renewed). The rivers of blood have no sombre connotations since they are associated with the words "nuevas" (renewed) and "incesante selva" (incessant wood). No word has implications of weakening or death; on the contrary, proliferation is implied: "sin final" (unending), "cruces" (crossroads), "una red que se intrinca" (a network which is intricate). The point of this ceaseless activity is questioned, "¿Desde dónde hacia dónde?" (Whence and whither?), and this would seem to imply that the potential of human life is beyond the finite scope of human perception: origins and end are known only through the example of others, and, moreover, individual beginnings and ends are engulfed in the greater reality of generations.

Generations are also seen as "eternity" as well as infinite proliferation. Finite human time, mortality, even Time itself, are subsumed within the greater everlasting power of Eternity, which is again envisaged in terms of an image of Nature, in the repeated idea of rivers:

> Eternidad de ríos estivales
> Que son un río solo como el mar. (350/51-52)

Rivers in full spate are another kind of absolute, as are the generations already mentioned, and as is Eternity *vis-à-vis* Time. Eternity is thus paralleled by generations who have existed over the years and who are seen as a symbol of greatness of similar magnitude to that of Eternity. The question which begins stanza 3 indicates that the parallel "single river/sea" is slightly equivocal, for its exact nature has to be clarified:

¿O más que el mar? Trascurre, se trasmite,
Más feroz que en su máscara de muerte,
Vida a estilo de vida.[15]   (350/53-55)

Once again connotations of death are carefully kept to a minimum by
the sense of the overriding vitality of life. "Vida a estilo de vida" (Life
in the manner of life) remains as an echo in the following lines, where
the way in which lives succeed lives is sharply emphasized:

Generaciones de generaciones,
Jardines sobre lechos,
¡Cuánto nacer innúmero hacia el sol!   (350/56-58)

The broad historical perspective of these first three stanzas of
section II narrows down to the appearance of the protagonist, once
again a living symbol of all who have gone before:

Y entre las criaturas,
Una vez ... Ah, yo. ¿Yo?   (350/59-60)

With greater concision Guillén indicates, by the progression from the
dots to the exclamation, declaration and final question, that this
protagonist, in addition to being a "peak", is one who stops to
question the exact nature of himself as a single entity. He is not a
solitary and self-sufficient individual but one who is dependent on
reality in both its past and present manifestations. He is adjusted to
his own limitations which, as in "Más allá", do not negatively
circumscribe his existence. One limitation is that of being mortal;
another is that of existence in a world not of his choice. However, the
positive nature of human limitations is indicated by his expression of
thanks:

Yo ajustado a mis límites:
El ser que aquí yo soy, sobre esta cumbre,
Bajo este firmamento
No escogido por mí.
¡Gracias!   (350/61-65)

The kind of existence suggested by this stanza is the essential one
which all human beings possess and which is frequently referred to in

---

[15] Compare the final line of "Nivel del río" (*C* 302). There is also an interesting
parallel with the compulsive life of the new-born child; see "El infante" (II, 7): "Luz de
carne, sonrisa corporal, / Suavísimos chispazos de una gracia / Con fuerza de misterio
sin final: / Vivir que sólo en más vivir se sacia." (*C* 387) (Light of the flesh, corporeal
smile, / Exquisite sparks of a grace / Which has the force of endless mystery: / Life
which is only satiated in more life.)

other poems of *Cántico*. Another kind of existence is implied in the following lines, a temporal existence which is handed down to the protagonist by generations of forebears and is seen as a gift from many unspecified people. He gives thanks for life, but to have a world in which to take part, to be a symbol of the generations of mankind, is a further gift to one who, literally, was "nothing and nobody" till being, life and language were bestowed by previous ancestors:

> Regalo para quien
> ¡Ah! nada merecía,
> No era nada ni nadie.
> Os debo a ti y a ti
> Mi don de ser a gusto
> Por entre tantos seres,
> Mis frases impelidas
> Por palabras que son de vuestras bocas.
>
> (350-51/67-74)

Thus, having reduced the perspective in these first stanzas of the poem, Guillén goes on to broaden it again until he arrives at his particular country – Spain.

That the protagonist and all men are composite beings is illustrated concisely in the next two lines. Ancestors are a source of glory and pride, the individual has the liberty or potential to make of life and himself what he will, and also the support and solidarity provided by forebears and specific nationality. The rest of this section considers the importance of the individual's past, specifically that represented by his ancestors, symbolized by the single subject pronoun "you" which indicates male forebears, those responsible for the continuation of mankind.[16] The symbolic ancestor is given attributes of still-lasting activity, as seen in the words "encendiste" (you lit), "energía" (energy), "Sin cesar" (ceaselessly). The recurring image of the river links with earlier lines:

> Sin cesar navegando en la corriente
> Sin principio ni término.
>
> (351/84-85)

Both essential and existential aspects of life are felt by each individual, the former in his thanks for the gift of life and the latter in the positive way in which he accepts the duties of work and parenthood. There are strong links here with the specific life and

---

[16] There is a comparison in Guillén's own family tree, for he was descended by direct male line from Jorge Guillén, b. 1502. See Joaquín Caro Romero, *Jorge Guillén* (Madrid: Epesa, 1974), pp.109-10.

work of the poet Jorge Guillén. "Tú encendiste la chispa suficiente" (You lit the sufficient spark) foreshadows the dedication to his father in *Y otros poemas*. In "Luz natal" the "spark of life" confirms Guillén in his role as poet and father, and all men in their own roles of worker and parent.[17]

If in stanza 8 forebears actively encourage the protagonist in his professional and personal life, in stanza 9 they are seen to represent a bulwark between life, "nuestra dicha" (our happiness), and adversity ("ese mundo / Terrible" [this terrible world]). Ancestors are known people who, though physically gone, are yet remembered and have influenced many later generations.[18] Like the protagonist of the present *Cántico*, the generic ancestor, referred to by the singular pronoun "you" and as "padre" (father) and "varón generoso" (noble man), has the same spirit to fight in the supreme game of life:

> Luchador de una lucha
> Que fuera sumo juego   (351/91-92)

There is also a very strong reminiscence of Michelangelo's *Creation of Adam*:

> Me aguardaba la tierra con el cielo
> Bajo tu poderío,
> Mano tendida hacia la criatura
> Nueva aún, expectante.   (352/96-99)

The change to the plural form of the pronoun "you" in the final two lines, connected with the first use of the word "Spain", would seem to suggest that the poem is moving towards a more specific consideration of one nation and its implications for a protagonist whose nationality is both particular and universal:

> Entre el destino y vuestro amor surgía
> —¡Oh supremo caudal aquí!— España.   (352/100-101)

However, "aquí" (here) is used to bring the past time of previous generations into the present, because life ("vuestro amor" [your love]) and destiny (of ancestors) have had a hand in the making of Spain and its present inhabitants.

Sections I and II of "Luz natal" have contained obvious references to Spain, and clear references to Guillén himself in the

---

[17] The ideas contained in the lines "el ansia hasta la obra / El amor hasta el hijo" (anxiety for my work / Love for my child) from "Luz natal" are elaborated in "Vida extrema" and "Más vida" respectively.

[18] Compare poem 34 in *Reviviscencias* (*OP* 507).

poem have been suggested. However, the universal connotations of the poem cannot be ignored. Section III contains the same kind of duality for, though one might expect Spain to be considered more specifically in view of the developments up to the end of section II, a wider sphere of reference is this time linked to language, and to man's various ways of expressing himself and his attitude to reality.

The world is made up of different nationalities but certain characteristics are always present. These are expressed, in stanza 1, through "alma" (soul), "espíritu" (spirit), "porte" (bearing) and "Esa inflexión —tan única— de voz" (that inflection – so unique – of the voice). Though different people speak different languages, what is supremely significant is:

Y la palabra. ¡Nuestra, la palabra!   (352/108)

This line is carefully separated from stanzas 1 and 3 and celebrates not simply the human voice, but the human's ability to make words which have meanings and communicative value. All the aspects mentioned so far make up life:

Vida común irreductible a idea   (352/109)

Language and life, though created over the centuries by many ancestors, nevertheless form an integral whole which cannot be encompassed in a single image or idea. No one person can define something into which so much has been instilled, except perhaps by the word "reality". This word, however, implies objects both organic and inorganic, animate and inanimate, and also the human being's ability to appreciate reality mentally, to have objective knowledge of it. In addition, reality is multifaceted, as is seen in the complex image of "air":

Entre muros y torres ved el aire:
Un aire de afluencias matutinas
Que también será ardor
Hasta por las penumbras y las sombras.   (353/116-19)

Air is a medium for sunlight and, because the latter belongs to a diurnal process, itself implies time, by which our days are measured. Sunlight also suggests heat, so that our day-to-day existence and the "spark of life" transmitted through generations of mankind are both implied in the coherence of these parallel images. Once again man is seen in terms of fire and also of its lifeless form, ashes. This fifth stanza takes the form of two questions which are serious attempts to put human life into perspective. How can something as mobile and vigorous as human life be imprisoned in mortality? Can man easily be resigned to death? What of mind and spirit – is that also to be consigned to dust? Will that "sufficient spark", which initiated so much, finally go out? All these questions could be contained in the formalized version of ancestry – History. But the protagonist implies, and here provides an answer to those questions, that history is only real insofar as it is in his living body – his life, actions, breathing, speech.

The sense of these two stanzas is recapitulated in stanza 7, again in the form of questions which are, even so, an answer:

> ¿Amarillentas ruinas?
> ¿Y el impulso que llega de vosotros,
> Los vivientes aún
> En esta pulsación que marcha sola
> Sin mí, tan mía, yo?   (353/128-32)

The concision of these lines is remarkable. The first question can be paraphrased: can we really consign reality in all its guises to senility and decay? The implied negative answer comes in the next question. The vital impulse which comes from ancestors is threefold. It is a "pulsación" (pulse) which is greater than the individual ("Sin mí" [Without me]), is nevertheless part of him ("tan mía" [so much mine]), and is expressed symbolically by the living individual ("yo" [me]). While stanza 7 ends with "yo" in a question format, stanza 8 begins with "yo" in an affirmative statement. There are no main verbs here, so that the pronoun implies all actions, both verbal and physical. The stanza starts with a reference which puts language on the same level as the history of mankind:

> Yo, bajo mis vocablos
> Resonantes de rutas   (353/133-34)

For it implies the past (development of language), the present (different languages according to nationality) and the future (where the individual's power to communicate may yet take him). Each individual inherits language and the liberty to pursue his own life in conjunction with others:

> A través de mi propia libertad
> Hacia lo todavía no existente,
> Hacia las tardes de una luz que espera,
> De un matiz que no vive nunca solo.
> ¿Habrá de ser mi mano

> Quien tal vez os colore,
> Trémulas tardes indeterminadas?[19]   (353-54/135-41)

His potential contribution to life is seen in a painting metaphor in the last three lines, which continues the idea previously suggested by "matiz" (hue).

Stanza 9 is a final statement for which the previous stanzas have provided a detailed illustration:

> Algo fue que es futuro:
> Incógnita filial,
> Juventud que no cesa.
> ¡Oh patria, nombre exacto
> De nuestra voluntad, de nuestro amor!   (354/142-46)

The essence of previous generations is an unknown quality which is described as "filial" and further clarified as unceasing youth, that youth symbolized by living individuals.

This section has confined itself to a consideration of the implications of language, reality, history and mortality for the individual. It ends with a widening perspective where all living individuals are seen as potential for future life. All these aspects are contained within the concept of "native land", where "will" implies the procreative instinct of past generations and "love" the present impulse to life.

The mention of the continuous undulating land at the beginning of section IV is a brief reminder that this poem has a physical, geographical setting. However, the second line goes on to clarify that the vision implied is that of a whole planet which is the fatherland for all men. Men of science have shown us that the world is round and constantly in motion. Men of letters, here Guillén, also show us that it is a unity of different lands and common anxieties. Section IV deals, therefore, with the social consequences which result from the existence of generations of men. The sphere of the world is an example of perfection for man to make use of. Physical and visual perfection exists in the world and man has the potential to recreate this perfection for himself. What follows in the subsequent stanzas

---

[19] Macrí, p.277, interprets the line "Habrá de ser mi mano ..." as referring to Jorge Guillén. I wrote to Don Jorge on this question of the "I" in *Cántico*, my term for it being the generic individual. His reply, in a letter dated 17 December 1979, confirms this: "El 'yo' protagonista – 'el hombre general', tiene usted razón – es el mismo de siempre en ese tomo /YOP/ y en el último – casi terminado: *Final*." (The 'I' protagonist – 'generic man', you are correct – is the same as always in this volume /YOP/ and in the last – almost completed: *Final*.) See also A.P. Debicki, *La poesía de Jorge Guillén* (Madrid: Gredos, 1973), pp.228-55.

shows that he can also destroy and negate his potential to create positively:

> Completa redondez
> Para nuestras dos manos.
> Pilas, moles, derrumbes
> Y polvo, polvo, polvo
> Si no el tizón y el humo.   (354/153-57)

It is also suggested that man's use of the earth as a habitat is purely accidental, that the earth is merely there to provide a solid basis for the water which covers two thirds of its surface. Various types of water are envisaged, ranging from the small quantity in a cistern or tank, through the surfaces of water disturbed by rain, to the saline expanses of our huge interconnected seas. The earth is thus a combination of natural phenomena and man-made structures. Upon its surface is man, in various continents, habitats and terrains, but always characterized by

> El sí, el no del animal que elige,
> Que ya se elige humano,
> Tan capaz de ser hombre.   (355/167-69)

These lines are another example of Guillén's ability to refine, in a densely structured metaphor, a complex series of relationships. "Yes" is man's negation, as a rational animal, of animality; it represents his positive decision to promote his *homo sapiens* nature. Man is the animal who accepts, with responsibility, that ratiocinative capacity which makes him the highest form of animal life. Once one makes a choice one has indicated, *ab initio*, one's potential ability to fulfil it. The *ab initio* qualification is necessary, however, for it is equally possible to distort and make mistakes:

> Es él también aquél, ya sobre tablas
> De fiesta y prepotencia.
> Mirad su catadura.   (355/170-72)

The "other one" is the individual who can become anti-human, and who is subsequently and logically portrayed in animal terms as a bull (power) and a lion (ferocity). This person is the tyrant/dictator phenomenon, particularly familiar in the twentieth century. The initial impression that he makes is, of course, good, otherwise he would never achieve power and control. Tragically, it is voice and language that he uses to sway listeners who will become followers. Guillén exploits the similarities of human and animal physiology to show how the evil side of such a person is not seen until it is too late. The smile which shows teeth and mouth and implies pleasant, credible words, changes. In animal terms it becomes a snarl, which shows the same mouth and teeth as weapons of destruction.[20] Moreover, the change from "Voz de halago" (enchanting voice) to "Airada contra el aire" (raging against the air) indicates that this dictator acts against the very source of life itself. What follows is inevitable:

> Escándalo, poder, pelea, crimen   (355/181)

Men are duped and stultified until they cease to be men and become "una abstracción con lujo de uniforme" (an abstraction disguised by a uniform). They become a crowd surrounding their leader who is, in fact, their natural enemy. Again, what follows is inevitable:

> Razones y razones, muertos, muertos.
> ¡Cómo pulula el incidente humano!   (355/184-85)

Once again both negative and positive aspects are seen together in "the human moment", where the word "moment" seems to imply strongly the ephemeral nature of these events when viewed in broader terms. History can never isolate misdeeds so that they may never occur again. Neither, fortunately, do good deeds cease to occur. Man will always be a unity of good and evil:

> No hay soledad de Historia.
> ¿Apartadizos? Juntos.
> ¡Compañía terrible,
> Dulce y consoladora compañía!   (356/186-89)

Having looked objectively at man, with no attempt to hide his evil side, Guillén goes on to pick out his supreme attributes – speech and the ability to hear it:

> Oíd: un hombre al habla.
> Manifiesto el espíritu.
> Es el habla común:
> Amorosa invasión de claridad.   (356/190-93)

The essence of language is that words have meaning which is discernible. One is forced to ask what distinguishes this stanza, which is an exaltation of language, from stanza 5, where language was the

[20] Guillén also uses the tiger and bull in "Cara a cara" and the bull in "El acorde" (*Harmony*, CL 15-19) as representatives of powerful and disorienting forces.

tool of the dictator. Here, however, Guillén is celebrating the gifts of speech and reason which alone distinguish us from animals, but *before* they are debased to become an instrument for political or aggressive manipulation.

In section V one can interpret various stanzas as having a specifically Spanish connotation. Spain is described as "native grace", but nevertheless part of the precisely spinning planet, the world. Stanza 2 is a delightful description of the clarity of Spanish light, which illuminates everything to such an extent that the protagonist feels he belongs there. Thus place contributes to being and nationality:

> Aquí soy consistencia de este valle   (356/203)

Here Guillén chooses things specific to the Castilian plain: "chopo" (poplar), "llanura" (plain), "Calor aún de viento" (still warm wind), "espigas" (corn ears). The heart lovingly gathers these visions into a treasure which is not simply an object but a living part of this human being. He recalls not only the cosmetic beauty of Nature – the flora and fauna which are eternally renewed – but also the fierce durability of Nature's harshness. Furthermore, in the question which follows, he is clearly aware of rather more substantial links between himself and the landscape. The rocks which have prompted him into awareness of nature's permanence are what he feels to be an "arcane call" which for him is something positive and helpful. He is conscious that his own skeleton can be equated with the rocks which give contour and shape to the natural world.

Stanzas 1-5 have traced the present effects of the place on the protagonist. The clarity and sounds of the present morning evoke the protagonist's own memory – that is to say, his recollections of his own time – whereas the rest of the poem has looked at a time scale beyond that of individuals. There is a sense of serenity here. Memory holds within it negative recollections, such as knowledge of crises, political stupidity, civil war; but there is a sense also that the protagonist's silent observation, even if slightly unwilling or "reticent", has nevertheless remained truthful and objective. Serenity is possible now, for mortality and nationality have been securely placed within the greater concepts of human durability (generations) and the universe:

> Sonando, despejándose,
> Ya la profundidad de la mañana
> Me conduce otra vez a mi memoria.

> Os rendisteis, mirada con silencio,
> Reticencia en repliegue que no oculta. (357/217-21)

What he sees in his memory prompts a question. What if strife, clearly seen as of man's making ("civil abismo"[civil ruin]), were all that were left to us? He is able to respond, with by now characteristic serenity, that whatever may be the adversities and chaos created by man, they will be perpetrated within the natural, lasting world of Creation:

> Abismo, sí, tal vez, de sol viviente. (357/224)

Why does he respond in such a way? Is it duty which impels him? The true source of his positive response is not, in fact, duty, but instinct, love, childhood links with one's home, the maturity and objectiveness of adulthood – all these call forth loyalty to the earth. Here "Earth" neatly straddles the Spain/World duality. His loyalty stems from nationality, but is given to the earth itself. This idea is repeated later in stanza 12:

> Confío mi esperanza a este planeta
> —En su presente forma de terruño. (358/253-54)

There are times when depression, problems and crises affect all men, but the overriding source of comfort is that the earth never ceases to exist – in all its positive and negative aspects. The world exists for the benefit of the protagonist who, nevertheless, does not take it for granted but rather participates in it, thereby helping to create the very thing which is a source of strength in which he can believe:

> Tú sólo existes, áspera, risueña,
> Para mi amor, para mi voluntad,
> Para creer creándote. (358/234-36)

Once again, "creándote" (by creating you) can be interpreted as a reference to Guillén the poet, but it also has a much wider implication, that of the reciprocation of man and Creation which is apparent throughout *Cántico*. This is reinforced by the next two lines:

> ¿Destino? No hay destino
> Cifrado en claves sabias. (358/237-38)

An individual's destiny cannot neatly be defined in a few words from some absolute source. Man's destiny is very simple, and yet very complex – and made by himself. It is to believe in a world by creating it, by being and living actively and positively within it.

The question of destiny has arisen naturally out of the process which establishes the earth as an eternal force and the position of transient man within it. The lack of an "encoded destiny" may constitute a problem, but Guillén shows in stanza 11 for whom and why this may be so. It is only a problem for "the inert", one who has no sense of active participation to raise him to the level of the ordinary hero who lives responsibly and actively. The former is only able to prophesy that destiny holds us all in thrall, to see an apocalyptic vision whose very negativity implies cowardice. The real problem is thus a multiple one – not destiny but rather something symbolized by those who respond fearfully to it:

> Problema, no, problemas
> Limpios de lagrimada vaguedad.   (358/243-44)

Moreover, the problems of destiny, existence, fate, man's purpose in the world, have been subjected to frequent and intense consideration, without it being seen that they have all been cleansed of their difficulties in the very process. All that we have is life, to be lived in conjunction with Creation and hope. The protagonist's response to this is a bold imperative. Let those who are blind to hope bury only the dead, but never hope itself, which exists beyond the confines of their mortal misery:

> Que los muertos entierren a sus muertos,
> Jamás a la esperanza.   (358/245-46)

Hope exists because life exists and will continue as long as humans do:

> Es mía, será vuestra,
> Aquí, generaciones.   (358/247-48)

The reference to "generations" recalls that parallel made between geological and genealogical durability in section I and echoed in the following lines:

> ¡Cuántas, y juveniles,
> Pisarán esta cumbre que yo piso!   (358/249-50)

Stanza 12 goes on to show clearly what kind of hope is being suggested. It is that which belongs, paradoxically, to mortality, which is not negative for Guillén. The choice of words is important here:

> Esperanza agarrada a la cautiva
> Sucesión: a través del tiempo, tiempo.   (358/251-52)

Time will always exist undamaged. Mankind ("sucesión"), though mortal ("cautiva"), will continue because of the lasting nature of generations already alluded to. The force of "sucesión" is pointed up by its adjective, from which it is carefully separated according to the demands of both metre and sense.

In the last four lines of section V, Guillén makes effective use once again of the word "aquí" (here), employed twice in different contexts:

> A pleno acorde aquí
> Todo mi ser apunta.
>
> Aquí, tan verde el agua hacia más agua,
> Siempre hacia su futuro, su infinito.   (358-59/255-58)

The first "here" is a reference to the world that the protagonist knows in his own mortal life. The second is not so much a reference to physical place as to spiritual and metaphysical awareness. This water is the life of mankind which flows onward to the future. It is not hedged about and diminished by mortality, as in a single individual's life, but is an infinite source: man begets man.

The importance of one's native land for the individual has been considered in section V of the poem, though it is always seen in the greater context of the "planet". The concept "native grace: Spain" is continued in the last section and the references to landscape are once more those of the environs of Valladolid, for the two rivers are the Pisuerga and the Duero. Moreover, there is a sense of "freshness", the physical counterpart to the mental and spiritual refreshment which has been made possible by the philosophical considerations of the poem. Nature is described in positive terms and reciprocation between protagonist and surroundings is suggested by phrases like "Vibración de riberas" (tumult of riverbanks), "cielos ... amigos" (friendly skies), "energía fluida" (flowing energy), "potencia guardada" (preserved power), "Se yerguen" (rise up), "tallos / Que verdean, se afilan" (stems which become green and grow tall). It is acknowledged that this very vitality will inevitably be diminished by winter, but for the moment "¡Primavera irrumpida!" (Spring the invader!) is the overwhelming effect. Clear skies, light and sun are the actual manifestations of Nature which make far-reaching vision possible. Once again "air" is the medium for vision, making the protagonist aware of what he is:

> Y el aire se me ensancha en luz natal,
> En eso que yo soy.   (360/283-84)

"Light of the universe", "light of this Castile" and "native grace: Spain" have been absolutes underpinning the protagonist's self-examination as a member of the human race. Light and air are fundamental to his existence and are symbolized in "native light". Thus the title's significance is explained. "Native" usually signifies something specific to an individual, most commonly in relation to place of origin. Here "native", used to describe light, implies not only nationality but something fundamental to the protagonist's life: air with which to breathe and light to provide physical and mental illumination. The specific is thus merged with the universal.

The Hill of St. Christopher is significant because it provides, in every sense, the starting point of both the poem and the protagonist's conclusions. Natural landscape, a symbol of eternal existence, has provided the protagonist, and by implication all people, with not only some basic guides to existential contemplation, but also the potential for serenity, a potential made real and effective by the development of the poem:

> Eminencia ofrecida como calma
> De nadie para todos,
> Local eternidad.   (360/287-89)

Man is thus able to make use of the world, as was suggested in section IV, in such a way as to make meaningful for himself as an individual the vast concepts of eternity and generations, to find his own "local eternity". The earth, uncontaminated by humans, shows itself to be an unblemished and intrinsic part of his existence:

> Y la tierra caliza
> —Sin surcos acerándose—
> Nos refiere a su término
> Familiar y no hollado,
> Término de planeta nunca antiguo.   (360/290-94)

"Vida extrema"

"Vida extrema" (Extreme Life, *C* 398-405) is written in eleven-syllable quatrains in ABAB full rhyme, disposed symmetrically in three sections of five, thirty-five and five stanzas respectively. It is similar to "Sol en la boda", "Anillo" and "El infante", all of which also comprise eleven-syllable quatrains in ABAB full rhyme.

Mention has frequently been made of the protagonist in these poems. In *El argumento de la obra* Guillén clearly describes the nature of the relationship between the protagonist and Creation:

> *Cántico* supone una relación relativamente equilibrada entre un protagonista sano y libre y un mundo a plomo.   (*AO* 25)

> (*Cántico* assumes there is a relatively balanced relationship between a healthy, free protagonist and a steadfast world.)

This essentially simple relationship is gradually made more complex as the scope and depth of *Cántico*'s vision is increased. In "El diálogo", for example, the protagonist is one of several friends and functions completely only in terms of friendship and dialogue with them. "El concierto" is a descriptive poem, where the effects of music on the protagonist lead to an awareness of the nature of music as man's supreme creation, and of the potential for human harmony that it symbolizes. In "A vista de hombre" and "Luz natal" the protagonist is in the forefront of the poem, but the poems are characterized by his efforts to see himself in a universal context. In "Las cuatro calles" he becomes an observer whose perception enables him to consider the nature of man's collective existence.

The protagonist/poem relationship in "Vida extrema" is very complex, for he is both objective observer, in sections I and III, and active but indirect participant in section II.[21] This complexity is necessary, for the poem deals with a primary action common to all men, that of articulating both individual emotion and the impact of surrounding reality. The protagonist within the action of the poem, that is, in section II, is the passer-by who speaks the following words:

> Porque de veras soy, de veras hablo:
> El aire se armoniza en mi garganta.   (402/95-96)

The poem is best described as a dramatic exposition of the idea that "extreme life" is man's ability to put his experiences into words: poetry (verbal harmony) equals Creation (visible harmony). The poem is "written" by an unidentified observer, most conveniently interpreted as the generic individual, the protagonist of *Cántico*. He

---

[21] Debicki believes that the protagonist of the poem is not the poet but rather an individual first presented objectively and then followed by the "direct presentation of his ideas at the end" (pp.68-69, n.12).

is watching his fellow men, symbolized by "the passer-by" and "another man", both of whom are shown in section I to be attentive and reciprocating, actively aware of selves and surroundings.

The following quotations are vital, as they provide in very concise terms some clues to the motives of the poem:

> Sea la tarea.
> Si del todo vivir, decir del todo.   (399/23-24)

> (Let the task be.
> If one is to live to the full, one must articulate to the full.)

> ¿El hombre es ya su nombre?   (404/145)

> (Is man already his name?)

The first quotation is the basis of the poem. If man lives attentively he must put into words both his emotional receptivity to the world which surrounds him and the reality of that world. This is symbolized by the last words of the poem:

> Gracia de vida extrema, poesía.

> (Grace of extreme life, poetry.)

The question in the second quotation above is provided with an implied "Yes!" by the whole poem. The "name" of man must be "*homo sapiens*", and "*sapiens*" must similarly be interpreted as man's ratiocinative ability which must always be active if he is to fulfil his role as a rational, and therefore superior, animal.

The protagonist/observer of the poem also contributes to the development of its central motif. This is to be seen most clearly in the repeated use of an extended water metaphor, which provides, within the poem, an internal example of the process of making poetry. Metaphor is a process whereby one set of linked words and ideas is used to describe a completely different object or objects for artistic purposes. In "Vida extrema" the sea and nautical vocabulary are used to describe a variety of aspects of one great object – reality. This is first seen in stanzas 3-5 of section I:

> ¿Todo visto? La tarde aún regala
> Su variación: inmensidad de gota.
> Tiembla siempre otro fondo en esa cala
> Que el buzo más diario nunca agota.

> ¡Inextinguible vida! Y el atento
> Sin cesar adentrándose quisiera,

Mientras le envuelve tanto movimiento,
Consumar bien su tarde verdadera.

¡Ay! Tiempo henchido de presente pasa,
Quedará atrás. La calle es fugitiva
Como el tiempo: futura tabla rasa.
¿Irá pasando todo a la deriva?   (398/9-20)

The afternoon symbolizes the entire ambience and its many different
manifestations are likened to drops in a lake or sea: "inmensidad de
gota" (immenseness of one droplet). The potential for man in this
context is endless; man and context are symbolized by "el buzo más
diario" (the most familiar diver) and "esa cala" (this creek)
respectively. Attentive man, both "the passer-by" and "another
man", wants to live life to the full ("*his* afternoon" in the greater
context of "*the* afternoon", or reality). However, individual lives are
subject to the passage of time, hence the question "¿Irá pasando todo
a la deriva?" (Will everything go adrift?), which expresses the fear
that the fullness of the present moment will be lost, if it is not fully
investigated and captured in some more permanent way.

The next metaphor occurs in stanzas 15-16 of section II:

El mar aquel, no un plano azul de mapa,
¡Cuánto oleaje en nuestra voz recobra!

Y es otro mar, es otra espuma nueva
Con un temblor ahora descubierto
Que arrebata al espíritu y le lleva
Por alta mar sin rumbo a fácil puerto.   (401/79-84)

The phrase "El mar aquel" (That sea) is an example of the process of
putting experiences into words. It symbolizes the afternoon, and
therefore represents more than the two-dimensional, visual presentation of the sea on a map. The exclamation continues the
metaphor: waves of additional meaning or significance break in the
mind's eye on hearing one thing described in terms of another. The
known thing, the afternoon or everyday reality, becomes something
more once the possibilities for describing it have been discovered.
This is an exhilarating and elevating experience, though clearly care
in matching one set of terms to another object has to be exercised for
the comparison to be a happy and meaningful one. "Sin rumbo a
fácil puerto" (Without a pathway to an easy port) implies this, and
remains faithful to the original metaphor.

Stanza 21 of section II provides a further extension of the same
metaphor:

> La brisa del follaje suena a espuma:
> Rumor estremecido en movimiento
> De oscilación por ondas. ¡Cuánta suma
> Real aguarda el paso del atento!   (402/101-104)

Here the sound of moving leaves is the "Rumor estremecido" (rustling noise) and the larger vision of groups of leaf-covered branches moving is implied by "en movimiento / De oscilación por ondas" (in oscillating movement through waves).

The final illustration of this far-reaching metaphor occurs in stanza 32 of section II:

> ¿El hombre es ya su nombre? Que la obra
> —Ella— se ahinque y dure todavía
> Creciendo entre virajes de zozobra.
> ¡Con tanta luna en tránsito se alía!   (404/145-48)

Here the interpretation of the question as to whether man fulfils his role is developed further. "La obra" (the work) is a symbol of man's continuous efforts to affirm both self and surroundings, and the hope is expressed that he may continue to do this, in spite of any of the difficulties suggested by the phrase "virajes de zozobra" (tacks and capsizings). The final line refers to the waxing and waning of the tides in conjunction with the phases of the moon. The alliance with time ("luna en tránsito" [moon in passing]) can be paralleled in terms of human creativity. Each literary trend, epoch or generation is a symbol of the continuing but ever-changing creative urge of man.

The different ideas expressed by this extended metaphor are all aspects of reality: general atmosphere, afternoon; the context of individual lives within the greater sphere of human life; the working of intellect and emotions together to produce the exact expression for one particular phenomenon – spring (see section II, stanza 20, which precedes the metaphor of waves/rustling leaves in stanza 21); the wider significance of man's creative effort not only in the past but also in future years.

The reference to the time element in the last example of the poem's extended metaphor is not the only one. It first occurs in the already quoted fifth stanza of section I. This stanza starts with a recognition that present time passes: the street is seen as "soon to be razed". Inevitably present time becomes the past, but one way of keeping it alive is to record it in thought and awareness put into more lasting form – written words –, a process which this poem exalts. Seen in this way, then, the final question of section I ultimately receives a negative reply:

> El orbe a su misterio no domeña.
> Allí está inexpugnable y fabuloso,
> Pero allí resplandece. ¡Cuánta seña
> De rayo nos envía a nuestro foso![22]
>
> El tiempo fugitivo no se escapa.
> Se colmó una conducta. Paz: es obra. (401/73-78)

"The orb" here refers to an idea from the previous stanza where the word "object" is used to describe the result of feelings having been put into words. The success of this is symbolized by "orb", which denotes the circle produced by words which in themselves recreate the initial emotional response. The process itself is described as a mystery but one which nevertheless contains a spark of illumination, the light of meaning which dawns in "the pit" of the mind's darkness. An initial response to something remains fugitive until it is expressed in a more lasting form, when it becomes durable, beyond the destructive power of time.

The idea suggested in the above commentary relating to "fugitive time" is continued in stanza 18:

> Palmaria así, la hora se serena
> Sin negar su ilusión o su amargura. (402/89-90)

Serenity, which is capable of accepting both possible immortality, through creative endeavour, and certain mortality, is one of the rewards for those who strive to fulfil their birthright of *homo sapiens*.

The symbol of man's rational and expressive faculties is the word:

> Palabra que se cierne a salvo y flota,
> Por el aire palabra con volumen
> Donde resurge, siempre albor, su nota
> Mientras los años en su azar se sumen. (402/109-12)

The stanzas which precede and follow stanza 23 quoted above deal with the durability of the word. The idea of mystery is repeated in stanza 22, "magia sustantiva" (substantive magic) and "Inefable el secreto" (inexpressible secret), but again there is no negative connotation. What was earlier implied in the verb "resplandece" (shines forth) is now expressed in the words "Su fondo" (its depth):

---

[22] Compare the final stanza of "Perfección del círculo": "Misteriosamente / Refulge y se cela." (*C* 90) (Mysteriously / It shines forth and conceals itself.)

all words have a meaning which is accessible and which is ultimately capable of comprehension. Words thus have an existence of their own which they retain over the years, irrespective of wordly events. Absolute clarity is the setting for "Vida extrema": the poem begins with the words "Hay mucha luz" (There is much light) and goes on to elaborate the idea of clarity of vision through attention and words. Significantly words are described here, in stanza 23, in terms of light ("Through the air") and their meaning or implications are described as "always new". Stanza 24 goes on to summarize the process of putting feelings into words in such a way as to juxtapose neatly a final action with infinite existence:

> Postrer acción, postrer defensa
> De este existir que a persistir se atreve.   (403/115-16)

"Vida extrema" deals not only with the verbalizing process but also with the phenomenon of the written word which is, of course, the former's most durable form. The written word needs a reader in order to be fulfilled:

> He aquí. Late un ritmo. Se le escucha.
> Ese comienzo en soledad pequeña
> Ni quiere soledad ni aspira a lucha.
> ¡Ah! Con una atención probable sueña.   (403/129-32)

Whoever reads is offering his attention for a time to a particular text and is referred to in consequence as a "good friend", for he provides the final and vital link in the chain which is thoughts – words – text – reader:

> Mejor el buen silencio que consigo
> Resguarda los minutos sin historia.   (403/135-36)

By reading one is joined with another time, that which saw the creation of the text. In stanza 30 the reader is described as having within him the deity who harmonizes his spirit. This "deity" is each individual's capacity as a creator, or rather re-creator, of the text in front of him, freeing words from their dormant state and allowing them to "dawn" again in his mind.

A final reference to time can be seen in stanza 4 of section III:

> Cal de pared. El día está pendiente
> De una suerte que exalte su carrera.
> ¡Algo más, algo más! Y se presiente
> Con mucha fe: será lo que no era.   (405/173-76)

The first two lines remind one of the beginning of the poem:

> Hay mucha luz. La tarde está suspensa
> Del hombre y su posible compañía.   (398/1-2)

Reality is dependent on man's receptivity and his response to it. "His potential companionship" has been shown throughout the poem in the numerous references to the process of mental assimilation and verbalization of the surrounding context. In the stanza quoted above, "luck" can be interpreted as the vital task mentioned in stanza 1 of section II:

> Sea la tarea.
> Si del todo vivir, decir del todo.   (399/23-24)

If this is carried out successfully then reality itself will be exalted. More is required of man than simple existence – reality requires our positive response. The reward of this is that reality will become more than what it was. Man's response to reality, in the form of the written word, will similarly enable him to perceive it in its infinite variety, and his faith in the communicative power of words brings this about.

The overall effect of the time references in this poem has been to show us that words are a source of strength and durability, through which we can come to terms with temporality:

> Eso pide el gran Sí: tesón paciente
> Que no se rinda nunca al No más serio.
> Huelga la vanidad. Correctamente,
> El atentado contra el cementerio.   (404/149-52)

In stanza 18 of section II "ilusión" and "amargura" were interpreted respectively as possible immortality and certain mortality. The following two lines of that stanza can be interpreted to support this:

> Ya no corre la sangre por la vena,
> Pero el pulso en compás se trasfigura.   (402/91-92)

Mortality is clearly implied by the reference to stilled life-blood, but the immortality of the writer is also implied in the pulse of another course of life: words. Words are not subject to time; they are those sounds that we utter, by means of our respiration and vocal chords, and they are also those that live in engravings, manuscripts, books – ranging from the inscriptions on ancient ruins to this very poem:

> Ritmo de aliento, ritmo de vocablo,
> Tan hondo es el poder que asciende y canta. (402/93-94)

There are two primary motives in "Vida extrema", symbolized by "Si del todo vivir" and "decir del todo". The first is to be seen in section I and in the generic individual's meditation in section II. The second is testified to by the whole poem, and both aspects are to be seen in section III. This begins with a secure and positive affirmation:

> Sí, perdure el destello soberano
> A cuyo hervor la tarde fue más ancha.
> Refulja siempre el haz de aquel verano.
> Hubo un testigo del azul sin mancha.   (405/161-64)

"Perdure" (May [it] endure) and "Refulja siempre" (May [it] always shine) are phrases which express not only hope but confirmed belief that man may continue to exercise his sovereign right of expression. This makes the object it exalts greater ("más ancha") and more permanent: "Refulja *siempre* el haz de *aquel* verano" (May the beaming face of *that* summer *always* shine) (my italics). Expressive man becomes throughout all time an important witness: "*Hubo* un testigo" (*There was* a witness) is immediately followed by the phrase "El testigo *va ahora*" (The witness *goes along now*) (my italics). Moreover, reality itself is an essential component of man's expressive nature (see section III, stanza 3). Without it his function as *homo sapiens* would be impossible:

> Impulso hacia un final, ya pulso pleno,
> Se muda en creación que nos confía
> Su inagotable atmósfera de estreno.
> Gracia de vida extrema, poesía.   (405/177-80)

This final declaration of faith in section III is an extended response to the question which ends section I, and both are characterized by a tone of objective observation.

The initial commentary on this poem went to some lengths to clarify the roles of "passer-by" and objective observer in "Vida extrema". One of the imperatives in section II is "¡Sea el decir!" (Let speech be!). This activity is carried out by both. In the case of the objective observer, as we have seen, it constitutes poetry in action, symbolized by the extended water metaphor. But it is more clearly seen in the words of the "passer-by" already quoted. His first utterance is a response to and acting out of the first two lines of the following stanza:

> Ritmo de aliento, ritmo de vocablo,
> Tan hondo es el poder que asciende y canta.

> Porque de veras soy, de veras hablo:
> El aire se armoniza en mi garganta. (402/93-96)

They represent the culminating realization of his nature as an expressive being. The various phases of this are clear throughout section II, stanzas 3-19:

> Quiere ser más el ser que bajo el viento
> De una tarde apuró su pena o gozo. (399/31-32)

> Atraído el vigía. Ved: se expresa. (400/41)

> ¡Alma fuera del alma! (401/65)

> Trascendido el sentir. Es un objeto. (401/69)

Man's sense of real being comes only in conjunction with the ability to articulate. Hence, in the stanzas quoted above, "de veras" (really) is used to qualify both "soy" (I am) and "hablo" (I speak). Man is only man when *homo* is fully in conjunction with *sapiens*.

A further reality of his existence, and a remarkable one as it can transcend time, is the phenomenon of the written word, man's efforts over the centuries to give visual form to a spoken utterance. As has been seen, hope has been expressed that man's work may "still endure, / Growing amongst tacks and capsizings". The "great Affirmation" is uttered in defiance of "the most grave Negation". It is after this point in the poem that the "passer-by" once again expresses himself, and in terms which echo, as it were audibly, what has been suggested earlier:

> —*Se salvará* mi luz en mi futuro.
> Y si a nadie la muerte le perdona,
> Mis *términos* me valgan de conjuro.
> *No morirá del todo la persona.*
>
> En la palpitación, en el acento
> De esa cadencia para siempre dicha
> *Quedará sin morir* mi terco intento
> De siempre ser. Allí estará mi dicha.
> (404/153-60; my italics)

An echo of Guillén's article "Anatole France" can be found in "Vida extrema", for the phrase "Eficacia técnica: eficacia humana" has relevance to it, as can be summed up in the following diagram:

Eficacia técnica ⟶ eficacia humana
ritmo de aliento ⟶ ritmo de vocablo

Efficacy is the key word – in technical terms, that of creating poetry which depends on attention to metre and rhyme for success ("rhythm of vowel sounds"), and in human, physiological terms, the co-ordination of respiration with air ("rhythm of breathing"): man must strive to make his conscious, expressive self as effective and immediate as his instinctive self.

"Vida extrema" is a poem whose thematic content is reflected in its technique. The additional gift of life – poetry – is celebrated, but at the same time the reader is aware of that gift actually being put into action. Terence Hawkes, in his book on metaphor, makes the following comment:

> Figurative language deliberately *interferes* with the system of literal usage by its assumption that terms literally connected with one object can be transferred to another object.[23]

The reader of "Vida extrema" is forced to ask what connection the water, sea and nautical vocabulary can have with the subject of the poem, which is indicated by the title. In connecting the metaphor with the literal subject he accepts the fact of "interference" and takes part in the re-creation of poetry, performing the fundamental "task" which the poem exhorts him to carry out.

"Vida extrema", then, is an exaltation of man's verbal powers and fits logically within the scope of *Cántico*. Further, it can also be seen as a preparation for *Homenaje*, whose subtitle "Reunion of lives" implies that the lives of both creative writers and their readers are united because of their collective dedication to the task which is exemplified by this poem.

"Las cuatro calles"

In "Las cuatro calles" (The Four Streets, *C* 419-23), as in "A vista de hombre", the city is of primary importance, though there is no direct link with a protagonist. In "A vista de hombre" the protagonist is singled out both by his loneliness and by his own pre-eminence – that is, his efforts to rise above circumstantial and existential problems. In "Las cuatro calles", however, there is no protagonist, although the poem directs every reader to look at this vision of a city in the context of the human beings who have made it. References to Nature

[23] Terence Hawkes, *Metaphor*, The Critical Idiom, 25 (London: Methuen, 1972), p.2.

occurred frequently in "A vista de hombre", either directly by description or indirectly by the use of images suggestive of its regenerative cycle. In "Las cuatro calles" Nature is also closely linked to the city. Thus, for example, the brilliant shades of sunset colour city walls and parallel the jewel-like window dressing of shops. In fact, the coexistence of city and Nature in "Las cuatro calles" is essential for our understanding of the rather difficult "salvation" suggested as possible in the last eight lines of the poem.[24]

A.P. Debicki makes the following rather brief observation on "Las cuatro calles":

> Este sitio (el encuentro de cuatro calles) viene a representar el vivir positivo en contraste con el caos de la ciudad y con los elementos negativos de la realidad moderna. Así, adquiere un valor simbólico, y relaciona la descripción de la ciudad con un tema más amplio.[25]

> (This place [the meeting of four streets] comes to represent positive life in contrast with the chaos of the city and with the negative elements of modern reality. Thus it acquires a symbolic value, and links the description of the city with a broader theme.)

Macrí points out the following similarity between this poem and "Plaza mayor" (Main Square, *C* 473), written in 1942 and 1944:

> El principio, con las cuatro calles que se anudan ... está tomado del final de "Plaza mayor' con la victoria de las mismas cuatro calles que confluyen en la unidad de la plaza.[26]

> (The beginning, with the four streets which link up ... is taken from the end of "Main Square" with the victory of the same four streets which converge in the unity of the square.)

The similarities of the end of "Plaza mayor" and the beginning of "Las cuatro calles" are entirely incidental, however, for the moods of the poems are very different. The meditative nature of the former and the questions it poses come from a serene, balanced protagonist. Any suggestion of urban chaos is negated by the image of the city's creator being "chance", which is nevertheless "a wise designer"; and though chaos may have been a kind of guiding principle, it is even so

---

[24] Macrí, p.195, believes that the city in Guillén's poetry represents a means with which to reflect the contrasts between man's world and Creation.

[25] Debicki, p.191.

[26] Macrí, p.206. The use of the words "the same four streets" is slightly confusing. Guillén informed Macrí that "Plaza mayor" refers not to one but to many Spanish cities (Macrí, p.193) and Macrí himself informs us that "Las cuatro calles" refers to the streets that lead into the Plaza de Canalejas in Madrid.

within the bounds of "this complete reality". The first question of "Plaza mayor" (*C* 473) relates specifically to the protagonist: "¿Adónde me llevarán?" (Where will they lead me?). The streets that are the subject of the question are closely linked to history, nature and everyday life in stanzas 3-4. It is for this reason that the second question is formulated in more significant terms, relating not only to the protagonist but also to the function of streets within cities over the centuries and in the future:

> ¿Adónde aún, hacia dónde
> Con los siglos tanto andar?

> (So much walking down the centuries,
> Even now where to, towards what?)

The last two lines of the poem, "De pronto, cuatro son uno. / Victoria: bella unidad" (Suddenly, four are one. / Victory: beautiful unity), must be an answer to the questions posed earlier. In Spain the *plaza mayor* is usually the place where the major civic and municipal offices are situated, but more importantly it is the place to which and from which all roads lead. In the apparent chaos, victory or order is to be found in the single unit of space at the metaphorical heart of the city. This interpretation is also valid in relation to the time element introduced in the poem. Towns have usually grown up round one place of central importance to the people, though over the years the areas of civic activity or commercial vitality may have varied, as is the case with the Plaza Mayor in Madrid. The *plaza mayor* will, nevertheless, always have these connotations of centrality and order, and the force of the final lines is thus clear.

The abstract, meditative tone of "Plaza mayor" distinguishes it entirely from "Las cuatro calles". The knowledge of which streets the poet had in mind is helpful here, though I believe peripheral. We are able to ascertain that they converge on the Plaza de Canalejas in Madrid, not a main square, although the idea of four streets leading into a single unit of space aids interpretation of the poem. This poem is much more closely linked to "historia fechada" (recorded history), specifically the city and men of our own time, and it is what man has made of his instincts as a social animal which can be seen here. Man has created a civilization over the centuries which is more and more urban, and "A vista de hombre" portrayed a lonely protagonist in the midst of such a context. "Las cuatro calles", for its part, shows us contrasts of activity and emptiness in a variety of ways, one of which is again a distressed human being, living out his existence according to the accepted precepts of urban life, but nevertheless solitary and possibly more troubled by loneliness because it is unnatural to those very precepts:

> Pero ese transeúnte, sin ningún otro al lado,
> En orden por su acera,
> ¿Dolorido no va
> También, más acosado
> Quizá?
>
> (423/113-16)

Successful existence in an urban environment depends on everyone living and conforming to a set of rules, having a social conscience, in fact, though this need not mean curtailment of individual freedom. The ordering of society must inevitably be arranged by the few for the many, though democracy is meant to allow the voice of the many to dominate. However, it is possible for control to be seized by the few, as was seen in "Luz natal". In "Las cuatro calles" it is economic and militaristic factors which are shown to be possible and, if we choose to look back over our history, real areas where this kind of subversive control can be exercised:

> Hasta los arreboles van heridos
> Por terribles caudales
> De números con ceros,
> Los ceros de esos hombres.
> ¡Ésos! Por estas calles transitan y sus nombres
> No ocultan.[27]
>
> (421/59-64)

and:

> Orden. ¡En orden! Bandas, rutilantes metales.
> Por entre los orgullos callejeros
> Se adivinan latentes los redobles marciales.
> ¡Aceros!
> Hay tanta brillantez que es ya siniestra.
> Ni la brisa lo ignora.
>
> (423/117-22)

The quotation above implies that the principles of ordered and systematic activity can be lost if "order", a necessary adjunct to urban life, is sacrificed to "system"; if principle, which can be interpreted by each individual, is sacrificed to impersonal, centralized control. Guillén makes clear his conclusions that such loss of

---

[27] In *AO* 27, these lines are preceded by "No falta el factor económico" (The economic factor is not lacking) and followed by "En el desorden está ya operando el mal, y la visión del mundo tiene que ser ética" (Evil is already working within the disorder, and the vision of the world must be ethical).

individual freedom ultimately leads to a situation where the governing factors of life are, in fact, nothing more than a great void:

> Ante todos se muestra
> La Oquedad ay, rectora.
> Nada al fin.   (423/123-25)

The commentary so far has been confined to negative human
activities, which are one important aspect of the poem. Man actually
creates his own "common anxiety" which can bring him to the very
edge of nothingness. It is for this reason that Guillén states: "Este
mundo del hombre está mal hecho" (This world of mankind is badly
made). A further comment from him is appropriate here:

> Los actos singulares o los grupos de actos que determinan la marcha y
> el aspecto de cada época ocupan un sitio muy visible: el de la historia
> fechada. La época de *Cántico* asoma de modo que permite circun-
> scribirlo cronológicamente.   (*AO* 37)

> (The single actions or groups of actions which determine the progress
> and character of each epoch occupy a very obvious place: that of
> recorded history. The epoch of *Cántico* appears in a way which allows
> it to be circumscribed chronologically.)

If "recorded history" is what has been discussed so far, how it can be
circumscribed is also expounded in the rest of this poem.

The poem begins with a description of four streets in an image
which implies strength. The place where they intersect is like a knot
which strengthens the network of individual threads. Each similar
place within a city thus creates greater strength in the network, and
the importance of the individual streets is emphasized:

> Nunca, ciudad, acalles
> Su inquietud. Es tu centro
> De suerte.   (419/3-5)

The disquiet envisaged within a city is that of busy turmoil and
activity of a positive kind:

> Oh lucha en el bullicio,
> Que precipita dentro
> De tanta confusión tanto servicio
> Sonriente   (419/6-9)

These lines are the beginning of a very long sentence remarkable for
its expansion outwards from the earthly bustle of a few human beings
to the concept of the whole of mankind, seen as

> espíritu sin dueño,
> Tornasol de un encanto
> Que es aire.   (419/16-18)

In between we see that the involuntary interaction between passers-by is what causes this: the expression on a face gives an idea of that person's character; some comment overheard shows the tenor of another individual's mind. It is not possible for there to be a single controlling power over all these different types, yet the metaphor to portray this is that of conductor and orchestra. Thus, once again, apparent chaos is seen in a positive light:

> No hay batuta
> Que dirija esta orquesta
> Desordenada.   (419/18-20)

Images from Nature are used to contribute to this positive vision. The light of evening gilds grey stone and is multiplied endlessly in all shiny surfaces. The sun's final light is seen as a "dominio" (control) which is "terso" (smooth) even so. It is a triumph of Nature that that which governs our very lives is such an acceptable and agreeable power. It has been suggested, however, that men, when in a position to control our urban lives, can become subverted from a strictly ethical performance of their duties. The beginnings of this are alluded to at this point in the poem:

> La atmósfera comparte su dulzura con todos.
> ¿Por qué en algunos hombres tanto silencio amargo
> Que delata el semblante?
> La paz es ya tangible. No hay cómplices recodos
> Hacia la disidencia. ¡Paz triunfal y adelante!
>   (420/39-43)

The implication seems to be that if some men are unwilling to accept a natural force of control, then they are more likely to respond to the possibilities for manipulation and chicanery inherent within man-made systems for ordering life.

The effect of the above quotation is to introduce a measure of uncertainty into the poem. Though the next lines continue in the tone set previously, a further interruption, this time the audible one of a car horn, gives rise to a further question:

> ¿Se ha roto el equilibrio en un segundo?   (420/49)

It is legitimate to query the nature of "equilibrio" as used here, as there has been reference to noise and bustle previously. The distinction lies in the way the earlier noise is qualified – "dentro / De tanta confusión tanto servicio / Sonriente" (into so much confusion so much smiling service), "entrada / Graciosa" (amusing way-in), "transeúnte disfruta, / Risueño" (passer-by enjoys laughingly), "orquesta / Desordenada" (disordered orchestra), "batahola pero nunca maldito" (hullabaloo, but never damned) – and in the fact that doubt has only just entered the poem. The car horn is a symbol, on a small scale, of the larger-scale problem implied earlier by "silencio amargo" (bitter silence), and its sound is what jogs the mind to ask the question.

Guillén goes on to juxtapose what are the two real protagonists of the poem:

> Mundo en esencia late, fabuloso,
> Mientras ¡ay! la ciudad
> Y sus torres mantienen contra el tiempo su acoso.
>
> (420-21/52-54)

"World in essence" and "city" once again represent the concepts of essence and accident already considered by "A vista de hombre". Clearly the evening setting of the present poem symbolizes the world and thus constitutes "essence". The city, man's creation, is therefore to be interpreted as accident or caprice, though one must be careful not to impute entirely negative connotations to this, otherwise the potential salvation offered by the end of the poem is nullified. The city is "accidental" insofar as it and its buildings "keep up their relentless pursuit against time". The essence of the city is its positive bustle of humanity in general, whereas the problematic aspect of the city lies in the fact that it can be seen as a challenge to Time and Nature. The only creation of man that is endowed with real greatness is music, as Guillén maintains elsewhere. The city is acceptable as a place in which man can live; it is only when some men convert it into a citadel for political animals that it is subverted into something negative. Creation and man's world are sharply distinguished in *Cántico*: "Nunca se confunden en *Cántico* Sociedad y Creación" (Society and Creation are never confused in *Cántico*) (*AO* 37). However, Guillén does make clear the essential aspect of the city which has already been seen in "A vista de hombre":

> Si la ciudad es, por una parte, profusión de atropellos y tropeles, representa sobre todo la exaltación de la energía humana. (*AO* 18)

> (If the city is, on the one hand, a profusion of outrages and thronging crowds, above all it represents the exaltation of human energy.)

That there is a kind of "essence" within the city is shown in the following lines:

> Palpita una verdad
> Entre accidentes, ruidos
> Y males,
> Peleas y dineros. (421/55-58)

Here the verb "palpita" (beats) recalls Guillén's belief in the validity of positive "human energy".

Though there are men able to distort economic factors for their own gain, Guillén urges us not to turn away and ignore them:

> Vedlos. ¡No, ningún sonrojo! (421/64)

In addition to these people, there are others who are aware of the positive and permanent influence of natural powers of control. For these, human destiny is clarified by the diurnal cycle: "Destino: cae el sol" (Destiny: the sun sets). For others it is linked to a belief in religion, the angelus bell being a symbol of a life ordered by Christian precepts: "Una campana / Profundiza, completa / La fe / De algunos en la tarde sobrehumana" (A bell deepens, completes the faith of some in the superhuman evening).

The benign influence of sunset shows everywhere in the streets, which the sun, formerly a "yellow moon", gradually turns into silver and grey as its powers wane:

> Balcones
> Hay felices sabiendo de ese ocio
> Flotante. Para todos se platea
> Su dorado esplendor con variaciones
> Más grises cada vez. (421/76-80)

Thus the inanimate buildings are an accurate reflection of an essential world, which some of their creators choose to ignore. The buildings are referred to as a "palace", and the hand which created them can be honoured for having taken part in a process which enables evening light to be reflected on to all things, particularly human beings who are beautified by it:

> Que inocente en cristales de palacio
> Con más ardor aún el crepúsculo vibre.
> Ya esa mano entrevista realza su topacio:
> Topacio con influjo en la belleza
> Tan difusa que entona
> Traje, velo, persona. (422/88-93)

Within the intrinsic beauty of the natural world, human life continues its varied activities, and in the lines quoted below the word "arrebato" should be interpreted as both rage and rapture, for these emotions are both part of the passionate impulse which characterizes life:

> Apasionadamente va la vida,
> Aunque retenga aquí su profundo arrebato
> Perpetuo.   (422/105-107)

Moreover, the exclamation "¡Calles en el quid del cruce!" (Streets at the very crux of the network!) indicates that the city streets which witness the events of human life are at the very heart of the essence/accident tension. However, they are silent, inanimate witnesses and can only reflect beauty or negation. The symbolic importance of the structure of city streets and squares is considerable. As at the beginning of the poem, connotations of strength and vitality can be deduced from the visual format of streets leading into a square, but so too can negative interpretations be made. For example, the effect of moving from the relatively narrow confines of a street into the vast space of a square can be disorienting – the apparently comforting presence of houses and shops on either side is suddenly removed and one is confronted with emptiness. The same kind of parallel is made in the poem with the inclusion of the solitary individual whose seemingly orderly progress may well be merely a brittle façade covering very basic loneliness and alienation. Also, of course, the whole idea of the "governing Void" at the very heart of urban existence is a further aspect of the symbolic richness of the poem's city setting.

As night falls there is no sense that it brings calm, quiet darkness, even though it is described as "loving night". A howling cat is pictured returning to the "solitude of the wild" in the night. The words "but" and "also" in the description of the solitary man which follows this surely invite some kind of comparison. A wild creature, domesticated by man, is still closer to its original state than man, here dominated by an ordered existence which has somehow manipulated and manoeuvred him far away from his ideal state of equilibrium.

In the vision of order and military display conjured up in the next lines, a clear contrast is implied between the sinister brilliance of steel and metal and the earlier beautiful brilliance of sunset on windows, streets and car roofs.

It has already been said that the streets which form the poem's title are at the centre of the essence/accident tension because they symbolize or make clear both aspects of it. What man has made of his world is shown to be bad. The question is then posed as to whether it was thoughtless trusting to luck which guided the construction of man's cities or, worse still, whether it was

> Error
> Sutil que en más desorden se degrada? (423/130-31)

Neither of these questions can be answered. Cities as monuments to man's energy have been built and continue to stand, and it is futile to try to ascertain the guiding principles of their construction. However, man within them has been seen in this poem as a positive "hubbub", and the whole envisaged as "this disordered orchestra". To this extent, then, there is something vital and essential which endures:

> Dura en las cuatro calles un rumor
> Tenaz que persistiendo, convincente,
> Resiste. (423/132-34)

We have seen that "a truth" is present within chaos and disorder. A further illustration of this is given in the last lines of the poem:

> Bajo tanto accidente
> Discorde, torvo, triste,
> Continúa el rumor sonando bajo el cielo,
> Tiranía también, y admirable: no miente.
> ¡Vivo soplo inmortal, feroz anhelo! (423/135-39)

The noise of city streets, which has been portrayed in a positive light, continues within two ever-present but distinct spheres, those of "accidente" (caprice) and "sky", the one man-made, the other natural. Man-made control has been shown to be open to abuse, to the point where it might be described as tyranny. Natural control, symbolized by the sun, has also been revealed, and the sphere within which it operates is, of course, the sky. "Tyranny", then, refers to the natural control exerted by Nature over man, a tyranny which is admirable because it is a cosmic and absolute truth. Human energy, manifested in the noise that continues resounding, is to be seen not only in the context of tyrannical man but also in the context of an equally "tyrannical" Creation. The "Void" created by man must be understood to exist within a greater and longer-lasting natural void – that of the sky, which even so is shown in other poems of *Cántico* to symbolize something true, perfect and comprehensible, and from which one can derive security of vision and place.

Macrí makes the following comment in relation to these final lines:

> Sabemos lógicamente ... que la salvación está en la Creación, pero lo que nos urge es asistir a la conversión, a la *transformatio* del Accidente en símbolo y realidad de la Creación.[28]

> (We know logically ... that salvation is in Creation, but what [he] urges us to do is to witness the conversion, the *transformatio* of Caprice into symbol and reality of Creation.)

However, the "capricious" aspects in this poem are surely those of man's making, for Society and Creation are never confused in *Cántico*. Guillén does not try to transform our world into that of natural Creation. That would be an evasion of reality, something which he constantly seeks to avoid. What Guillén is concerned to do in *Cántico* is to put all things into perspective, to make sense of them by an act of attention and observation, so that balanced vision and a quiet mind are the reward. He sees things as they are. He does not try to transform the negative into the positive but to balance them, a task only possible by having faith in Creation. This is a natural world which surrounds us with "objects, compact with their own being, in accord with their meaning, faithful to their essence" (*AO* 13), against which we must measure ourselves and through which we may also come to terms with what we are.

The final line of the poem, "¡Vivo soplo inmortal, feroz anhelo!" (Living immortal breeze, fierce desire!), recalls the much earlier lines:

> espíritu sin dueño,
> Tornasol de un encanto
> Que es aire.   (419/16-18)

It refers to the "essence" inherent in the collective group of mankind, made up of countless different individuals, whose need of "air" for life is paralleled by and extended into "Living immortal breeze". Man's breathing, voices, words – in short, energies – show both his eagerness for life and his fierce desire to live it. In order to realize the full potential of this, we cannot allow ourselves the luxury of despondency. We must never envisage our lives as worthless and futile within the world we have made, but must enlarge our vision

---

[28] Macrí, p.209.

and see ourselves in the context of Creation. Only then is it possible to make sense of apparent chaos.

Conclusion

The poems that have been examined in this chapter have considered various aspects of human life. Man's creative energy is constantly alluded to, and music is seen as his supreme accomplishment ("El concierto"); so too can the city be a symbol of the positive essence of his abilities ("Las cuatro calles"). His relationship with and need of other human beings is made clear in "El diálogo"; and acute awareness of what it means to be an individual, open to loneliness and isolation even within the collective group of mankind, is the basis of "A vista de hombre". "Luz natal" effectively categorizes both nationality and universality as the patrimony of each member of the human race; and "Vida extrema" shows us an additional life-force, special to humans, that of verbal awareness and dexterity. The four major themes alluded to earlier in this chapter are all to be discerned in these poems, as they are in the other major poems that Guillén selected for his definitive *Cántico*.

The poems analysed are works of art which all bear witness to a state of maximum awareness on the part of the protagonist, and prove to us as readers the nature of the "road" that has gradually been established. The clarity of natural light is an important element in several poems. Indeed, "afternoon" and "morning" are often active participators in the poems, with the result that the pathway of experience that each poem catalogues is correspondingly effective. It is not a narrow ribbon with parallel verges which goes on endlessly in front of one, but rather a vast circle encompassing protagonist and reader. Our natural boundaries are elemental ones of horizon and sky. The extent of our vision, the horizon, leads us upwards, in an exhilarating fashion, but ultimately back to ourselves. There is no need to travel on without sense of purpose, no cause anxiously to pursue the chimera of the future, for our lives can be just as conscientiously lived by a constant awareness of self in relation to surroundings. If we are thoroughly involved in this relationship we will live constantly in the present in such a way as to elevate this time to always, a time of constant and self-renewing presence. Hence the inclusion of the quotation from Unamuno at the end of *Cántico*:

Sumersión en la fuente de la vida,
Recio consuelo!

(Submersion in the fountain of life,
Robust consolation!)

Past and future can only have real meaning when seen as subordinate
to the present – the past contributing to the present and the future
stemming from it, though always conditioned by what has gone
before.

In "A vista de hombre" the eminence of the protagonist lies
both in his solitary and insomniac state and in his attempts to come
to terms with his situation. Future equilibrium is anticipated and
achieved in this poem by the protagonist's own efforts, whereas the
conclusion which is most difficult for human beings to accept after so
many centuries of civilization is that offered by "Las cuatro calles".
Human tyranny is wearily and sadly acknowledged. The very word
tyranny has negative connotations and symbolizes, almost entirely
now, something evil which we strive to overcome. However, man,
when he creates music, has shown his ability to create a perfection
which harmonizes exactly with that offered by Creation. What
Guillén suggests in "Las cuatro calles" is that we must find the
courage to believe in an admirable and true "tyranny", that of the
natural world, which rules far more effectively and absolutely than
anything man has managed to create, and with which he can and
must live in harmony.

The world *Cántico* places before us is in some ways ideal, but
not evasive. The idea of a magic transformation of reality is
something in which Guillén resolutely refuses to indulge. He
establishes an ideal, non-evasive vision, and the major poems
analysed suggest above all the component parts of this vision. They
cover all areas of man's existence and constitute a means (faith) to an
end (life). Once one's way is clarified and one has faith in the
direction in which it leads – a true affirmation of self and
surroundings –, then adverse circumstances need be only momentary
problems which can be negotiated positively. If the supremacy of
Creation itself is accepted, then courage to face the tyranny of our
own worst creations can also be found.

Having established this series of balances so emphatically in the
final edition of *Cántico*, Guillén can allow *Clamor* to have its own
moment, and even so find a still, clear centre of calm within it.

CHAPTER 4

CLAMOR: SIX PILLAR POEMS

Introduction

When the three separate volumes which comprise *Clamor* were published, they aroused great interest among literary critics. In particular *Maremágnum*, the first of the books, caused considerable differences of opinion. There were two basic responses: first, that it was a recantation of the studied optimism of *Cántico*; second, that it was a continuation of *Cántico*, but with the emphasis placed on social concerns, rather than on the abstract aestheticism found in *Cántico*.[1] However, Guillén himself made clear his intentions with regard to his poetry in two interviews with Claude Couffon, where he stated:

> He emprendido un nuevo libro, *Clamor*, cuyas proporciones serán análogas a las de *Cántico*. En este último ya había aludido yo a ciertas fuerzas que considero negativas para el estado de plenitud en la vida. Se trata del mal, del desorden, del azar, del paso destructor del tiempo, de la muerte. En *Clamor* quisiera desarrollar estos temas, pero no ya en su forma general, como en *Cántico*, sino de una manera concreta, vinculada a la vida contemporánea y a la historia. Esto no implica por mi parte un cambio de actitud, sino sencillamente que ha llegado el momento para mí de evocar estas fuerzas. *Clamor* será, por consiguiente, el complemento de *Cántico*.[2]

> (I have embarked on a new book, *Clamor*, whose format will be similar to that of *Cántico*. In this latter book I had already alluded to certain forces which I consider detrimental to the state of plenitude in life. I

---

[1] See F.D. Wardlaw, "A Thematic Analysis of Jorge Guillén's *Clamor*", Diss. Duke 1977, pp.7-36.

[2] Claude Couffon, *Dos encuentros con Jorge Guillén* (Paris: Centre de Recherches de l'Institut d'Etudes Hispaniques, 1963), p.17.

mean evil, disorder, chance, the destructive passage of time, death. In *Clamor* I wanted to develop these themes, but not in their general form as in *Cántico*, but in a specific way, linked to contemporary life and to history. This does not imply a change of attitude on my part, but simply that for me the moment has arrived to evoke these forces. *Clamor* will therefore be the complement of *Cántico*.)

Guillén is acutely conscious of the way he constructs his poetic works. As chapters 2 and 3 of this book have shown, all the editions of *Cántico* are a gradual consolidation of his initial attitudes towards reality, and of the creation of poetry as a means of expressing the beauty of that reality. But the word "initial" should not be interpreted as meaning attitudes which would change radically or profoundly. On the contrary, the slow gestation of *Cántico* indicates that this is Guillén's primary stance; once the possibilities of joy have been fully catalogued and convincingly elaborated, then the poet – and, of course, the reader – is in a position to acknowledge the crises and horrors of man's world, to confront death and mutability in all their terrifying contingency, and yet not be diminished by such a confrontation. *Cántico*'s subtitle, *Fe de vida*, has a very real and vital function. It is the prime and everlasting declaration of Guillén's belief in the value of life, no matter how fiercely it may be assailed. The reader convinced by the validity of Guillén's exposition of this in *Cántico* must similarly accept his statement that *Clamor* is its complement.

Clamor means clamour, outcry or protest, and because of its contrast to *Cántico*, a hymn of joy or praise, indicates that this outcry gives expression to all those negative forces previously mentioned which belong in man's existence, bound as it is by historical time, as opposed to the eternal present enjoyed by the protagonist in *Cántico* and only briefly assailed. The realities of Creation have already been sung, and now Guillén turns his attention to the negative realities of man's world, those with which he struggles in his day-to-day existence. *Maremágnum* means noise, confusion, disorder, and the poems of this volume refer to the social disorder and confusion of contemporary life. The quotation from Juan Ruiz, "Non es todo cantar cuanto ruïdo suena" (Not all noise that sounds is song) (*CL* 22), which precedes the poems, warns that what follows will be the dissonance and confusion hinted at in *Cántico* but given full rein here.

Whereas *Maremágnum* refers to the collective and social time of our age, in . . . *Que van a dar en la mar* time is that which concerns the individual:

...el suceder del tiempo, no tanto en su desarrollo histórico como en su desenvolvimiento general. Es el melancólico tiempo que pasa, y, como siempre, el curso temporal con su carga de recuerdos de pasado va hacia un futuro que acaba individualmente en la muerte.

(Couffon, p.26)

(...the passage of time not so much in its historical evolution as in its general development. It is melancholy time which passes, and, as always, temporal flow, with its burden of memories of the past, goes towards a future which ends individually in death.)

Guillén adds that the poems are meditations on the past, memory, lost youth, the approach of old age, the dead and death itself. This central book is what he calls "un cancionero amoroso" (a loving song-cycle) in memory of his first wife. Here he evokes the death of someone very dear to him, but also refers to death in non-human circumstances, as in "Muerte de la rosa" (Death of the rose, *CL* 232), "Muerte de unos zapatos" (Death of some shoes, *CL* 245), "Muerte en la escalera" (Death on a stairway, *CL* 247). Casalduero refers to this second volume of *Clamor* as a tragic elegy which is "una serena, madura, viril aceptación de la vida, de la vida tal cual es, con un sol brillante, velado a veces por una suave melancolía" (a serene, mature, virile acceptance of life, of life as it is, with a brilliant sun, veiled at times by a gentle melancholy).[3] Emotions vary from the anguish of the solitary widower to a most moving stoicism, to be found particularly in the short three- and four-line poems, or *tréboles* (Clover Leaves), of the central section. Underlying the whole of this second book is the implication of its title. Taking Jorge Manrique's words, from the "Coplas por la muerte de su padre" (Lines on the death of his father), Guillén indicates that the temporal movement through existence to non-existence, with its consequential difficulties, is the main concern of the volume.

The third book of *Clamor* takes its title from a quotation from Antonio Machado: "Es más difícil estar a la altura de las circunstancias que *au-dessus de la mêlée*" (It is more difficult to be equal to circumstances than to be above the conflict). Guillén says that the poems concerned are

signo de una posición muy afirmativa y debe entenderse como una especie de imperativo ético ... No es posible abandonarse al apocalipsis, al derrotismo, a una final anulación. La vida, la

---

[3] J. Casalduero, *"Cántico" de Jorge Guillén y "Aire nuestro"* (Madrid: Gredos, 1974), p.258.

continuidad de la vida, tienen que afirmarse a través de todas esas experiencias y dificultades. Por eso, aquí, en este libro se presenta más bien la condición general del hombre, porque la realización del hombre es la meta a la que todos nuestros esfuerzos deben tender. Nosotros no somos más que una tentativa hacia una plenitud propiamente humana.   (Couffon, p.27)

(an indication of a very affirmative stance and must be understood as a type of ethical imperative ... It is not possible to surrender to the apocalypse, to defeatism, to final annihilation. Life, the continuity of life, must be affirmed throughout all these experiences and difficulties. For this reason, here, in this book, it is rather the general condition of man which is presented, because the achievement of human-ness is the objective towards which all our efforts must strive. We are no more than a collective effort towards a plenitude which is essentially human.)

    Each section of *Clamor* is as carefully structured as the sections of *Cántico*. In the first Sudamericana editions the indexes have certain poem titles in capital letters, and these are placed symmetrically throughout the various subsections. One significant difference in the overall structure of *Clamor* is that two subsections in each of the three books comprise one major poem each. Wardlaw refers to these as the "ideological pillars of the particular work",[4] a description which is particularly relevant, since the two poems provide a key to the overriding concerns of each book, with the other major poems, the remaining poems and the *tréboles* providing further details and elaborations. As the choice of major poems analysed in chapter 3 was conditioned by those new compositions singled out as major poems by capital letters in the index of the 1950 edition of *Cántico*, so these six "pillar" poems from *Clamor* – "Luzbel desconcertado" (Lucifer Disconcerted, *CL* 72-93), "La hermosa y los excéntricos" (Beauty and the Eccentrics, *CL* 138-55), "Lugar de Lázaro" (The Land of Lazarus, *CL* 202-19), "Huerto de Melibea" (Melibea's Garden, *CL* 366-85), "Dimisión de Sancho" (Sancho's Resignation, *CL* 435-45) and "Las tentaciones de Antonio" (The Temptations of Anthony, *CL* 491-505) – form the basis of this present chapter.[5]

    What is remarkable about these poems is that they are all closely connected with areas of man's knowledge of existence. They range from the biblical sources of Lucifer, Sodom and Lazarus to the

[4] Wardlaw, p.3.
[5] All quotations of poems in *Clamor* are from the 1977 Barral edition, Barcelona.

literary sources of *La Celestina, Don Quijote* and Saint Anthony.[6] Clearly Guillén has taken care to introduce into a book of poems which discuss man's world various aspects of his mythological and literary inheritance. All six poems have a separate protagonist, and Guillén's choice of a variable protagonist, who is individually known to the reader, is significant for the latter's response to the poems. In *Cántico* the generic individual who is the protagonist of the poems stands for all men who have the potential to be and act like him. In *Clamor*, man's world is the unique subject, and contemporary man the reader who is given a vision of his own society and attitudes and ultimately learns from them. Guillén is still concerned to create a pathway of experience, so he uses Lucifer, the Queen of Nations, Lazarus, Calisto and Melibea, Sancho Panza and Saint Anthony to provide *exempla* – human ones created by human beings. As he himself says:

El horizonte de esta poesía antes y ahora es un modesto horizonte
siempre terrestre y humano.   (Couffon, p.27)

(The horizon of this poetry, now and as before, is a modest horizon,
always human and terrestrial.)

It would be wrong to suggest that Guillén's poetry in *Clamor* is an example of moral didacticism, but the poems are a progress followed not by a pilgrim but by his secular counterpart, whose goal is not a holy place in the religious sense, but the noble one of human-ness. It would seem that Christianity provides for Guillén an allegory of the human way of life. In *El argumento de la obra* he writes:

La Creación se revela de tal modo que puede postular una vía posible
hacia un Creador. Por de pronto, henos ante la presencia terrestre. A
su exaltación se limita *Cántico.*   (*AO* 22)

(Creation is revealed in such a way that it can suggest a possible route
towards a Creator. For now, we stand before earthly presences.
Cántico is limited to the exaltation of them.)

And in *Dos encuentros con Jorge Guillén* he says:

Se puede estar con Dios o sin Dios, pero nunca contra el posible Dios.
                                                       (Couffon, p.27)
(One can be with God or without God, but never against the possible
God.)

---

[6] Saint Anthony can be loosely classified within the literary group of sources since his beliefs and philosophy are to be found in *The Life of Saint Anthony* produced by his follower, Athanasius.

So, biblical sources are a valid means of illustrating certain aspects of man's existence, since they are well-known and commonly accepted. Significantly, the first three pillar poems, in order of their appearance, have biblical sources, and the final three have literary sources. Guillén chooses first to relate man's experience by means of what could be called primary sources, and secondly through literature created by man as a symbolic interpretation of aspects of his existence.

The four major themes, Life, Harmony, Time and Creation, are also to be discerned in *Clamor*, and they are developed in a variety of ways. Life as a theme is the process by which man attempts conscientiously and courageously to live. Two supreme examples of this are found in "Dimisión de Sancho" and "Las tentaciones de Antonio". Sancho and Anthony both achieve self-knowledge through their experience in life, Sancho through disillusionment and Anthony through the potential desire within him to attain supremacy and mystic isolation. In their individual struggles with surroundings they show the reader that they have both travelled along a road to self-knowledge and are indeed "equal to circumstances". In "Lugar de Lázaro" life and love of earthly existence are the main subjects, while in "Huerto de Melibea" life and love are exalted. However, both poems have death as the inevitable outcome, dictated obviously by the established biblical and literary sources, but also as a logical part of ...*Que van a dar en la mar.* "Luzbel desconcertado" and "La hermosa y los excéntricos" both show perverted life-styles, the first in Lucifer's determined rejection of God's harmony, and the second in the ambiguous and unnatural sexuality of the people of Sodom.

Harmony is clearly to be found in the dénouement of "Dimisión de Sancho" and "Las tentaciones de Antonio": it is part of the lovers' enclosed world in "Huerto de Melibea", and of Lazarus' life when he returns from the dead. In "Luzbel desconcertado" harmony exists by virtue of Lucifer's vehement denial of it. Harmony is also to be seen in the natural sensuality of the Queen in "La hermosa y los excéntricos". However, the titles of both these major poems indicate that balance is absent from each: Lucifer is "des-concertado" or de-harmonized; the people of Sodom are "excéntricos" or ex-central. These poems clearly show confusion and disorder, hence their importance as the main supports of *Maremágnum.*

Creation is the background against which man plays out his life, and thus is an acknowledged but vital part of each poem.

Lucifer's reaction to it is predictable, and he talks of Creation in words and phrases familiar from *Cántico* but debased by his sarcasm and inability to believe in them. In "La hermosa y los excéntricos" the world of Sodom is seen on a beautiful sunny day and the atmosphere is one of happiness and festivity, similar to but a perversion of that in "Sol en la boda" in *Cántico*, in that all is clearly debased by the "eccentricity" of the Sodomites. Creation in . . . *Que van a dar en la mar* is very much the terrestrial one of this world. In "Lugar de Lázaro" it is Bethany, the place on earth that Lazarus loved with his life. In "Huerto de Melibea" Guillén chooses to depart from Rojas in so far as he emphasizes the place in which Calisto and Melibea meet. Rojas' belief that the air which surrounds man is "alien and strange"[7] contrasts totally with Guillén's decision, in his re-creation of the former's work, to stress the orchard, a place of natural harmony, which conspires to be an active participator in the human harmony that the lovers symbolize. Thus Guillén chooses to emphasize the earthly reality of each of these poems, a reality which is to be seen as a consolation because those who live, love and die, do so within the parameters of human mortality.

The theme of time is implicit in all the poems, as the subtitle *Tiempo de historia* indicates. The six pillar poems all have a specific moment in time to which their source belongs. The biblical sources come from the Old Testament, Isaiah, 14.12 (for the source of the word Lucifer/Day-Star relevant to "Luzbel desconcertado"), Genesis, 14, 18 and 19 (for the source of the history of Sodom), and from the New Testament, Saint John, 11.1-44 (for the miracle of the resurrection of Lazarus). The literary sources belong to the time of their creation, *La Celestina* (1498 or 1499), *Don Quijote*, Part II (1615), and *The Life of Saint Anthony* (early fourth century). Each poem is also "contemporary", of course, created by Jorge Guillén during the years from the late 1940s to 1963. Moreover, there is the historical time of man's existence and evolution, which forms the general background to all the poems of *Clamor*. In "Dimisión de Sancho" the relatively short duration of Sancho's sleep in section II gives rise to the longer-lasting effects of his subconscious, and therefore timeless, communion with and participation in the greater context of the universal harmony of the earth. This marks the beginning of his journey towards self-knowledge, the end of which

---

[7] See Stephen Gilman's introduction to *La Celestina*, 2nd ed. (Madrid: Alianza, 1971), p.21.

sees him in complete involvement, spiritual and physical, with "daily truth". Similarly, in "Las tentaciones de Antonio", the time during which Anthony dreams of his two potential selves – the one that desires to destroy for the purpose of personal supremacy, and the one that desires to be part of a mystical, and therefore inhumanly isolated, union with God – again serves to lead him along the path towards self-knowledge. He moves from "the actual moment" towards the possibility of "levels of human involvement which are well-shared", a situation where the individual's desire for supremacy and isolation is negated by a sense of community with other human beings. In "Huerto de Melibea" time is only the moment enjoyed by the lovers, their separation bringing distress and disorientation. There are several auguries which relate to the untimely end of the lovers, giving the poem a fatalistic element which is nevertheless balanced by the justification of love among human beings as a time of happiness and harmony which must be exalted rather than mourned for its transience. In "Lugar de Lázaro" Guillén gives a frightening portrayal of Limbo in which the soul exists after death. Lazarus' return to normal life calls forth from him a moving celebration of earthly life, as well as an equally moving confession of his wish that life after death could be the same as this terrestrial one. "Lugar de Lázaro" juxtaposes the timeless limbo of spiritual essence and mortal human life, and finally chooses to exalt the latter.

"Luzbel desconcertado"

In his article "De la *Divina Comedia* a *Clamor*", Luis F. Costa points out that the title *Maremágnum* and the poem "Luzbel descon-certado" (Lucifer Disconcerted, *CL* 72-93) imply connotations of a potential Hell.[8] Clearly, Guillén's use of Lucifer as a protagonist in *Maremágnum* is to investigate in detail the viewpoint of one who denies the harmony of Creation, an investigation which fits ad-mirably into the scope of this first volume of *Clamor*, given that its vision of the world is one of chaos and confusion. Lucifer is thus an important ideological symbol in *Maremágnum*. However, Guillén is careful to show, by Lucifer's use of debased *Cántico* language and by his determined rejection of God and Creation, that though powerful and persuasive, Lucifer cannot present a clear picture of harmony resulting from his condemnation of it. He is "disconcerted" initially

[8] In *Homenaje a Jorge Guillén* (Massachusetts: Dept. of Spanish, Wellesley College/Madrid: Insula, 1978), p.155.

because he has been expelled from God's ordered harmony and, finally, because his outrage has led to the awful realization that he was part of God's plan from the very start:

> La extensión lógica de su pensamiento es que él mismo es también el complemento de la Creación, que así logra su completa armonía; su rebelión fue también parte del gran diseño.[9]

> (The logical extension of his thinking is that he himself is also the complement of Creation, that he thus brings about its complete harmony; his rebellion was also part of the great design.)

Yudin describes this poem as "a self-destructing monologue"; it becomes an excellent exposition of the dangers of what Casalduero calls "la desviación de la inteligencia" (the deviation of the intelligence), and a warning to like-minded human beings that the exaltation of Nothingness is a futile "actitud nihilista y contraria al orden natural" (nihilistic attitude, contrary to the natural order).[10]

In the poem Lucifer seems to be looking down on mankind and, on the one hand, criticizing it sarcastically, while on the other trying to deny harmony at the very moments when he is most aware of it. The first words that Lucifer utters are "Yo, yo . . ." (I, I . . .), which are the first indications of his subsequent self-glorification in splendid isolation. He naturally allies himself with the dawn, as the other meaning of "Lucifer" is "Day-Star", so that immediately the reader contrasts those poems about dawn in *Cántico* which herald the arrival of harmony and clarity with this poem where dawn proclaims the arrival of the archetypal figure of evil. Lucifer accepts the early-morning cockerel's call as a suitable fanfare, reminding the reader forcibly of "Gallo del amanecer" (Dawn cockerel, *C* 344), and Guillén's comment that the cockerel is a caricature of the "I, swollen with pride, eternally damned".[11] Lucifer directs his sarcasm at both the sleeping human beings and the trust that that sleep implies. This introduces Lucifer's adversary, referred to first simply as "Him", and also his own narrow concept of the relationship of men and creatures with God:

> Pero ¿le importa a Él
> Que esas desventuradas bestias —hombres

---

[9] Costa, p.157.

[10] See F.L. Yudin, *The Vibrant Silence in Jorge Guillén's 'Aire nuestro'* (Valencia: North Carolina Studies in the Romance Languages and Literatures, 1974), p.59; Casalduero, p.256; Debicki, p.161, respectively.

[11] Geist and Gibbons, p.107.

Y gallos—
Descansen, cacareen?
Le bastará la adulación rezada.   (72/10-14)

Lucifer's first criticism of God is that it is vanity which causes Him to require adoration through prayer from man, and this vanity is seen by him as a poor second to his own pride:

¡Ay, vanidad de Dios!
Que me acusen de orgullo: lo prefiero.   (72/15-16)

In stanza 2 the mist accompanying dawn is a perfect opportunity for Lucifer to query the existence of Harmony, if one aspect of it is a confusing lack of clarity:

¿Y dónde la armonía?
Ostentación confusa
Lo desordena todo.   (72/19-21)

He goes on to make the usual claim that God would have been better advised to have conformed with the rebellious angels. According to him, God would then have avoided being associated with Creation, which he sees as

Esta plétora torpe,
Siempre caos que mal se disimula ...   (73/24-25)

In stanza 3 he summarizes the events which led to his downfall by first imputing to God the pride and vanity normally associated with himself. This is bolstered by his belief that his own greatness lies in the fact that he foresaw God's plans and discovered His motives, which he ascribes to selfishness. His own subsequent state, that of an outcast and eternal wanderer, is described by him as a privilege: he believes his own rebellion was sensible clear-sightedness, not sin. In this stanza we see Lucifer's ability to rationalize, to present his own actions in a favourable light and to cast doubt on the motives of the Creator of the world. It is the beginning of the "deviation of the intelligence" referred to by Casalduero.

In stanza 4 Lucifer acknowledges the way in which man sees him. The tradition of the rebellious angel has been developed into a myth which teaches man to see Lucifer as a perverted god-figure: because God refused to understand his excellent motives, so men, whom Lucifer sees as God's subordinates, similarly refuse to acknowledge the potential good of Lucifer's aims. He goes on to say:

Me recrean humano,
A su imagen más zafia.   (73/42-43)

It is precisely this aspect of the mythology of Lucifer which makes him such an excellent choice as the first major protagonist of *Maremágnum*. Man is only able to re-create mythical figures in the terms of the language and iconography with which he is familiar, those which pertain to himself. If man is able to do this, is he not also able to indulge in the sterile rationalization of nihilism uttered by Lucifer?

Thus far, Lucifer's criticism has been rational and sarcastic, but the thought that man re-creates him in a crude, human likeness infuriates him. The pride for which he was cast out from heaven surfaces in violent indignation which paints an even more critical picture of mankind. The concept of expiation is seen as cruelty, and his description of men as "civilizados" can only be derogatory:

> ¡Yo, que soy ángel, fatalmente el ángel
> De la suprema luz,
> Como si fuese un hombre
> Complacido en el fuego,
> En un sagrado fuego expiatorio,
> Verdugo que gozara
> Con esa crueldad
> De los civilizados!   (73-74/44-51)

Stanza 5 is addressed to mankind, whose inability to hear him is another cause of his indignant fury. Once again he refers to man as a unique example of the failure of his adversary's creation. This stanza is a preface to the next five, written in five- and six-syllable quatrains, in contrast to the free composition of the previous verses. The monotony of the rhyme (*abba*) and rhythm, and the content, sound like a catechism, the expression of Lucifer's perverted vision of man and Creation. The first and last stanzas of this group contain references to Hell in relation to man's situation – firstly the hell of man's own making ("Sois el mal eterno" [You are eternal evil]), and finally the Hell of God's making, the entire earth. Lucifer sees earth as the Dance of Saint Vitus, where the uncontrollable, spasmodic movements characteristic of this disease are symptomatic of chaos, a chaos which is symbolized by the sole cry which he believes is typical of man: "¡Guerra, guerra, guerra!" (War, war, war!). So chaotic, uncontrollable movements and persistent destruction are Lucifer's vision of the earth and its inhabitants. In the second stanza in this group he suggests that the cause of man's personal hell is God, because He persuades man to praise Him. He goes on to envisage a self-perpetuating situation, in the third stanza, where man praises

God and God encourages him to do so, the better to enjoy His own glory. The words "encienden" (inflame), "resplandor" (splendour), "alumbre" (illumine), "llama" (flame), "purifique" (purify) have accepted meanings within Christian doctrine, and refer to the light of goodness and the flames of purification, though Lucifer uses them to imply the torrid light and damnation of the only hell he believes in – earth. Man's frailty is implied in the fourth stanza, where his need of purification causes the mutual dependence of God and man – a sign of weakness for one who exalts solitary pride.

The contrast between the end of the final quatrain and the beginning of the last stanza of section I is great. Having described man's only utterance as a belligerent shout, he refers to the dawn time as "el sueño y la paz" (sleep and peace) which the sleepers enjoy, although he calls them "infelices" (unfortunates). This is because Lucifer alone is aware of man's warlike nature, something which he believes is "sin cesar latente" (ceaselessly latent). He describes dawn as it makes houses visible, houses which contain inveterate evil:

> Albergues
> De previstas maldades.   (75/82-83)

Can there be anything more monotonous than the constant trickery and fraud which constitute Creation? he asks. His indignation increases in the last lines of the first section, where he incredulously compares himself with man, who thinks him evil, when he, Lucifer, never attempted to deceive God, only to show Him the truth. He is contrasting his own goodwill which called forth punishment, with man's deception of God, which elicits only absolution. Lucifer is condemned to wander, as a fugitive in the outskirts of a "patria" (homeland) which he believes is rightfully his. The last two lines juxtapose the two antagonists of heaven. Lucifer exults in his uniqueness, echoing the first words of this section, but the phrase "el Máximo" (the Supreme One) suggests the futility of pride in himself.

If section I allows Lucifer full rein to express his hatred of Creation and to exult in his own superiority, section II begins with him recognizing his impotence. He is destined to be seen by man as a one-dimensional figure, because his counterpart, in alliance with man, always appears omnipotent. God, "el Otro" (the Other), prevents him from having any real control over man. The first lines of stanza 2 seem to contradict this:

> Aquél, en ese piso,
> Me será fiel.   (76/101-102)

However, Lucifer can only have putative control over man. Man himself commits foolish acts, but he is not incited thereto by Lucifer. This section deals with the suicide of an individual, and his gradual sense of alienation from his human world causes him to see all in terms of emptiness and futility. As a result, Lucifer presumes solidarity with him. Clearly this can only be *a posteriori*, for man has first to commit himself to negation. The process of his alienation is shown in stanzas 2-3. First the individual refuses to compromise with existence. He rejects dialogue and communication (the kind celebrated in "El diálogo" in *Cántico*), and he denies the validity of life. The world seems to be an empty desert where he is unable to accept anything as purposeful. At this point Lucifer is able to predict that this state of being implies a gradual loss of vitality. Fear of this state causes terror in the individual, but because of his negativity, he sees only a void, which inevitably confirms his doubt and alienation.

In stanza 4 the window, an image from *Cántico* of positive and successful reciprocation, is now used in a negative context:

> La ventana susurra
> Su tentación. El aire ahora diáfano,
> Tan profundo, no miente.   (77/121-23)

The window becomes a temptation because although it shows to the individual the same diaphanous atmosphere found in *Cántico*, in this context it provides confirmation of the void for a mind no longer able to perceive anything else. In "Una ventana", in *Cántico*, a sane, balanced protagonist looks out at the world and is thrilled by what he sees. In "Luzbel desconcertado" an alienated individual, who lacks clarity of vision, sees only a world which confirms his dark pessimism. The incontrovertible logic of alienation takes over completely, and the deranged individual's desperation is described as "luminous", an adjective which is as effective in this negative situation as it is in the positive context of *Cántico*. Perversity in man, tragically, is as enlightening as its opposite, and thus finds its due place in *Maremágnum*. Since logic and enlightenment of a negative kind are so convincing for this alienated individual, their only possible outcome is suicide, life taken unnaturally as a confirmation of lack of belief in the validity of that life. The tragic futility of this action is clear in Lucifer's description of the suicide as "Saeta hacia lo oscuro" (Arrow towards darkness).

Further confirmation of Lucifer's impotence is found in stanza 5. His belief that the alienated individual would be faithful to him is dashed by the suicide, which, according to him, is the action of a noble, quixotic fool. He can no longer hope for a living, alienated human being to help him in his crusade against God. However, the tragedy still serves a useful purpose for Lucifer, if only because it constitutes one more element of failure in God's Creation:

> En presencia del Músico sin par,
> ¡Cómo va fracasando la Armonía!   (77/135-36)

Lucifer uses the accepted phraseology of *Cántico* – Creator equals "The Musician", Creation equals "Harmony" – but with a sarcasm which stems from hostility. His final comment is an exhortation to man to pray, for that human reaction to death is a consolation for a Creator whose world is not perfect.

In section II then, Lucifer's ability to influence man to follow nihilism is seen to be spurious, though he is able to use man's own foolishness as proof of the inefficacy of God's Creation. Section III, however, begins as follows:

> A todos nos aflige el mismo error
> Del Pródigo   (78/138-39)

For Lucifer, God's creation of man and the complexity of the Universe is a sign of weakness. Singularity is strength for him, hence the question:

> ¿Para qué pervertir
> La Nada, maravilla perfectísima?   (78/143-44)

Lucifer is dedicated to the perpetuation of Nothingness, which is perfection for him. The declaration that abundance is abhorrent to him can be seen as a deliberate glorification of himself. He categorically denies any wish to recruit followers, as power resides in his own isolation and nihilism:

> Yo, yo soy el más fuerte.
> Yo podría ... ¡No quiero!
> Atenerme a este arranque
> Sin sucesión me embriaga.
> Todo el impulso dure en mí, latente,
> Invulnerable, límpido.
> Yo soy más que mis obras,
> A mis pies y nonatas,
> Tendidas sin cesar
> Hacia mi poderío de perfecto.   (78/145-54)

Stanzas 2-6 are quatrains, with nine syllables in the first and third lines and five syllables in the second and fourth, and with a rhyme scheme of *AbAb*. These stanzas seem to be a paean of diabolic nihilism. They are Lucifer's personal set of commandments. The first exhorts honour to unfulfilled potential; the second denial of the truth; the third, isolation of vitality; the fourth, maintenance of silence and concealment of one's beliefs, and finally, honour to "la esterilidad / Del exquisito" (the sterility of the affected one). The language in which these lines are written gives the impression of a Satanic litany, where words and phrases reminiscent of Christian prayers and moral laws are effectively debased to reflect Lucifer's perverted vision.

These stanzas serve to strengthen Lucifer's belief in himself and he returns to the contemplation of man. His sarcastic commentary reveals existing aspects of our present civilization:

> Saldrán a recibirte con sus flores,
> Sus pestes y sus átomos
> Tres o cuatro políticas en busca
> De tus felicidades,
> La estolidez gentil
> Y sus cabezas de profuso monstruo,
> La cruzada y sus crímenes,
> Dos distinguidas civilizaciones
> Que en sus aras te ofrecen
> Glorioso privilegio de holocausto,
> El azar, la injusticia,
> Sus máscaras,
> Y en torno la miseria,
> La constante miseria con su aroma
> De espíritu corrupto:
> El fracaso de Dios.   (79-80/179-94)

As a description of our man-made society these lines are uncomfortably succinct and accurate, yet they are uttered by Lucifer, the archetypal figure of evil! By constructing his poem in this way, Guillén is effectively evoking a picture of man's world, while at the same time deliberately excluding the pure faith that characterizes *Cántico*. These lines show the kind of hell that man has created for himself and which Lucifer justifiably isolates and criticizes. Moreover, he wants no part of it, for it symbolizes a kind of evil which has none of the glory that he sees in himself. His own strength lies in solitary, proud rebellion, the kind which man has neither the strength nor the commitment to follow. He carefully distinguishes himself from the devil whom man occasionally invokes and at times seems implicitly to follow. He is an independent force in opposition to God and on a par with Him, not a subordinate caricature used simply by man as the deity of black magic. Self-glorification is Lucifer's intention here, and he does so in words that are once again a debased reflection of *Cántico*:

> Mi luz es mía, mía. De fe, de certidumbre
> Me colma.   (80/203-204)

Lucifer has no followers, he has no direct power to cause chaos in man's society, but he is glad that that chaos exists:

> Y el rumor de las calles en el centro
> Forma al fin un vaivén en discordancia
> Que, *por fortuna*, quiebra la Armonía.
> (80/207-209; my italics)

Section III develops as an exercise in self-glorification, after Lucifer's failure to recruit the alienated individual in section II. Thus he moves logically and rationally through his commentary on man and Creation and his own position in relation to them.

The idea of Harmony, the final word in section III, is continued in section IV, where it is seen as a gilded cage which imprisons man. His prayers, his acceptance of Creation and his own position, infuriate Lucifer who considers man's passivity and inertia as the only suitable glorification for God. In stanza 2 he declares:

> Cante, cante el esclavo,
> El esclavo armonioso,
> Con armonía bien sujeta a un Dueño,
> El Dueño de la música,
> La música de un orbe sometido.   (81/220-24)

The orderly progression of these lines, from the slave (man) to the master (God), shows Lucifer's knowledge that harmony exists. But he can deny it because it all sounds so lifeless, false and impoverished. The harmony of the spheres, a human way of visualizing the perfection of the universe, is intolerable to him.

These two stanzas provide Lucifer with fuel to intensify the fire of his pride. Stanza 3 glorifies him once again as a source of illumination. His intelligence is sufficient to break down the harmony and symmetry, to open the doors of the gilded cage and make way for his own supremacy. The future verbs of these lines (pp. 81-82) imply as yet unfulfilled actions, but their potential is sufficient to make Lucifer feel happily part of the chaos and confusion of the city on which he gazes. The time is now midday, and he associates it with the height or plenitude of noise and disorder in the city:

Estrépito,
Contradicción, contraste, mediodía
Del sol sobre los ruidos.   (82/236-38)

Midday is only a short-lived time of full light, whereas Lucifer, whose
other name is Day-Star, believes himself to be "unlimited light".
Because midday lasts only briefly within the diurnal order, he
denounces it as darkness, because it is part of the order which holds
man imprisoned; it is part of the divine fraud:

Yo, yo denunciaré la gran tiniebla
Del orden,
Desgarraré los vínculos ficticios,
Lanzaré la verdad
Contra el embuste sacro.   (82/240-44)

In stanza 4 he hails criticism as his Goddess, because it is the only
thing which can create disorder and dissension. She controls a
universe of her own beyond the puling, unanimous hymns of praise
offered by man. Lucifer again refers to midday on earth and again
debases it. For him this time of full light is in fact one of "condemned
shadows", indicating his belief that God's world is a sham; that
Lucifer alone is able to see that the absolute light of midday serves
merely to show the darkness of condemned mankind.

In the last lines of stanza 4 Lucifer again refers to windows, but
he rejects their function as providers of visual access to the intrinsic
truth of the external world, for he believes that the mind, or
intelligence, is the only valid "inventor" of that world. As a result, he
is able to claim that it is a transitory thing, a mere spark which will
inevitably alter. Obviously this declaration is an indication of his
own intellectual perception of the created world as something which
is worthless and whose demise, moreover, can be accelerated by
humans who, like him, rebel against Creation. In stanza 5 Lucifer is
aware of such men and his description of them is consistent with his
negation of Harmony, for he refers to rebels as "bold hearts who
dominate", and to Creation as "the crisis". His vision of their victory
is again voiced with a future verb, for in stanza 6 he claims that the
unrebellious man will not prevail, referring to him sarcastically as
"faint-hearted".

Stanza 7 begins with the word ";Clamor!" (Clamour!), an
exclamation which expresses Lucifer's delight at the outcry that may
be raised by human rebels, his potential followers. The noun is
repeated seven times in the next lines, accompanied by words
expressing his vision of man: "opresos" (oppressed), "perdidos"

(lost), "rabia" (rage). He sees mankind as an army becoming more and more enlightened by the most perfect light (his own, as its leader), a light which shows up the divine deception and illuminates the "truth which sets men free". The rhetoric of this stanza is that which might be used by a crusader in a holy war. Only the context shows the language in fact to be debased.

Lucifer, as the leader of the malcontents, urges them in stanza 8 never to be swayed by the sweet blandishments of those who believe in God. Again his rhetoric is simple and obvious and it ends with a militant cry exhorting the destruction of Creation and its supporters, since God is cruel and impassive. Here Lucifer plays the part of a revolutionary leader, stirring his followers to rebel. However, the dream is not fulfilled, and the rhetoric of the previous verses is revealed as a sop to his sense of self-importance.

The high point of excitement is suddenly over when we reach stanza 9. Lucifer is left merely enjoying the confusion of the city, a microcosm of the macrocosmic chaos which he would like to create, and the final question again implies his impotence, for the fact that he has to question indicates that he cannot ordain:

> Ciudad,
> Inventado atractivo,
> República del ágil.
> El maremágnum vibra, se refunde,
> Lo absorbe todo.
> > ¿Triunfa?   (84/298-303)

Man's creation, the city, is an ideal setting for this potential subversion so much desired by Lucifer. Human life, particularly in this century, is characterized by speed and pressure to move and act quickly. In this final stanza man is symbolized by a car, speeding everywhere but with no purpose, no faith to justify such frenzied activity. Tragically, man believes that there is some kind of validity in this highly-pressurized life-style, and the stanza ends with Lucifer laughing to himself that such folly should be so much part of man.

These ten stanzas form the central portion of the poem. In it the time-scheme has progressed to midday, calling forth Lucifer's impassioned denunciation of Creation as a divine fraud. Lucifer himself also rises to the heights of his power, both from the point of view of the chaos he envisages as a result of a future rebellion on earth, and with regard to the rhetoric he uses. Up to this point Guillén has remained faithful to the order of events and details of the rebellion of the angels and of Lucifer's subsequent exile. Lucifer says and does everything that one expects, and Guillén takes the opportunity to add his own interpretation of the significance of Lucifer as a force for negation, by giving to him language similar to that used in *Cántico*, effectively showing that words can be an expressive and emotive tool whoever uses them.

Lucifer's pride in himself, evinced by section IV, is again seen at the beginning of section V. Pride and his conviction that he is inviolate ultimately lead to his downfall in this poem. Continuing to watch mankind with casual and supercilious idleness, he describes a ceremony of civic homage to a distinguished poet. The words of the Governor and the poet are set out in dialogue form, reflecting a similar structure in sections I and III. All that the Governor says, in admittedly sycophantic language, is ridiculed and rejected by the poet. The latter is a creator, and one who cannot possibly support the praise being lavished on him. Costa suggests that in this section Lucifer ridicules God. However, a comment by the "poet", in the same format as all the others, indicates that he belongs to a particular historical time, and cannot therefore be taken to represent God:

> ¡Primero
> De mi país, qué ludibrio,
> De mi tiempo nada más![12]   (87/360-62)

Nevertheless, for Lucifer the poet is an analogue of God insofar as he is a creator. The poet is proud and narcissistic and refuses to accept praise because it is not a sufficient recognition of his grandeur. Lucifer's pleasure at this scene lies in the fact that the poet is disillusioned: he has to accept the fact that his work is not destined for immortality. For that to happen his poetry would have to be thoroughly understood, and his failure clearly reveals him as non-divine:

> Eso ya concluído le traiciona:
> Materia en que jamás encarna el soplo.   (87/376-77)

Lucifer's words recall biblical references to the Word made flesh and, indeed, God's breathing of life into lifeless things at the creation of the world. Earlier in the poem he mocked God's creative power; in this section he finds convincing evidence that man as a creator is a failure too.

In section VI we see further examples of creators. The first is

[12] In a book published after Costa's article appeared Guillén says that this scene is a comic one, with no implied reference to any contemporary artist. It is included as another criticism of pride, "the great sin of the spirit". See Geist and Gibbons, p.111.

God, likened to a painter, producing "Bocetos / De realidad mal hecha" (Sketches of badly-made reality). Because the viewer of His created realities is Lucifer, all the images describing Creation are negative: the sun illuminates only weariness and is like a painter's varnish, artificially bright. Such obvious artificiality, Lucifer believes, must surely be repugnant to the intelligent.

In stanza 2 he describes one such person. Like the suicide victim of section II, this young man sits at his window and cannot help but enjoy the repugnance he feels for a world full of illogicality and chaos. Again the window is accepted as a means of showing up Creation in all its confusion:

> ¿La ventana propone tierra y cielo,
> Creación corregida
> Por sus más afamados residentes?
> Inútil.
> Al ventanero, lúcido,
> Le atormenta una angustia.   (88-89/398-403)

He cannot accept what he sees and takes refuge in intellectual superiority. He begins to write, recording in philosophical terms his alienation from the world. There is the glory of creation in this, even though it is a restricted glory and the fruit of real anguish. Lucifer, however, is cynical about the extent to which the young philosopher will commit himself to his beliefs:

> Tampoco ya le importa.
> ¡Adiós!
> Se irá, se irá al café, que no está lejos.
> Náusea metafísica se vence.   (89/417-20)

Because the philosopher shuns action and restricts his alienation to the written word, he becomes a creator who is repugnant to Lucifer:

> ¡Criatura! Sumisa,
> Acabará por reforzar el orbe
> Que niega aún: concurre laborando.
> ¡Traidor!   (89/421-24)

The philosopher, in his creativity, is a traitor to the cult of Nothingness and, therefore, ultimately no ally for the protagonist.

Lucifer has thus watched two human creatures who, though imperfect, are nevertheless unlikely subjects for the negation he wishes to instil in man. Section VII begins by following the pattern already established. After failure, Lucifer boosts his morale by self-glorification:

Me busco en mí. ¿Quién más inatacable?
Ceñido de fulgor, fulgor yo mismo,
¿Cómo podría soportar la noche
De ese "infierno", su fondo
Tenebroso de penas
Humanas, humanísimas   (90/425-30)

As Lucifer sees God's control over man, existence on earth is like that lived in concentration camps. He is proud of the fact that he has no such camps, a final recognition that in fact he has no place within the "chaotic" system of Creation.

Stanza 2 begins with a question that indicates not only Lucifer's sense of solitude, but also his purposelessness. He is tormented by a frustrated desire to be the active promoter of negation. Although he equates himself with the astral bodies which orbit the universe, he denies that such regularity of movement could possibly be considered harmonious:

Cánticos no me engañan.   (90/445)

He is in possession of a reflector, the distorting lens of his own character, with which he is able to shatter the "round emptiness" of the sun, the force which controls the harmony of the earth.

The following stanzas finally reveal the purpose of the title of this poem, a poem about a Lucifer who is not only out of harmony with Creation, but also disconcerted:

Si este universo no se justifica,
¿Por qué me afecta a mí, resplandeciente
Desde mi propio rayo?
Un dolor me corroe, lo confieso.   (91/450-53)

Stanzas 4-8 are quatrains, with assonance in lines 2 and 4, and syllabification ranging from one to nine per line, long and short lines alternating. Thus section VII contributes to the structural pattern, in which sections I, III, V and VII are organized in similar formats. This group of five quatrains is a mournful song of uncharacteristic sorrow. Lucifer laments his isolation from the stars and his lack of affinity with the firmament; the probability that the things man sees are as beautiful as he believes them to be; the power of God which inversely affects his own ability to be powerful; the fact that God exists with such power and validity and that he himself is not in that supreme position. The fifth quatrain shows that it is this final lament which is the source of Lucifer's grief:

> Me duele, me duele
> Sin cesar
> Que seas, que existas, oh Ser
> Tan actual.   (92/470-73)

In stanza 9 Lucifer admits to being overwhelmed by these conflicting sensations:

> Y este dolor —¿también amor? quién sabe—
> Me abruma
> Como una dependencia.   (92/474-76)

Both Costa and Yudin refer to the fact that Lucifer destroys himself at the end of the poem. He has consistently denied the efficacy of God's Creation, criticized man as a condemned slave, and used self-glorification as a ruse to disguise his impotence. Stanza 3 of the final section is the turning point, for once he questions his own vehement denial of Harmony, then he is implicitly accepting its existence. When he asks himself if the pain of isolation is also a manifestation of love for that from which he is isolated, he finally eclipses his own misguided splendour. The verb "abrumar" (to overwhelm) is a cognate of "bruma" (mist or fog): the "angel of supreme light" is obscured by the mist of ontological uncertainty.

Lucifer continues his lament in stanza 10 by acknowledging his impotence ("Triste el ángel sin coro" [Sad the choirless angel]) and his distance from the splendour to which he once belonged. He has no rightful place nor purposes, and even his traditional role as the tempter is, as we have seen, a spurious one. Man, whom he so virulently despised, has freedom of choice, a gift – from a true Divinity – which Lucifer has no power to assail. Even the suicide victim and the philosopher carry out their actions within the logic of Creation. In stanza 11 Lucifer tries once again to fan the flames of his own hatred of Creation, repeating the idea that it is chaos. But he has to acknowledge, in this paradoxical mist of sanity, that such a system as Creation is good:

> ¿Y no es mejor así: que luche todo
> Bajo la inteligencia irreductible?   (92/489-90)

The acknowledgement implied by this question rules out any further rebelliousness:

> Enmascarar no puedo mis verdades.
> No lo permite el Otro.
> Él me obliga a vivir en el enfoque
> De mi clarividencia   (92-93/491-94)

His clear-sightedness is such that the more he considers himself, the more that part of him that wanted to be supreme is destroyed. He is chained and humiliated within his own unredeemable evil.

Just as Lucifer's moments of Satanic fury occurred at midday, so the light of knowledge dawns as the day wanes. Dusk falls over a city whose chaos is not malignant. The rhetoric of the earlier passages is gone, and he admits to admiration that the electric street lamps, put on in opposition to the natural darkness, nevertheless are an embellishment of dusk. As Lucifer's light gradually wanes, so the light of the constellations is seen, proclaiming God's glory by their acceptance of His organization of the Universe. The appearance of Venus, the evening star, is Lucifer's signal to depart, and the poem ends with his deliberate negation of the glory he has just acknowledged. Lucifer's self-destruction occurs because he refuses to accept what rational consideration has made him aware of:

> Venus está. Se anuncia el orfeón
> De estrellas, las tan fieles, que proclaman
> La gloria de Quien es.
> Venus, adiós.
> > ¿La gloria?
> > > No. La niego.   (93/508-13)

His final words, "No, no", remind us of the beginning of the poem. "I" and "No" are characteristic of Lucifer; he glories in himself and in his own subjective vision, refusing to accept objectively and completely the patent glory of Creation around him.

The natural progression of light from dawn to dusk, which, though in the background, accompanies the development of Lucifer's thinking, remains unaffected by his attack. Creation can withstand the most concerted assault on its principles, even destroying those who lead the assault. The words "harmony", "symmetry", "canticles", "midday", "window", "luminous", "Musician", "light", "sun", "dawn", "dusk" and "orb" remain with their positive connotations, because the one who debased them is annulled by his own irrational denial of the context in which they exist. Moreover, the poem in which these events have evolved is a monumental denial of chaos. Symmetry, order and invincible creative endeavour here, too, put to rout Lucifer and all he stands for.

"La hermosa y los excéntricos"

In "La hermosa y los excéntricos" (Beauty and the Eccentrics, *CL*

138-55) the Queen of Nations symbolizes natural, normal sexuality surrounded by the abnormal sexuality which characterizes the people of Sodom. It is a strange poem, partly because of the juxtaposition of the natural and the unnatural, partly because one is not sure of the stance or identity of the narrator. Wardlaw mentions a narrator who, by the end of the poem, is more and more confused as to the nature of reality.[13] Costa writes of an anonymous narrator,[14] who could even be Lot (who was saved from destruction because he was Abraham's brother's son), for on the arrival of the strangers who destroy Sodom at the end of the poem, he is sitting in the gateway of the city in which he lives. Further helpful information for the sources of Guillén's poem can be found in Genesis, 17, which recounts the renewal of the covenant between Abram and God. The Lord changes Abram's name to "Abraham", meaning "Father of a Great Multitude", and Sarai, his wife, is given the name "Sarah", meaning Princess. God also makes Sarah "a mother of nations". These biblical references seem to imply that the Queen of Nations has the same righteousness and goodness as Sarah. Moreover, Sodom is destroyed to preserve goodness and eradicate wickedness. Clearly, however, any biblical parallels there may be with "La hermosa y los excéntricos" must be used only as a helpful analogue to the background of the genesis of the poem.

"La hermosa y los excéntricos" is written in prose in sections I, III-VII and IX. Sections II and VIII are in verse, which celebrates the beauty and naturalness of the love between the Queen and King of Nations. The prose of the other sections varies in structure from groups of four lines in section I and groups of three lines in sections III, IV, VI and VII, to groups of five lines in section IX. Section V has five subsections of three groups of two lines. Macrí suggests that the prose passages refer to the activities and descriptions of the populace of Sodom, but this fails to take into account the central prose section referring to the King and Queen of Nations.[15]

The poem begins and ends with the word "Sodom" and reveals the essence of that city, the attitudes of the inhabitants towards one another and to the visiting Queen. After the naming of the city, the first thing which is emphasized is the time of day. As in *Cántico* where the day is an important part of the poems' thematic sense, so in this poem the afternoon is an integral part of the festivities:

---

[13] Wardlaw, p.43.
[14] Costa, p.157.
[15] Macrí, p.323.

> Sodoma. La tarde está de fiesta bajo un cielo
> de pocas nubes, amigas de aquel ocio, de aquella
> luz tan derrochada como un ocio.   (138/1-3)

Guillén goes on to create a picture of festivity, pleasant idleness, warmth and colour. However, certain aspects of the description are strange. Having established the idea of leisure, he goes on to say:

> Es la relajación de muchas atenciones sometidas   (138/4)

"Attention" was "latent" in "El diálogo" and in "Vida extrema" man was described as "the attentive one". The fact that the attention of the Sodomites is "subordinated" can only refer to their subjection to sin. This day of festivity is a time for relaxation, but, as the rest of the poem shows, still a time when sin is their main preoccupation. The colourful festivity is evoked as a companion, but it is also seen as superfluous. The whole of the afternoon, the entire time of the festivity, is described as "substantial frivolity", a time given up to enjoyment and diversion, with no real purpose. Physical enjoyment is all for the crowds who have gathered to say farewell to the Queen of Nations. The latter is described as a true sovereign because of her beauty:

> Reina por derecho y por calidad: hermosa.   (139/27-28)

However, the accoutrements which give the impression of beauty yield to the inner beauty, or radiance, that the Queen possesses. Her regal position and nature distance her from the crowd, though her expression is friendly and smiling. Such an attitude is an indication of the essence of the Queen, and to express this Guillén uses the traditional image of the eyes as windows to the soul:

> Iluminación que conduce hasta los ojos, entre
> verdes y ya grises. Si de estatura directora,
> ¿cómo tan esbelta, ahincada en su poderío?   (140/35-37)

In stanza 13 her beauty is described in terms of fruits and vegetables, emphasizing both her animal grace and her natural loveliness:

> ¡Qué frutal por la piel, y con su riego
> de sangre-savia, tan animal y vegetal!   (140/39-40)

Concha Zardoya interprets these lines as a "dehumanization that exalts feminine beauty, by means of its vegetablization".[16] However,

---

[16] See Concha Zardoya, "*Clamor* I: Stylistic Peculiarities", in *Luminous Reality*, ed. Ivask and Marichal, p.157.

dehumanization and exaltation of feminine beauty seem to me to be contradictory. Recourse to the world of flora and fauna to express physical human beauty belongs to a tradition that goes back to the Song of Solomon, a tradition that Guillén is clearly following in this poem. The luminous beauty of the Queen is like a gift, for it is a reminder of her essential character and disposition:

> Llamando está un relieve en simple desnudo,
> aunque vestido —o por eso: todo hacia la persona,
> hacia su empaque de inmediata persona.   (140/41-43)

The idea of the immediacy of feminine beauty, symbolized by the Queen, is repeated in the next stanza. Moreover, it is femininity which is sacred to males; the attractiveness of the Queen lies in the fact that she is a perfect example of heterosexual love. As such she represents both lover and loved one, and her sole reason for existence is her absent King.

This section has set the scene of the poem. The unnatural gaiety and idleness of the Sodomites have been made evident, and the Queen of Nations has been described in great detail in such a way that she represents perfect human love: she is the "culmination of the world". She is also "la tan destinada" (so destined), following "el rumbo perpetuo ... a un hombre" (the eternal pathway to a man), which provides a contrast to the finite pleasure of those around her. The exclamatory praise of the narrator is clearly expressed, and his enthusiasm is such that he breaks into song, the only suitable medium by which to celebrate the significance of natural love.

The phrase "the eternal pathway" indeed implies natural love, rather than the short-lived unnatural sexuality characteristic of Sodom. The song forms section II of the poem and corresponds to section VIII, giving the work a symmetrical structure. The verses are quatrains of alternating long lines (from eight to fourteen syllables) and short (from two to six syllables). Macrí claims that the lines "Secreto imán del instante / Sin fin" (Secret magnet of the endless instant) refer to woman, though the whole of this song is developed in such a way that it can be interpreted as the expression of love by both a man and a woman.[17] Stanza 1 is a declaration that the entire being of the lover, both physical and mental, is directed towards the expression of their united love. Stanza 2 sees the union of the lovers as a place where the one person flourishes in the love of the other. Stanza 3 repeats the idea of the first, with the addition that each lover

[17] Macrí, p.319.

is a magnet who is able to create for the other endless moments of
ecstasy. The certainty of the lover's innate knowledge that their
union is a place and time of spiritual serenity is the basis of stanza 4,
while the fifth describes love in terms of "destino" (destiny) and
"salud" (health) and the beloved as "suerte" (good fortune). Stanzas
1, 3 and 5 use philosophical terms to describe the nature of love, while
stanzas 2 and 4 equate the lovers with such natural phenomena as
crops, sun, and the flowering of nature, with the seclusion of love
referred to as a "nido justo" (perfect nest) and a "retiro" (secluded
place). The way in which this song is expressed is direct and straightforward. There is nothing in the vocabulary or imagery to suggest
strangeness or perversion, for this section symbolizes the perfect
expression of love in the midst of Sodom.

     In section III the narrator continues to observe the Queen's
progress as she moves through a crowd of people of varying attitudes
of curiosity, enthusiasm and hostility. Furthermore, the activities of
the Sodomites are described in more detail:

>   Hortensia escapada de su jardín, un adolescente
>   gesticula, rápido, rítmico, ante un adulto con
>   peso de doctor muy docto. Se entresonríen.   (142/76-78)

Following her commentary on dehumanization as an exaltation of
feminine beauty, Zardoya writes:

>   The same type of vegetablizing dehumanization, applied to an
>   eccentric, appears in the same poem: "Hortensia . . ."[18]

However, Guillén is not describing this eccentric in the same way as
he describes the Queen. The young man has escaped from his rightful
place, and the analogy with Hortense, the *goddess* of gardens, serves
to show that he is a homosexual, attracting an older man. Both are
beyond the bounds of natural sexuality. Guillén's use of references to
nature in this poem is entirely appropriate, as he carefully distinguishes between normality and abnormality through this usage.
Moreover, the place where Sodom was situated was in the plain of
Jordan, a well-watered and, therefore, fertile plain before it was
destroyed by God.

     Further descriptions of Sodomites follow, including a couple
where the younger of the two dominates and controls the elder; an
elderly man with "mandíbula vehemente y manos ya despóticas"
(vehement jaws and already despotic hands) who surveys the crowd

---

[18] Zardoya, p.157.

in the hope of attracting someone; an exquisitely dressed individual who receives the adulation due to "la Perfección Andrógina" (Androgynous Perfection); a person of indeterminate sexuality; and someone whose solitude indicates that he is, for a Sodomite, abnormal, for he merely watches and is not actively involved in the perversion. After this detailed account of the crowd the section ends with further exaltation of the Queen, again expressed in terms of the natural beauty of heterosexuality:

> ... mujer hermosamente
> destinada al hombre, más hermosa que la flor, más
> hermosa que el mar!   (143/104-106)

The commentary in section III is that of the narrator, but in the following section the Queen, devotedly directed towards her lover, looks at the crowd and sees clearly their true nature:

> Muy sagaces, sus ojos distinguen a muchos o
> los presienten. ¿Una muchedumbre, un solo
> caudal de agasajo? Ellos y ellos. Ellas y ellas.   (144/110-12)

Thus she is separated from the Sodomites and sees them as clearly as the narrator. The abnormality implied at the end of the lines quoted is confirmed immediately: a woman of high social standing is brazenly calculating likely people to seduce; two young women gaze yearningly at the Queen, but submit to the prevailing atmosphere, which encourages "eccentricity". The following lines describe the beauty of the place, with natural perfumes filling the air. A large, dominating, middle-aged woman comes near to the Queen:

> La Equina, ruborizándose, tan próxima a esta
> Reina, contiene su impulso imperioso y desvía
> la mirada, ahora dura —mientras se rinde.   (145/128-30)

In these lines normality and abnormality come face to face, with the latter unable to recognize the supremacy of the former.

The presence of the Queen has served to increase the bustle and agitation of the Sodomites, who all know that the festivities provide an opportunity for sexual pleasure. At the end of this section the Queen is referred to again. She alone has the true power to seduce, though her sexuality, unassailed by the crowds, is directed solely towards her lover. Here the King of Nations is mentioned for the first time, and in section V, the central section of the poem, the lovers' refuge is described.

The palace imagined by the narrator is a place which reflects the harmony of two united lovers, where love takes place in seclusion, in contrast to the public display of the Sodomites. The way in which the narrator phrases his description is reminiscent of poems like "Salvación de la primavera" and "Sol en la boda" in *Cántico*. The lovers create "a single happiness":

> Hacia esa cima del aire vuelven los dones y
> el ansia de los dispuestos al gozo que junta.
>
> Prende en acorde cabal a dos pulsos una armonía
> sumada a los cielos por glorias infusas.   (146/148-51)

The central trio of couplets are an extended exclamation in praise and celebration of a "Relojero terrestre y celeste" (earthly and heavenly Watchmaker). This Being, both earthly and divine, is celebrated because in his wisdom he created love as a necessary force between human beings. He also gave to love those limits, boundaries and confines expressed by the word "rigor" (rigour). Love is described as

> esa invasión de la
> vida en la vida, placer por alud de tumulto,
>
> Articulado prodigio con dirección a una crisis
> de trasformaciones: más mundo y maduro! (146-47/154-57)

"Rigour" is a significant term, broadly encompassing all the ideas incorporated in these passages. It implies harmony of thought and desire between the lovers, but above all it refers to the uniqueness of heterosexual love, and contrasts strongly with the widespread, public display of abnormal sexual instincts evinced by the Sodomites.

The third group of couplets refers to woman, paralleling the first trio. She is referred to as "so feminine", again emphasizing her sex, and she gives herself up to the eternal, living power of love. The Sodomites confine themselves to the gratification of their own desires, and remain distant from the kind of submission to a natural force suggested here. Her surrender symbolizes "coherence", because physical desire and femaleness (her "destiny") are joined into a coherent whole where the satisfaction of human desire reflects the woman's conformity with the way she was created.

The fifth and final trio refers to the two lovers and parallels the second trio. It begins with a statement which gains impact from antithesis. The lovers' lives are made more profound by their involvement in a humble, ordinary emotion. It is this final trio which clarifies Guillén's choice of "Watchmaker" to express the concept of

a creator of love in mankind. The word inevitably suggests connotations of time, and this is seen as the supreme asset of love. Love's
climax is a short-lived ecstasy, which nevertheless has infinite
implications for man:

> ¡Qué largo el minuto,
>
> Qué breve de historia la raya tan simple que,
> siendo infinita, niega el final y su punto!   (147/165-67)

Love's meaning for man is that through its grace he becomes a part of
cosmic harmony:

> Hacia su Rey va una Reina. Astros sonantes.
> El hombre en su amor es el músico.   (147/168-69)

These lines are also a reminder that this section is created by the
narrator's imagination. The lovers form an island of perfection,
prompted in the narrator's mind by the distasteful scenes that he has
witnessed among the Sodomites. The contrast which he has described between the Queen and the residents of Sodom creates an
awareness of the absolute harmony of normal love. As a result, the
subsequent descriptions of the Queen, in section VI, indicate her
supremacy not simply as a ruler, but also as a being made supreme by
acquiescence in her heterosexual destiny:

> La Reina preside y se impone a la tarde, a su
> pululación sumisa o insumisa, y por su virtud:
> mujer hermosamente destinada.   (148/171-73)

The remainder of section VI comprises further descriptions of
the inhabitants of Sodom, with the Queen a mere observer of all that
goes on around her. In spite of her obvious moral and sexual
supremacy, the activities of the Sodomites continue to be as depraved
and immoral as before. Clearly the narrator alone responds to what
the Queen represents.

Several references have been made to the season of the year –
the month is June – and Macrí interprets this as a symbol of
"Sodomite ambiguity".[19] However, June is the mid-point of the year,
a time of plenitude which corresponds symbolically to the perfect
sexuality of the Queen. The inhabitants of Sodom, of course, are
unaware of such symbolism:

> ¿Para qué afanarse entre los destellos
> y las sombras del estío inminente?   (143/92-93)

---

[19] Macrí, p.323.

Section VII begins with another reference to the season of the year: "spring tinged with summer". We see too that the day has progressed, and that the land is enveloped in the shadows of evening. The second stanza in this section is as follows:

> Aquel señor —con un niño— disfruta, concorde:
> Reina en toda su autoridad cuando él acata
> la supremacía del Encanto.
> (150/207-209)

His pleasure in the evening would appear to be, partially, a response to the presence of the Queen, who paradoxically symbolizes heterosexuality, and who is likewise a representation of purity:

> ¡Dominio de la más valiosa: dádiva constante,
> energía de júbilo con participación de claridad,
> torre de esplendidez!
> (150/210-12)

The tower is a symbol of her moral excellence, which raises her above the Sodomites who are all around her. The nature of their abnormality is clearly shown by the description of one woman as "disoriented, or with successive orientations". Herein is expressed the entire problem of Sodom. There is no single, good and guiding principle – that of love:

> ¿Dentro de qué refugio de melancolía —tal es
> su abandono— quedarán consolándose, lejos
> del amor?
> (151/226-28)

As the Queen leaves the city, the ritual of farewell reaches the height of ceremonial, whereas around the Queen there is "a vibrant profundity", a symbol of cosmic harmony. As with sections III and V, section VIII is not a description of a scene observed by the narrator. It is a poem which shows the consequences of perfectly attuned love between man and woman. Earth will shine and be seen in heaven; in other words, normal man is good in the sight of God. The future stretches ahead uninterrupted and time ceases to be an enigma, for the same path, mortality, is followed by all. Emotions are balanced and, because of mutual understanding, are a gift which ensures future happiness. The rest of the world, sunk in moral turpitude, must eventually give way to such harmony. Section VIII ends with the following stanza:

> Entre las tentativas inferiores
> Se cumple
> La ya fabulosa, mayor realidad:
> Por fin su relumbre.
> (152/255-58)

The way in which this entire section is phrased suggests universalized concepts of love and harmony, repeating both the structural organization and the thematic content (universal lovers) of section II. The Queen of Nations is a symbolic representation of that perfect love which, when it occurs, enables the world to have meaning:

> Va a refulgir en el cielo estrellado
> La Tierra.   (152/241-42)

When it does occur it shines clearly amongst the abortive attempts to achieve that love which take place all around. The implications of this section are that man's future is assured when he can imitate what the Queen exemplifies: each man and woman can be a father and mother of nations, as God intended them to be.

The fact that sections II, V and VIII occur surrounded by the activities and unnatural persuasions of the Sodomites is a clear indication that what these sections celebrate does not exist inviolate. The final section of the poem concentrates entirely on Sodom alone. The people who live there disintegrate into permanent abnormality, because they are not part of the Queen, who is now referred to as the Bride:

> Y la Esposa
> impaciente se va tras el Esposo, a lo largo de
> viñedos que la recogen y cantan.   (153/261-63)

These lines are reminiscent of the "Cántico espiritual" of San Juan de la Cruz, and as the title of the great mystic's poem implies, the lovers are part of a spiritual harmony very different from the human and physical preoccupations of the Sodomites. Guillén is careful to emphasize that the city is part of the known human world, as his insistence on the presence of a blackbird proves. Time slips away from these inhabitants in the details of daily life; each minute is lived as though it were the last, for there is no concept of future, no sense that the passage of time in a life is the opportunity to achieve fulfilment of a lasting kind. The narrator's perception of this sterility causes him to lament the frivolous attitude he sees around him:

> ¡Ay! Doncellas y donceles, donceles-doncellas
> en transición ¿hacia qué porvenir, qué horizonte?
> Encrucijadas de una crisis nunca frívola o casi
> nunca, penosa, ardorosa, difícil, esforzada, ¿hacia
> qué término jamás plenario?   (153/274-78)

The inhabitants of Sodom are a symbol of ambiguity. The

narrator's questions in the lines that follow indicate his inability to understand their essential nature:

> Todo es y no es. Pero ¿qué es? (154/286)

As the day draws to a close peace and calm seem to descend on Sodom:

> Es lento y apacible el tránsito. ¿Qué sucede?
> Nada. (154/287-89)

The people of Sodom continue to be as they always have been and there is no evidence of God's wrath:

> ¿Poniente de fuego celestial? No. Castigo, no.
> Las parejas circulan entre sus propias llamas.
> Entre sus llamas se consuman y se consumen.
> Indolentes o impetuosas —aproximaos, no hay
> soplos de infierno— las parejas se pierden. (154/291-95)

Guillén's use of "flames" to mean passion here also has an intentional symbolism. The passion in which they indulge is an actual, real experience of damnation which the Sodomites perpetuate, isolating themselves from normality. They have brought about their own destruction, and the arrival of strangers in Sodom is merely the prelude to an event which has been orchestrated by the people themselves.

For Guillén, wilful promotion of evil is a more potent force than any supernatural self-destruction or divine retribution. Mankind is a combination of harmonious and eccentric beings, and the biblical myth of the destruction of Sodom is a useful symbolic parallel for a wayward intransigence which leads to the sterile, chaotic and meaningless life-styles of man's civilization.

"Lugar de Lázaro"

In . . . *Que van a dar en la mar* the two poems comprising a section each are the first and last poems of the whole volume, whereas "Luzbel desconcertado" and "La hermosa y los excéntricos" are the second and penultimate sections of *Maremágnum*. Together with the central section of . . . *Que van a dar en la mar* "Lugar de Lázaro" and "Huerto de Melibea" provide lengthy illustrations of the meaning of life, love and death on both universal and personal levels.

In section II of "Lugar de Lázaro" (The Land of Lazarus, *CL* 202-219) Guillén reproduces faithfully the biblical story from the

Gospel according to Saint John. However, rather than giving the
poem the simple title of "Lázaro", Guillén chooses one which
indicates that Lazarus' place or situation is the most important
aspect of this re-creation of the biblical miracle. Furthermore,
Guillén's poem is remarkable for its lengthy first section, which
details the experiences of Lazarus' soul in Limbo. In section III we
are supplied with much more detail of his response to earth after his
resurrection. In the following section Guillén interprets Lazarus'
own thoughts and discoveries about life after his experience of
lifelessness, and also his attitude towards God's gift to mankind, the
possibility of life after death. Thus Guillén's poem is far more than a
re-creation of the Gospel story of Lazarus. It is a creation, in its own
right, of particular relevance to mankind because we see a human
Lazarus coming to terms with an experience no other person has
ever known. Man's fear of death stems from the fact that it is
something which is not only inevitable but also impossible to have
intimate knowledge of. We can only accept that it occurs and, if
possible, hold to the belief that there is life of some kind after death.
Christ's resurrection of Lazarus is a miracle recorded by Saint John,
and ordained by God, for the specific purpose of providing
consolation for the fear of death. Hence its importance within the
Bible, and hence also Guillén's inclusion of such a theme in a body of
poetry which catalogues man's experience of life in its every aspect.

Section I of "Lugar de Lázaro" is written in unrhymed eleven-
syllable lines. It is divided into seven subsections, which are signalled
by a divided eleven-syllable line, and each of which will be referred to
as a stanza for reasons of clarity. The first of these stanzas begins with
a statement that death has occurred. Its blunt but compassionate
simplicity is a moving vision of death in language which is consistent
with Guillén's view of life in *Cántico*:

> Terminó la agonía. Ya descansa.
> Le dijo adiós el aire. Ya no hay soplo
> Que pudiese empañar algún espejo.
> No, no hay combate respirando apenas
> Para guardar el último vestigio
> De aquella concordancia venturosa
> Del ser con todo el ser.   (202/1-7)

In "Luz natal" light and air were seen as vital components of
human life, and Guillén maintains that idea in this poem. When
breathing stops, the image to express it is the "farewell" of air. In the
second stanza the corpse no longer partakes of the light of earth;

death renders the translucent body opaque. If the first stanza's statement about death is characteristically abstract and serene, the images of stanza 2 describing the dead body and what that state represents are more emotional in tone:

> Sin la perduración arisca de la piedra,
> En una piedra el cuerpo va trocándose.   (202/13-14)

The body is described as a "sad bulk", a "heap" and a "stone", all of which suggest substantiality, something which Guillén is at pains to emphasize in this second stanza. He implies that confronting a corpse makes one realize that the dead person is suddenly distanced:

> Muerto.
> De repente, lejano. ¿Dónde, dónde?   (202/17-18)

However, he resolutely refuses to move into a consideration of where the spirit may be now that physical life is ended. He goes on instead to describe the dead body as being surrounded by the living, and proposes the idea that death causes an involuntary betrayal. Body and spirit are irrevocably separated by death:

> Yace alguno
> Que ya no es él: traición involuntaria.
> A través de la muerte no hay posible
> Fidelidad.   (202/20-23)

The corpse is once again seen as something which no longer represents the identity of Lazarus, and Guillén emphasizes the strangeness of this for the mourners. Gradually the dead body becomes more substantial as death stills and stiffens it, smoothing all traces of character from the face. Almost inevitably, it seems, this extraordinary stillness and solidity force a reminder of the differences between life and death:

> No hay medida común para esa
> Calma sin tiempo y la inquietud variable
> De estas horas —las únicas— en curso,
> Trémulas entre manos de viviente.   (203/32-35)

Life for human beings is mortal and the passage of time is something fragile, in comparison with the calm stillness of death. This stanza has consistently stressed the substantiality of the dead body, something which impresses the mourners with its strangeness, yet it constantly tempts the onlookers, symbolized by the unidentified observer, to wonder about what has occurred, to question where the dead man is now.

The third stanza considers the soul and the place in which it finds itself. It is described as waking up, as though from sleep, for this is the first time the soul has had any independent existence. However, it finds itself in a strange place whose main characteristics are blurred contours, greyness and distance, something of which the soul has intuitive awareness, rather than absolute knowledge:

> Se despereza,
> Gris, un refugio de temblor cansado.
> Le preside la paz en sombra de una
> Lejanía que intuye acaso el muerto.   (203/38-41)

In the next lines Guillén effectively demonstrates the difficulty of arriving at knowledge of the situation by suggesting ways of describing it and then denying them. It is hard to come to terms with spacelessness and timelessness when there are no clearly visible objects to aid perception:

> Nubes serán ... No, no lo son. ¡Girones
> Suaves! Pero ¿son suaves? No se palpa
> Nada. ¿Qué existe fuera? Fuera, ahora,
> Alcanzar el espacio es muy difícil.
> ¡Si se determinase una presencia!
> Entre los bastidores más borrosos
> Flota mal el presente de aquel mundo.   (203/42-48)

In the above lines it is impossible for the soul to apprehend its own position with regard to both time and space. Much is insinuated, nothing is known. All that is sure is that there is consciousness of a final state:

> Algo sigue: conciencia sí se salva,
> Conciencia de algún término imposible
> De eludir o negar.   (203/51-53)

In stanza 4 Lazarus is clearly conscious of utter solitude and of pure spirituality. Solitude is described as a catastrophe but not something of which he has emotional knowledge. There is no pain even though all his physical characteristics are absent. The soul exists as pure consciousness, and though all is lost, the knowledge of permanent formlessness increases:

> Perdido, todo.
> Y perdura — perdura todavía—
> Este no recobrarse hacia su forma,
> Lázaro apenas siendo y recordándose
> Para sentirse mínimo en un borde,
> Harapiento despojo de un pasado.   (204/63-68)

In this fifth stanza Lazarus' horror lies in the fact that he now encounters himself in non-existence. As the process described in this section is one of discovery of spirit, Guillén relates it in terms reminiscent of "Más allá" in *Cántico*. Waking is paralleled by the stirring of the soul's consciousness. Once "awake" the soul affirms itself in its discovery of loss and solitude, so different from the "realities" in stanza 4 of the first poem of *Cántico*. The soul wanders with no direction, no end. Again Guillén negates the possibility of there being any definition of time or space:

> Inhabitante ahora —si es "ahora"   (204/72)

>   El muerto vivo asciende
> —O desciende, ni rumbo ni altitud   (204/81-82)

As Lazarus attempts to affirm himself as a soul, all that he discovers is his "formless" existence in Limbo:

> En su nombre se busca el que fue Lázaro,
> Y entre las nieblas, entre las tinieblas
> —¡Oh seno de Abraham!— se identifica,
> Informe, tan ex-Lázaro por Limbo,
> Morada de neutrales y de justos   (204/75-79)

The exclamation, as Wardlaw says, "serves in its irony to underscore the horror of life after death".[20] Guillén sees life after death as an experience of confusion and darkness, contrasting utterly with the glory experienced by Lazarus the poor man, who was carried after death by angels into the bosom of Abraham, a place of solace and security. In addition to formlessness, Lazarus is no longer the man identified by his name; he is "anulado" (annulled), he no longer exists in a real place ("pura sombra de ningún sol" [pure shadow of no sun]) but one which is "desmemoriada" (unrecorded). If his name no longer has meaning, then similarly Limbo provides nothing to aid perception. To describe this void Guillén has to use words of communicative value for the reader, and perforce reminds us that Limbo denies communicative value to all things and is therefore an "unrecorded region". At the end of stanza 5 the question "¿Qué le importan a Lázaro la Tierra, / Los hombres?" (What do the Earth and men matter to Lazarus?) serves to emphasize his complete alienation from all things known in the past.

Stanza 6 begins with the following statement:

---

[20] Wardlaw, p.69.

> Tan ajeno es ya lo ajeno
> Que se hunde, se extingue en el olvido.   (205/86-87)

These lines bring together both the dead man and the living. Each has become alien to the other because of death, the "fatal, obscure shipwreck". On earth life continues in the bodies of the living, whereas life for Lazarus has ended there:

> Todo queda entre zarzas corporales.
> Todo falló entre el polvo y las pasiones.   (205/89-90)

Guillén's choice of the image "corporeal brambles" to express life (breath caught in the mass of human bodies) is excellent, for it contrasts strongly with the formlessness of Limbo. The clinging dust of the earth and emotions, which are symbols of life, function in the same way. Life is seen as a "Más Acá inasequible" (unreachable Nearby), though Guillén goes on to diminish the impact of the meaning of "inasequible", for the effect of Eternity on the soul is to remove all desires, all memory of human life; even the living are as the dead for Lazarus. He is now no longer a man but one of the "potencias preparadas / A plenitud celeste" (initiates prepared for heavenly fulfilment), and as such nothing on the earth has meaning or value for him:

> Sobre el suelo
> Del Globo —diminuto, sin matices,
> Sin relieve asidero ni horizonte—
> Discurren las hormigas, los parlantes
> Que ignoran casi siempre a los ausentes   (205/98-102)

Thus Guillén finally clarifies the effect of death on both the dead man and his soul and on the living. The latter forget the dead, for the simple reason that they are "absent". For the dead, the earth no longer has any objects or shapes which are an aid to perception ("Sin relieve *asidero* ni horizonte" [With neither *graspable* shapes nor horizon]). In the last lines of this stanza Guillén uses two verbs beginning with the prefix "entre", the meaning of which emphasizes the absolute distance between the living and the dead. The latter are "Muy poco entretejidos" (hardly entwined) in life, which is described in terms of emotions, light and flora – all things from which the soul is irrevocably parted. The living are described as "los que transcurriendo se entreviven" (those who passing through time survive together).

In stanza 6, then, Lazarus and the living are seen as permanently alienated. Lazarus is described as being resigned to this situation, and the section ends with an exclamation which is the narrator's perception, as a living being, of life after death:

> ¡Qué pureza
> Terrible, qué sosiego permanente,
> Espíritu en la paz que aguarda al Hijo!   (205/108-110)

Here the poet introduces for the first time the beginnings of the biblical story of Christ's resurrection of Lazarus, at the same time suggesting that for both Lazarus and those who knew him the miracle of resurrection and the possibility of life after death were not yet real, as the question "¿Le espera Lázaro?" (Is Lazarus awaiting Him?) indicates. In this first part of the poem Guillén has created a situation which catalogues the horrors of the void into which the dead are apparently cast. The dead body remains to all intents and purposes as real as the living man, except for its strange stillness, but Guillén also emphasizes the mourners' knowledge that death has occurred and includes a veiled reference to a possible "Beyond" for the spirit. The experience of Limbo is cleverly portrayed by the use of vocabulary which, although it belongs to the world of the living, is made an effective tool to describe nothingness.

Section II is in *romance* form, with Christ's words having a slightly different rhyme scheme from the rest of the section. Guillén follows very closely the New Testament source, but also incorporates his own interpretation of the significance of Christ's action for mankind. In a manner reminiscent of parts of section I Lazarus is described as "tan borroso" (so indistinct), and Christ is shown surrounded by his followers, who are described as

> Los que le siguen en todo,
> Y también los errabundos
> Sin fe, compasión ni arrojo.   (206/117-19)

He again reminds the reader of the distinction between the living and the dead by describing Lazarus as "solo / Por entre fajas y vendas" (alone amongst linen bands) and the living as "los otros, / Libres en aire con luz, / Luz desde aflicción a lloro" (the others, free in light and air, light from sorrow to grief). When Christ approaches the tomb Lazarus is visualized as lacking both identity and soul, recalling the detailed references to the eerie solidity of the dead body. The four days in the tomb are seen as a "Rumbo hacia su final destrozo" (way towards his final annihilation), reminding the reader again of the formless void in which Lazarus' soul awoke. After Christ calls him to rise up from his burial place, Guillén continues his re-creation of these events by celebrating the significance of them for mankind. Christ's words, uttered at a specific time and in a particular place, in fact have an eternal significance:

> Palabra que eternamente
> Lanzando está aquella Voz
> —Eternamente suprema
> Sobre deidad y varón—
> A los hijos de los hombres
> Necesitados de amor.   (208/180-85)

Christ's love of mankind, Guillén claims, is as necessary a part of man's make-up as the sun is necessary to Creation. Without the sun, which is the one thing which enables the world to exist, Creation would be valueless. Without the love of God, shown to man by Christ, man's existence would become nothing more than a futile search for an impossible immortality:

> Amor tan ineludible
> Como el resplandor del sol
> En mediodía más fuerte
> Que la desesperación
> Del hombre a caza del hombre,
> Sin vislumbrarte, Señor   (208/186-91)

With the miracle of the resurrection of Lazarus, God's love is shown in its greatest significance, just as the sun at midday is a time of plenitude and displays the wonders of Creation in absolute light. Christ's words, calling Lazarus from the dead, bring to man the eternal possibility that his mortality may be overcome:

> Para todos esperanza
> De plena consumación.   (208/192-93)

Section III is the longest in "Lugar de Lázaro". Structurally it parallels section I in that it has no rhyme scheme. Thematically, it details Lazarus' experiences after resurrection and as such is as original as section I. "Ser" (to be) is the verb used to describe him, just as "apenas siendo" (scarcely existing) referred to his experiences in Limbo. He does not share his experience of the void with his living companions, because it was a purely spiritual awareness and as such is impossible to express in linguistic terms. In section I there was no "medida común" (shared measure) to equate life, transient mortality, with death. So in section III there are no "comunes términos / Humanos" (shared human terms) to which Lazarus can have recourse to explain the inexplicable to fellow human beings.

In stanza 2 his previous experience is described as "dangers" and "catastrophes", but the routine of life enables him to return quickly to normality. The words "Volver a respirar / Es la delicia humilde" (To breathe again is humble pleasure) are a profoundly impressive insight into the simple but real implications of his return to life. There is no difficult search for orientation in time and space, as the soul experienced in Limbo. The simple act of breathing is the key which unlocks all the marvellous complexity of life. Florence Yudin's interpretation of this poem lacks her usual insight. Lazarus' lack of communication with his family and friends she interprets in the following way:

> Lázaro's silence, the incommunicable language of God with man, is now his unique wisdom. Having experienced the Final Silence, he must make a return to the world of words: "... vivir es siempre cotidiano, / Y volver a respirar se aprende pronto". The matter-of-fact tone serves as a fitting contrast to the metaphysical purport of the secret wisdom.[21]

The reason for her misinterpretation lies in her attitude to the significance of silence in the poem. She seems to ignore the horrific experience of Lazarus in Limbo and also the tenor of his long prayer in section IV. The tone of the lines quoted above may be matter-of-fact, but this is because they are a prelude to a revelation even greater, in this re-creation of the miracle of resurrection, than any details of the soul's experience in Limbo might be.

Lazarus, in his return to life, shows none of the characteristics of death. He is "natural ... Sin palidez sublime" (natural ... with no otherworldly paleness), and becomes intimately involved with the details of daily life which, in contrast to the blur of Limbo, actually reinforce his sense of being alive. The description of this feeling includes a reference to "roots", which recalls the "raíces manchadas de mantillo" (roots speckled by fertile humus) from which Lazarus was so completely separated in section I. There is also a reference to "words", indicating that his sense of belonging incontrovertibly to life lies in the fact that language and the noise of people speaking around him signify that he pertains to a specific time and place:

No hay mayor entereza:
Ser en pleno —con todas las raíces—
Por entre los vocablos que son patria:
Estas calles y calles de rumor
Que es música.

[21] Yudin, p.69.

> Y la voz de María,
> Y el silencio de Marta,
> Que se escucha también,
> Y pesa.
> Todo es sencillo y tierno   (210/218-27)

A more personal aspect of Lazarus' sense of belonging lies in the simplest act of living, symbolized by the bread on the table:

> La casa,
> Y en la casa la mesa,
> Y a la mesa los tres ante su pan:
> Volumen de alegría
> Común sobre manteles
> O madera de pino.   (210/231-36)

Lazarus is rarely alone, never seeks solitude, and finds his real being in companionship, something which deepens his sense of being human in a specific place:

> Hombre en esta Betania de su amor.   (211/246)

Stanza 6 goes on to emphasize the details of place, ranging from the ground beneath Lazarus' feet to the trees and flowers that he sees. It should be noted that these very details specify shapes and perfumes: the broad spread of the elm, the straight line of the cypress tree, the sharp perfume of jasmine and orange blossom. From the scent of the flowers Lazarus becomes more strongly aware of his supreme attribute as a human being – the experience of the passage of time. The momentary perfume of the flowers, described as "attacks" and "moments of fragrance", reminds him of other times when he was aware of them:

> Aroma con un fondo palpitado,
> Tan íntimo,
> De tardes con jazmín, con azahar,
> Vivas en emisiones instantáneas.   (211/258-61)

Stanza 7 broadens this theme of time to see it as "la corriente / Del vivir incesante" (the current of incessant life). Each new day renews Lazarus' sense of vitality, and the passage of time is thus a pleasure to him, rather than sorrow. Here he is once more, like the protagonist of *Cántico*, in the centre of his mortal existence, in perfect accord with his own particular time and place:

> Y Lázaro circula
> Según

> Su justeza espontánea,
> Humildemente a gusto:
> Interior al rincón que le dio el Padre.　　　(212/273-77)

Lazarus' simple pleasure in his awareness of the passage of time is shown in stanza 8, while in the following stanza the idea of life as a "current" is repeated, though its finiteness, too, is specifically referred to. Lazarus' conformity with mortality is expressed in the image of him as a "buen navegante por su propio río" (good navigator along his own river). Old age and death are portrayed in images intimately connected with the human experience: "Ondas, canas, adioses . . ." (waves, white hairs, farewells . . .), words which recall the compassion and simplicity of the very first lines of the poem. The phrase "Lázaro erguido" (Lazarus erect), at the end of this stanza, creates an impression of a man standing resolutely and calmly to face the eventual end of life, symbolized in the depiction of dusk, where the line "*Actual* y *ya* extinguiéndose" (*Here* and *already* dying away) (my italics) summarizes the temporal concerns of these stanzas.

In stanza 10 it becomes clear that the horror of Lazarus' experience in Limbo does not affect his ability to be completely immersed in life, neither does he feel any sense of importance because of the singularity of that experience. The stanza ends with a further reference to his identity, which stems from his temporality:

> . . . Lázaro es Lázaro
> Sobre días y días
> Terrestres, fugitivos.　　　(213/308-310)

He is surrounded by his family, a symbol of human tenderness, and is familiar with Christ's frequent presence. His attitude to his mortality shows on his face, not in lines of worry or bitterness, but in the serenity of patient acceptance, and the positioning of the words "De arrugas" (of wrinkles) and "Paciente" (patient) emphasizes their importance as examples of this particular individual's conformity with life:

> Todo va entretejiéndose en la red
> De arrugas
> Adonde va a parar
> El tiempo de aquel hombre:
> Tiempo bien esculpido,
> El semblante de Lázaro
> Paciente.　　　(213-14/319-25)

Lazarus' physical presence and the fact that he bears no visible reminder of his death cause people quickly to forget what happened to him. The second half of this twelfth stanza records small details of his actions to emphasize his reality, which is that of an "earthly creature of his God". The penultimate stanza of section III finally refers to Lazarus at times when he actually recalls his experience of death, and the last stanza is a statement to the effect that he does suffer as a result:

> De paz no goza el hombre que recuerda
> Para sí, para dentro, lo indecible.
> Único en el retorno de ultratumba,
> Se interroga, compara, sufre, teme,
> Se encomienda a su Dios,
> Suplica.   (214/345-50)

The whole of this third section is an imaginary creation on Guillén's part of Lazarus' response to receiving the gift of life for a second time. It has exalted, in a quietly meditative way, the pleasure of regaining life and experiencing once more the essence of what makes human life special, its passage through time. As a prelude to section IV, where Lazarus gives voice to his own reactions, stanza 14 of section III amounts to a specific rejection of any possible thought that he has experienced something wonderful. On the contrary, though he loves his mortal existence with renewed fervour, he cannot enjoy a sense of peace as a result of returning from the dead. His experience is incommunicable. As a consequence of it, he can only do what other Christians do when confronted with death and the unknown beyond: he suffers, he knows fear, and he commends himself to God.

Section IV is in *romance* form, making it a parallel structure to section II, and it records Lazarus' own response to his experience in the form of a prayer offered privately, and with great pathos, to God. He sees his resurrection as a miracle of such extraordinary rareness that it causes confusion and bewilderment. Guillén's use of the word "lumbre" (light) to mean miracle, and "deslumbramiento" to describe Lazarus' reaction, is particularly effective since the latter has two meanings: one is "brilliance", but the other – with a negative sense suggested by the prefix "des-" – indicates that he does not feel enlightened and secure because of his knowledge of life after death, but rather bewildered and confused. He feels greatly privileged to have had such an experience, since he is unique amongst men who know nothing of the silence he knew. But he refers to the silence of

Limbo as "atrocious" – not something that can be interpreted as a situation to which he "longs to return", as Yudin suggests.[22] In fact the noises which surround Lazarus serve to remind him of the secret silence he experienced, which he feels increasingly constitutes a threat or a danger ("Con relieve de nublado" [with the appearance of impending danger]). For Lazarus noise means life, and as a result of it he is able to delight in each new day and the life which dawn reveals to him. The things of the earth, from dew and wind to travellers from foreign places, reinforce his love and praise of God. But simultaneously those same things prove to him that the earth is the only experience that makes him real too. He humbly recognizes this, but stresses his mortal state, a combination of spiritual strength ("mente" [mind], "fervor" [fervour]) and physical weakness ("piel" [flesh], "flaquezas" [frailties]). In words that remind one of the famous lines in the last stanza of section I of "Más allá", Lazarus proclaims his faith in the only thing that gives him objective knowledge of his earthly existence:

> Y gracias a tantas formas
> Firmes que se me demuestran,
> Soy —porque estoy.   (216/394-96)

Lazarus follows this exaltation of mortality by declaring his belief that in life after death he will continue as a being of flesh and blood, of physical as well as spiritual reality:

> Habré de resucitar
> Con mi espíritu y mi cuerpo:
> La promesa ha de cumplirse.   (217/405-407)

This, then, is Lazarus' understanding of the experience of resurrection – a continuing life of body and spirit.

He breaks off at this point, realizing that what he wants is not what is laid down in the Scriptures. He claims that he does desire the bliss of heaven, but questions exactly what part of his nature it is that hopes for this. There is the part of him that enjoys earthly existence, who is resurrected each day with each dawn, and the part of him which has experienced life after death. In stanza 4 he opts firmly for the former as his real desire:

> Si fuera
> Yo habitante de Tu Gloria,
> A mí dámela terrena.   (218/434-36)

[22] Yudin, p.69.

He hopes that heaven may be a continuation of earthly life. He cannot conceive of being immortal:

> ¿Qué impulsaría a mis manos,
> A mi carne resurrecta,
> Cómo sería yo aún
> Éste que contigo sueña,
> Mortal? Mi ser inmortal
> ¿Sería mío?   (218/445-49)

Lazarus only *knows* human, mortal life; his knowledge of life after death is "the inexpressible"; it cannot be made real by words, or shared with others. Such a confession shames him and he tries by further prayer to rectify his misguided view. Yet the prayer is an alternative formulation of what he has just confessed. He hopes that heaven may be a place where precisely those aspects of life which make him joyously mortal may remain:

> Que la sacra excelsitud
> Como una Betania sea,
> Y la bienaventuranza
> Salve las suertes modestas
> En que un hombre llega a ser
> El hombre que Tú, Tú creas
> Tan humano.   (218-19/455-61)

In the final stanza Lazarus again confesses to being mistaken. He describes himself as lost, but not dissociated from God. In this turbulent mental state Lazarus is fully aware of his wish to live on in his earthly form, at the same time as he wills himself to accept God's purpose. His final statement is full of pathos:

> Mi sitio ...
> Es éste donde soy quien
> Soy mientras hacia los cielos
> Me empuja, casi cruel,
> Una exigencia de cumbre,
> Sumo lugar, sumo bien,
> La revelación del Hijo,
> Y el alma se va tras Él.   (219/476-83)

But what an extraordinary conformity this is! Lazarus was chosen by God as a symbol of life after death, a symbol to give hope to all mankind to offset the fear of death and nothingness. He alone experiences a return to life, an experience so full of joy and reality that he wants never to relinquish it. Man's desperate desire for life after death becomes something for Lazarus which is cruel, but which he humbly accepts:

> Que su luz sea mi guía.
> Quiero en su verdad creer.   (219/484-85)

What Lazarus experienced, in Guillén's re-creation, was Limbo –
which paradoxically reinforced his love of mortality. He wants to
believe in Christ's truth, but knows as no other man can his
propensity to wish that that truth should be exactly the same as the
life he has lived with renewed vigour on earth. Lazarus' final stance is
an act of faith, in conformity with God's will, but one which is
arrived at in full knowledge of the difficulties such faith implies.

"Lugar de Lázaro" is an intensely human poem, and a fitting
start to the second volume of *Clamor*. Although Guillén uses a line
from Jorge Manrique as the title for this second volume, a line which
purposely calls to mind mortality, he begins with a poem which is an
exaltation of that mortality. The differences between the poem and
its biblical counterpart are obvious, and the source material takes up
a very small part of Guillén's creation. Rather than a symbol of
divine love, Lazarus is a symbol of intensely human aspirations. The
poet shows in his portrayal of the dead body and of Limbo that
attempts to know death before it occurs are futile; he shows, in
sections III and IV, that life is supremely precious because it can be
known to the full. Even after a unique experience, Lazarus is more
strongly convinced of this and more tragically confused by the
symbolic meaning of his resurrection. Man's only real and meaningful experience is life and the passage of time, and he has language to
make that experience more real. He does not have the words to
explain the unexplainable and, therefore, should not long for
knowledge that will in some way prepare him for the unknowable.
Lazarus is indeed a symbol for mankind, but in Guillén's work his
experience is converted into a warning. He does not enjoy the peace
that mankind mistakenly assumes is the gift of knowledge of life after
death. It is his very mortality that comes to seem precious to him, and
it is precisely this aspect of his unique experience that is offered to us
for particular consideration by Guillén.

"Huerto de Melibea"

"Huerto de Melibea" (Melibea's Garden, *CL* 366-85) has an
epigraph from Fernando de Rojas – "Todo por vivir" (All for life) –
which indicates that everything in this poem is created to reflect an
overwhelming desire for life, an epigraph in which the infinitive

"vivir", used in preference to the noun "vida", stands as a positive contrast to a story which the reader knows ends in death. Luis F. Costa begins his commentary on this poem with an interesting analysis of the rhyme scheme of the opening section where lines 9-10 break with what he identifies as the favourite Guillenian rhyme scheme for *décimas*, thereby reflecting a major theme of the poem, that of plenitude prematurely dashed.[23] The initial rhyme scheme, in effect, echoes the story of Calisto and Melibea, whose lives are ended suddenly and tragically by accidental death and then suicide. "Night" serves as a narrator to introduce the poem. Gullón suggests that "Night" enables the lovers' conversation to take place "dejando a un lado escenario, situación y tiempo" (leaving aside setting, situation and time).[24] However, it should be noted that this imaginary addition to the story of Calisto and Melibea is there specifically to give details of place and time. Two further points of interest in the differences between Guillén's re-creation and Rojas' original work, apart from the former's emphasis on the harmonious conspiracy of the garden with the lovers, are that the poem is neither comedy nor tragicomedy. Neither is there the violence and evil which are an important part of Rojas' work. Yudin's commentary stresses the silent order of Creation in harmony with the lovers, and also the lovers' enjoyment of the palpable silence which surrounds them in the garden.[25] Casalduero compares the poem with "Lugar de Lázaro" on the basis that night is an important element in each. Lazarus leaves the darkness of death to take up life again, while "Huerto de Melibea" symbolizes a night which, though ending in death, is nevertheless transcended by love.[26]

The first speech by "Night" sets the scene, and in doing so, immediately establishes differences between Guillén's creation and Rojas' original. Although Guillén's poem is in dramatic form, his choice of "Night" as a character of equal importance to the lovers enables him to create a scenario which describes, in a way that Rojas does not, the place where the lovers meet as a symbol of cosmic harmony. Another re-creation of the story of Calisto and Melibea is to be found in "Las nubes", the ninth section of Azorín's *Castilla*. However, Azorín departs radically from *La Celestina* by imagining Melibea and Calisto as married, with a beautiful daughter. At the end

[23] Costa, pp.159-60.
[24] R. Gullón, "Huerto de Melibea", *Papeles de Son Armadans*, 4 (1956), 90.
[25] Yudin, pp.28, 47.
[26] Casalduero, p.258.

of the section this girl, Alisa, is seen in the garden, where the arrival of a falcon brings with it its owner. Calisto, seeing these events, knows exactly what will transpire in his daughter's conversation with the young man. Azorín's purpose is to emphasize the eternal repetition of man's life within time:

> Sí: vivir es ver pasar: ver pasar, allá, en lo alto, las nubes. Mejor diríamos: vivir es *ver volver*. Es ver volver todo en un retorno perdurable, eterno; ver volver todo —angustias, alegrías, esperanzas— como esas nubes que son siempre distintas y siempre las mismas, como esas nubes fugaces e inmutables.[27]

> (Yes; to live is to see things pass by: to see the clouds pass by, there, high above. It would be better to say: to live is *to see things return*. It is to see everything come again in a lasting, eternal return; to see all come again – anguish, joy, hope –, like these clouds which are always different and always the same, like these fleeting, unchanging clouds.)

Guillén's purpose in his poem is similarly to remind the reader that love is an eternal force, as is the dawn which returns each day. Defence of love, symbolized by Melibea's suicide, is in itself a positive response to cosmic order, even though her death is precipitated by human error.

The first words of "Night" refer to the harmonious forces of Creation:

> Del instante en silencio parten hacia lo oscuro
> Las fuerzas que se acrecen deseando,
> Formando su futuro:
> El mando
> Que habrá de presidir el mediodía.   (366/1-5)

The passage of time, from darkness to daylight and plenitude at midday, is thus the framework within which the world exists. It is also that in which human life evolves, and "Night" returns to this idea in her final speech. Within the sphere of this harmonious movement, voices are heard, those of Lucrecia and Melibea. Having set human lives in this context of order, "Night" returns to consider the moon. Its light brings to the garden illumination similar to that of daylight; it is a source of pleasure for mortals who are guided by it, for the still moon is a beneficent augury of the dawn to come. Harmony, silence, seclusion, love and clemency are introduced in these first lines:

> Todo, todo converge hacia un objeto

---

[27] Azorín, *Castilla*, 7th ed. (Buenos Aires: Losada, 1969), p.93.

Ahora
Más deseado aún que conocido.
¿A nadie le revela su secreto?   (366/14-17)

The "object" mentioned in the lines quoted is an abstract reference to
what is about to take place. It can be interpreted as a fusion of Life
and Love, experiences which Calisto and Melibea actively desire but
of which they as yet have no absolute knowledge. Both desire a love
more permanent than that snatched clandestinely in the garden. Both
want a life which is a public demonstration of that love. But neither
knows to what ends either Love or Life will take them. The question
"Is its secret revealed to nobody?" is only answered by the dénouement of the poem, when Melibea learns that the secret of life is love.
After Calisto's death, she realizes that the secret of love is life, and
both are enjoyed, the poem implies, in life after death, a life where the
lovers exist in another "garden" similar to their earthly one, but
unassailable by chance events.

The philosophical considerations of this section are interrupted
for a second time by the introduction of a young girl:

Ved cómo esa doncella
Con voz que es ya centella
Da a lo oscuro sentido.   (366/18-20)

Her voice and words illuminate and clarify her purpose in the garden
with her maid. Here Guillén's decision to describe Melibea's voice as
a "spark of light" which gives sense to darkness presages the conversations between the lovers. Their love is expressed and given
meaning by the words in which they proclaim it to each other, and
also in Calisto's declaration that Melibea's voice and very name are
symbols of his good fortune.

The first conversation between Melibea and Lucrecia records
Melibea's impatience for her lover, which as in *La Celestina* Lucrecia
tries to calm by song. In Melibea's first speech she believes the stars of
heaven share her grief at her lover's delay, but in her final speech she
affirms her knowledge of his imminent arrival, and envisages their
happiness in terms of cosmic and eternal joy:

Donde Amor nos guardará
—Seguros dentro del huerto—
Con alegría de gloria
Que a los dos sostenga eternos.   (369/81-84)

Guillén follows *La Celestina* by showing the women singing
alone and then together. Lucrecia's first song refers to flowers

becoming more beautiful when the lover arrives, and to the noise of the fountain sounding because the lover who hears it gives reality and meaning to its existence. In terms of imagery these stanzas parallel those that she sings in *La Celestina*. The song sung by both women refers to time which detains the lover, but which will be in harmony with them when they are together. The verbs are in the future, reflecting the known joy which is to come, for the words of love that will be spoken will be like a divine illumination of the darkness. This idea reflects the imagery and meaning of the words spoken by "Night" previously. When Melibea sings alone, her words contain none of the mild annoyance that she shows in *La Celestina*. On the contrary, she declares the pleasure she gains from loving Calisto and again refers to truth being the import of her lover's words. Thus Guillén partially follows Rojas but adds his own interpretation of Melibea's emotions. He retains the sense of harmony developed in the words of "Night" and emphasizes the lovers' participation in cosmic order.

In the second speech by "Night" the earth is described as muting its own voice so that nothing will prevent the lovers meeting:

> Las voces y el silencio de la Tierra
> Van fundiéndose en vasto
> Rumor de fondo oculto.
> El ansia enamorada así no yerra
> Su término.
>
> (369/85-89)

"Night" follows this with the first presentiment of disaster, for she hints that the end to which the lovers move may later be inauspicious. This remains as nothing more than presentiment, for the impulse of love continues with no knowledge of future happiness or pain. "Night" implies that love is divine in its perfection: within the circle of destiny the lovers will find joy. The stanza ends with an exclamation, full of desperate hope: "¡Oh fugitiva perfección, detente!" (Oh fugitive perfection, stay a while!). This second speech has emphasized the unity of earth with the lovers, but has also envisaged future happiness as surrounded by the possibility of destruction.

In the conversation between the lovers which follows, Calisto bewails the time when he is absent from Melibea as "Un gran remordimiento de retraso" (A great remorse of slowness). His daylight life is like that of a ghost, for his only real existence is that experienced with Melibea:

¿Puedo llegar a ser si tú no eres,
Si no estás de verdad ante mis ojos,
Si mis manos te buscan
Y en la luz no te encuentran?   (371/119-22)

During the day all Calisto's senses are dormant, until the night falls
and he is impelled by a force greater than himself towards Melibea.
She in turn affirms her constancy in words which are images of time,
which by paradox imbue their temporary happiness with an
everlasting significance. Calisto recognizes that such an existence is
impossible and confesses to a presentiment of death:

A veces me arrebata en una onda
—Pero yo la rechazo—
Una furia de mar hacia más agua,
Más agua ...
            de un olvido.   (373/157-61)

The traditional image of the sea as death is continued when Calisto
suggests that his whole life, this love for Melibea, is like the
experience of a shipwrecked sailor:

A no ser que yo viva
De mi naufragio, siempre naufragando.
Aquí respiro.   (373/165-67)

When Melibea offers him peace and repose with her, Calisto willingly
enters a world where the normality of the dawn belongs to
"outsiders" and where the two lovers can sink into the darkness,
symbol of their clandestine love. He goes on to liken Melibea to a safe
port for himself, the shipwrecked sailor.

Their final conversation re-establishes the imagery of voice and
words which symbolize absolute existence. Melibea only exists
because of her love for Calisto:

Sin ti no hay Melibea.
Contigo nazco, me conozco, siento
Mi sangre como un río que es un don.
....
Amor, amor, regálame,
Cíñeme con palabras envolventes.   (374/192-99)

The words of love become symbolic actions of love, and both
confirm the existence of the beloved. The section ends with Calisto's
earnest wish that the world could be reduced to the harmonious
garden which not only symbolizes their love but is also a synonym for
Melibea.

In the third speech by "Night" the harmony in love achieved by Calisto and Melibea in their conversation is paralleled by the silent garden which is submerged deeper into the cosmic harmony which surrounds it:

> El huerto, recogido
> Bajo sombras sin voces,
> Se ahonda en este olvido
> Que el mundo le reserva.　　　　　(375/209-212)

It is part of the "gran pulso recóndito" (great recondite pulse) of Creation, and its trees fuse in a protective circle around this part of the earth, around the human lovers. Secrecy is maintained by the natural silence and stillness which actively contribute to the essential harmony that has been achieved. With an exclamation, "¡Triunfad en claro, círculos mayores!" (Triumph openly, greater circles!), "Night" exults in this universal harmony which, though mysterious, has nevertheless proved the existence of Love, as exemplified in the love of Calisto and Melibea:

> Amor, de amor capaz,
> —Si no lo arrasa todo con el oculto filo
> De pronto violento—
> Extiende este sigilo
> De paz.　　　　　(376/230-34)

The image of circles being cut by a sharp, straight line foreshadows the separation of Melibea from Calisto, but the overriding sense of the final lines is a re-emphasis of the harmony, universal and individual, that has been achieved:

> Amor: los astros giran en torno de este huerto. (376/238)

The second conversation of Calisto and Melibea begins with exclamations of wonder by Calisto. His world of love is Melibea, and she is the centre of it. His interpretation of his recumbent state as that of being "tendido / Como para morir" (stretched out as though to die) is further evidence of his morbid presentiments, but, as in the previous conversation, Melibea denies such thoughts. Having described her as his horizon, the outer limits of his world, he goes on to depict her as the "goal" of his existence, something the more tangible for being real. The constant fluctuations in his speech between life and death reinforce the impression that existence for him is life in Melibea's presence and death in her absence. However, she sees their love as a light which will never hide them from each other. During the day the shadow of the cypress tree provides her with a small reminder of the darkness which envelops their meetings. Thus Melibea constantly finds positive interpretations for Calisto's gloomy presentiments. For her there is no sense of time when she is with him, the warmth of his body is like the light of day for her and their physical and spiritual closeness represents immortality. For Calisto, however, time is very real and carries him remorselessly to the next day and abhorred separation. His outcry of fierce sensuality is rebuked by her because such words "darken the night", have a destructive force which contrasts with the meaning of their words of love. She declares her faithfulness to him, even though they are separated during the day, a loyalty which symbolically outshines even the brightest moonlight:

> Estoy más lealmente
> Desnuda para ti —bajo mi ropa—
> Que aquella tan desnuda de allá arriba,
> Entregándose al huerto.   (379/299-302)

For Melibea physical contact brings about the possession of the essence of the loved one. Here she utters her first negative thought, one which expresses her horror of life without the closeness of Calisto. The latter takes up her words, referring to the thought of spending his days separated from her, dreaming either of his own death or that other death following the climax of sexual union. In either situation Calisto sees himself as "Rendido, loco, muerto" (Exhausted, mad, dead). Melibea stops these thoughts, pointing out both her presence and her love, and also the presence of night, the one thing which makes possible his meetings with her. When voices are heard, the silence of love – and the especial life within it – is broken. Calisto rushes away, and further noise of shouts and groans makes Melibea realize that the harmony is gone:

> ¡Oh fortuna
> Sin ley!
> Fui tan feliz que tengo miedo.   (381/350-52)

Melibea's final words indicate mistrust of such perfect happiness, but only when Calisto's precipitous flight from her has already introduced a sense of human error.

The fourth interpolation by "Night" continues the idea of destroyed harmony:

> No oigo bien el murmullo de esa fuente.   (381/353)

In the opening section of the poem the light of the moon was seen as the "fountain of love", and Lucrecia later referred to the fountain as a ceaseless activity caused by the lovers' appreciation of its sound. The fountain thus has connotations of both light and sound, forming part of the lovers' harmony. When that harmony is broken, the noise of the fountain, which like Melibea's voice is light and sound, is no longer clear. "Night" suggests that it is destiny which causes the sudden intrusion of the world in the shape of the people who invade the silence of the garden. Several times Calisto refers to people as "the others", signifying their non-involvement in his and Melibea's world. Now that the world has been violated, now that the magical silence of the garden has been broken and transformed into the ordinary silence of the world beyond it, destiny and chance are expected to play a part:

> Corre tanto el destino
> De algunos seres a su desenlace
> Que en el silencio se precipita de repente
> La expectación del mundo. (381-82/354-57)

The private world of Calisto and Melibea's life and love has been made public by a rash act. "Night" questions whether one single mortal can destroy a harmony of such perfection that it is divine, whether a chance and fateful action, a symbol of chaos, can have the power to ruin "the remaining harmony". These questions are not answered directly, but the word "Rigor" (Rigour) serves to show that what destiny has dictated will be fulfilled, and "Night" returns the reader once more to the story of *La Celestina* by announcing the death of Calisto.

The fourth section of conversation is between Lucrecia and Melibea, and as with Rojas, so here there is a long speech by Melibea which begins by repeating the substance of those questions asked by "Night":

> ¿Es posible que esta gloria
> Se haya quebrado de un golpe? (383/381-82)

The circle of their love and life has been broken by a single blow, as was foreseen by "Night" in her third speech. Now, in contrast to her sense of real existence brought about by Calisto's words of love, Melibea is pierced by the words and voices around her. Although Calisto lies dead on the ground he no longer exists for her – not even as a dead man, for his voice no longer illuminates anything and makes it real. Melibea herself ceases to exist, surrounded as she now is by noise and separated by Calisto's death from the only air and light that made her live. She describes herself as in a double exile: firstly because Calisto is dead, and secondly because she is alienated from her very self. She believes that a door has been closed by his death and now the secrets of love contained within her must remain hidden. The phrase "¡Si tuyos son, serán míos!" (If they are yours, they shall be mine!) is the first indication that she will take her own life, and, as in *La Celestina*, she mounts the tower from which she will be able to see Calisto. In death he represents a haven to which she aspires:

> Yo he de volar hacia ti,
> Sumirme en el oro enorme,
> Vivir de revelación
> En la cima del gran orden,
> Salvada, sí, para siempre,
> Mi boca en tu boca.   (384/409-14)

Thus Calisto in death becomes, as he was in life, the way to absolute harmony, where life and love are forever enjoyed. Once again the mouth, which in mortal existence uttered the words of love which bestowed life on the lovers, becomes a symbol of communication on an eternal level. Calisto is also and once again a symbol of illumination:

> Ponme,
> Calisto, mi amor, de nuevo
> Triunfante, dentro del orbe
> Que alumbrarás para mí,
> Donde me aguardas.   (384/414-18)

Images of light and sound are here coherently incorporated into a vision of life and love which continue in unassailable eternity, the same, only more surely founded, as their love and life on earth.

Melibea knows that her death will cause the same kind of anguished sense of separation for her parents as her present state causes herself, irrevocably isolated from Calisto. The word "corte" (cut) here is a reminder of the images used to describe the destruction of harmony earlier in the poem ("hidden knife-edge", "blow", and the clamour of voices which pierce Melibea after Calisto's death). She talks of her own destiny, death, in terms of rivers running to the sea, recalling both her own and Calisto's words earlier. She sees her future happiness as being with Calisto, and their reunion is described as a high place far away from her present earthly existence:

el monte
Que nunca habrán de cubrir
Estas manchas que corrompen
La luz de tu paraíso.   (385/434-37)

Calisto's state is described in terms of light and paradise, and the image of stains to express earthly existence without him indicates that the intrusion of the world into the lovers' secret haven renders it sullied and worthless. In throwing herself from the tower, Melibea initiates the reconstruction of their paradise by referring to Calisto in terms of "love" and "garden"; she commands him to gather her into the circle of harmony which will be re-created by her death.

The final speech by "Night" brings the reader, literally, down to earth. The orchard is now empty both of human beings and of life and love. The cypress tree, which for Melibea had earlier been a means of recapturing her nocturnal Calisto by day, is now seen in the traditional way as gloomy and funereal, without love to lend it a special essence. The world was formerly surrounded by silence and calm, and its reciprocation with the lovers was reflected by verbs like "to linger", "to converge", "to fuse", "to affirm", "to deepen", "to associate", and "to reabsorb". Now, in contrast, it is "yerto" (rigid) and the victim of a solitude made the more real by the absence of people and emotions. The deaths of the lovers are tragic for those who remain, making them even more aware of their mortality. But the questions which follow imply that the lovers were not destined to suffer tragedy:

¿Ha destruido Amor a sus enamorados?
¿Fueron ellos los libres sin fortuna,
A ciegas tan nocturnos, lastimosos?   (385/447-49)

These questions, reminiscent of Pleberio's anguish at the end of Rojas' work, are clearly given negative answers by the whole of Guillén's poem. Love did not destroy Calisto and Melibea: a precipitous action caused by a chance event did that. Love is in fact the force which reunited them. They were not "lucklessly free, blindly nocturnal", because their liberty as individuals led them to love, the expression of which was illumination. The final lines echo the ideas expressed at the beginning by "Night". Dawn is returning, bringing about the reunion of the world with harmony ("los nuevos acosos / De la Atracción" [the new urgings of Attraction]). The fountain can now be heard clearly, and a new day, symbolizing love of life, is beginning. Love has been redeemed by Melibea's action, hence the final question:

¿Quién no defendería a quien amara?   (385/456)

Guillén has made effective use of the well-known story of Calisto and Melibea. By adding a further character, "Night", to comment on the scene, he contributes a philosophical gloss to the life and actions of the two main characters, and in doing so elevates them as symbols of absolute love. In this, of course, he distances himself totally from the comic and didactic tone of Rojas' work. That this fifteenth-century source can be made an illuminating example of the triumph of love and life over death is of great significance within a book of poems which discusses man's world, something essentially transitory. Unlike Azorín, Guillén calmly accepts the finality of the death of the lovers, but makes of it a symbol of permanence. Thus Melibea can assert:

Yo, yo no pasaré.   (372/150)

"Dimisión de Sancho"

The poem "Dimisión de Sancho" (Sancho's Resignation, *CL* 435-45) follows very closely indeed the episode in chapter 53 of the Second Part of *Don Quijote*. The lines chosen by Guillén as an epigraph for his poem allude to the suddenness with which Sancho loses his long-coveted governorship of the Isle of Barataria, an episode which marks the end of an elaborate and cruel game played at his expense by the Duke and Duchess. The fact that the whole Barataria episode is a trick leads to Sancho's being taken out of his normal sphere of existence; he is, as Costa suggests, distanced from his authentic self.[28] Wardlaw, Yudin and Costa all agree on the basic theme of the poem, Sancho's recovery of his natural role as a result of the simulated attack on him by his servants. Wardlaw speaks of Sancho "struggling with his surroundings" and thereby becoming aware of his own limitations.[29] Yudin's commentary is based upon silence as the source from which Sancho "emerges renewed from his crisis; instead of the trauma of dissociation, he is at last one with his image".[30] However, one of the major points to remember is that the inimical circumstances in which Sancho finds himself lead first of all to disillusionment, a profoundly human experience, out of which he is able to construct an equally human solution. He may well be

[28] Costa, p.160.
[29] Wardlaw, pp.105, 106, 109.
[30] Yudin, p.25.

immersed in "the trauma of dissociation", but instead of trying to strengthen his position as governor, he in fact deliberately intensifies that dissociation because he realizes it to be the key with which to achieve normality. For Debicki, Sancho is a symbol of man's need to find his own understanding of the value of life.[31]

Section I begins by setting the scene, the simulated attack on the castle by Sancho's servants. The calm of night is suddenly menaced by the din of the attackers' cries. The verbs "cae" (falls) and "se desploma" (crashes down) serve to emphasize the noise by giving it an almost physical presence. Stanza 2 continues this emphasis with the use of the words "irrumpen" (erupt) and "sobresaltadas" (frightening) to describe the sudden onset of noise. That this confusion is complete and effective is indicated by the following lines:

> Violencia total
> Robustece su cerco.   (435/12-13)

The organization and orderliness of the servants' plan is efficiently indicated in the first four lines below which greatly reduce Cervantes' prose original:

> Los guiará el Señor,
> Capitán de improviso,
> Y ya entre dos paveses,
> De pie —paralizado.
> La rígida figura se derrumba.
> Adversidad: el suelo.   (435-36/19-24)

The use of the word "Señor" is ironic, for Sancho is governor and, therefore, "Master" to the servants, yet they plan this attack to belittle him. In stanza 4 Guillén is careful to stress the nature of this attack. It represents the kind of cruelty and viciousness that only human beings can perpetrate, and as such renders the attackers a special kind of animal:

> La brutal pesadumbre
> De una masa con saña sólo humana:
> Brutos pies de animales
> Que sólo pueden ser —miradlos— hombres.
> Y se encarnizan miserablemente,
> Revoltijo soez   (436/26-31)

The familiar plural imperative exhorts all of us, as readers, to see the

---

[31] Debicki, p.41.

true nature of these attackers, who constitute the adverse circumstances of life with which all men have to come to terms. In spite of his armour, therefore, Sancho is defenceless against this particular attack. The question "¿Muchedumbre?" (Crowd?) and its answer "Son pocos —de los muchos" (They are but few – of the many) indicate that the unfaithful servants are a symbol of the treacherous nature of mankind. Sancho is described as a "supuesto inferior" (presumed inferior), for the servants know that his position is owed solely to the malicious scheming of the Duke and Duchess, but Guillén's reference to the servants as "los peores" (the worst ones) effectively balances the reader's view of the scene. In stanza 6 Sancho is now portrayed as "Un cuerpo de galápago / Que entre sus conchas sufre y se retrae" (A tortoise which suffers and withdraws into its shell), which Costa believes to be a sign of the narrator's sympathy. In fact, the image is borrowed from Cervantes,[32] and it serves to show that the ridiculous picture Sancho presents supports the servants' view of him as inferior. He has ceased even to be a man and becomes a mere plaything.

In stanza 7 the harshness of the attack gradually abates, and in another image taken from Cervantes the exhausted Sancho is depicted as a boat beached broadsides on the sand. "Relative peace" now descends on him, but he rejects the praise offered to him in victory. In the Cervantes original Sancho's speech indicates that he knows very well that he has been the victim of a cruel game, but here there is no direct speech and he is merely described as having "El alma pesarosa entre aflicciones" (His soul sorrowful in afflictions). At this point he faints away into further unconsciousness, and the use of the verb "se desvanece" (fades away) here is important, since section II goes on to show that the man who was ambitious in his desire to become a governor fades away during sleep, and Sancho subsequently awakes to a new sense of what he must do. Sleep is thus effectively used as a pause between the old and the new Sancho and serves as a time of renewal, recalling the poem "La rendición al sueño" from *Cántico*, whose final question, "¿Hacia la seña / Clara / De otra verdad?" (Towards the clear sign of another truth?) (*C* 154), is particularly appropriate to Sancho's situation.

The sleep of section II is "of great calm". It is

> como una crisis
> Que todo lo remueve y lo recoge

[32] See Cervantes, *El ingenioso hidalgo Don Quijote de la Mancha*, ed. Luis Andrés Murillo (Madrid: Castalia, 1978), II, 442.

—Todavía sin luz—
En tierra, subterráneo
De profunda frescura esperanzada.   (438/74-78)

The "crisis" of this sleep, unlike the real crisis of the day, is one where in spite of the darkness Sancho achieves serenity. The unconsciousness of his sleep is one which indicates Sancho's trust in a supreme power, where the darkness of his daytime experience is illuminated by his own innate knowledge of his real self. Stanza 2 emphasizes the silent harmony of a situation where human beings are held captive within a greater network, that of Creation. Sancho has an essential existence which is linked to forces greater than that represented by the mocking servants and the elaborate trickery of the Duke and Duchess:

El cuerpo inerme del dormido existe
Con una gravedad
Sumisa a ignotos númenes y números.
Todo está en firmamento.   (438/88-91)

This essential existence is termed "gravedad", meaning not only dignity, but also gravity or weight; he is thus in the centre of Creation, part of its cosmic inspiration ("númenes") and harmony ("números"). Further lines from "La rendición al sueño" are a perfect illustration of what is happening to Sancho:

descansa
Mientras a su universo
Consagrándose está.   (*C* 154)

(he rests
While he consecrates himself
To his world.)

In stanza 3 Sancho is described as "lost", but the power of this particular kind of sleep is such that he "finds himself", discovers who and what he really is. Thus section II portrays sleep as a time of gravitation within the cosmos where Sancho moves towards the acquisition of self-knowledge.

Section III begins at dawn, and stillness and quiet characterize this awakening, in contrast to the noise and confusion of section I. Stanza 3 emphasizes the silence, and Yudin sees these lines as "the interplay between silence and self-affirmation [which] shapes the dramatic climax in the poem".[33] Guillén's structuring of this stanza is remarkable, for each line begins with the important words which trace the beginning of Sancho's self-knowledge:

---

[33] Yudin, p.25.

> Amanece en silencio.
> El hombre
> Se descubre a sí mismo
> Despacio
> Mientras, una vez más,
> El sol consigue mundo.   (439/104-109)

Sancho's process of self-discovery begins at the same time as the daily discovery of the world by the sun. His sleep is an unconscious time of meeting and finding his true self; daylight is the intellectual awareness of who he is.

Sancho's silence moves his attackers to respect and imposes a limit of dignity beyond which they cannot go, a silence that cannot be broken by mockery and taunts. The "limits" described here are another example of the delineation of form discussed in chapter 2 of this book. Here, silence gives form to something worthy of respect, and the attackers, themselves stunned into silence, allow Sancho the opportunity to reassume his essential being. The possibility of discovering "essence" through "accident" is here once again portrayed.

In section III Guillén shows Sancho's self-discovery to be a slow and solitary process, and in section IV it is described as a road to a destination yet unknown. Sancho is seen as "aún sepultado" (still buried), the adjective here having a figurative meaning, that of Sancho entombed, or enveloped, in the silence of dawning self-awareness. The question "¿Hubo como una muerte?" (Was there a kind of death?) continues the idea initiated by "sepultado", but the only "death" that has occurred is that of verbal communication. No part of Sancho's character has "died", and in fact the contrary has occurred. The next question, "¿Habrá resurrección / A esta luz albeada?" (Will there be resurrection in this dawn-light?), asks whether Sancho's experience can lead to enlightenment and real self-knowledge, that most difficult achievement for mankind. The comment which follows, "El alba es manantial" (Dawn is a spring), recalls the previous section, where Sancho discovered himself at the same time as dawn appeared. Dawn, signifying both spring and source in the line quoted, means that this can be a time of clarity and purification for Sancho, a time when he may also come to know his own origin, his own *raison d'être*. Once again natural light and self-enlightenment go together.

In stanza 2 Guillén describes the actions that take Sancho along the road to self-discovery. Now the attackers are "los otros, / Con embarazo ahora observadores" (the others, limited now to being observers), and his sense of security is symbolized in the kiss of peace he bestows on Dapple, his simple donkey who instinctively knows his true character, and is so different from the human animals who were the source of his crisis. In the Cervantes original, Sancho equates his present misery with having left his humble state and followed the dictates of ambition, and all this is implied in Guillén's lines showing the donkey's recognition of Sancho:

> Se dirige, por fin,
> A quien sabe más cerca
> De su amor, su destino. (440/133-35)

Sections II, III, IV and V are similar in structure, being composed of three, four, four and three stanzas respectively, in unrhymed lines and varied metres. In section V the donkey is shown as a companion whose loyalty is a source of comfort. Sancho's soul is "aliviada" (relieved) now, in contrast to the former "pesarosa" (sorrowful). The donkey symbolizes "un vivir compartido" (a shared existence) and "la diaria verdad" (daily truth) and thus leads him to "su propia existencia / De Sancho verdadero" (his own existence as the real Sancho).

In stanza 3 Sancho saddles up and prepares to leave. The tone is one of simplicity and objectivity, and the final phrase, "A los hombres alegra / Poner los pies en su real camino" (To set out on one's rightful road is a joy to men), is similar to "Volver a respirar / Es la delicia humilde" (To breathe again is humble pleasure) from "Lugar de Lázaro". The obvious sincerity of such lines is another indication of the deep-seated faith in life which sustains Guillén's view of human society even in the darkest moments of *Clamor*.

Section VI begins with Sancho's anticipation of a serene future because of his memory of the past. Such memories have validity now that he has regained his true character. His vision of the life of a simple rural man follows accurately the original in *Don Quijote*. Stanza 2 makes of Sancho's experience a universal truth:

> Un hombre es esa urdimbre de menudas
> Costumbres
> Y cosas que se palpan
> Entre impulsos ajenos
> Entonces al embuste
> De irreal perspectiva:
> Ínsula sin un mar,
> Gobierno, leyes, vara de sapiencia,

> Vanidad en vacío,
> Torres de una ambición que se nos hunde.   (442/167-76)

In contrast to the splendour of the imaginary governorship, the donkey symbolizes truth and brotherhood. When the servants try to persuade him to stay, Sancho stops them, for he has learned from his experiences, and, in a speech which uses the popular sayings so typical of the original Sancho Panza, he declares his intention to hold to his simple former life. The remaining stanzas of section VI are a close re-creation of the Cervantes original. Guillén's addition of the phrase "La carretera es recta" (The highway is straight) reinforces the purpose of the modern poet's choice of this episode from a seventeenth-century text. The road of life is straight and secure now that Sancho has achieved self-knowledge. As an *exemplum* of one of the most problematic areas of man's personal development, Sancho is a friend to all who read of his particular crisis.

In section VII Sancho and the donkey are following the road of reality, in freedom:

> Sancho ha tocado tierra,
> Tan evidente y tan simple. Sancho es Sancho,
> Y en su puesto, ceñido por sus límites:
> Realidad entrañada,
> De veras plenitud bien asumida.   (444/208-12)

"Sancho has touched the earth" is meant not in the simple sense of having recovered from the fantasies which led to his governorship, nor yet in the sense of being once again the down-to-earth man he used to be. It is more precisely understood by the statements of section II, where Sancho is described as being part of the greater harmony and order of the Cosmos. The idea of man being circumscribed by limits, seen in *Cántico*, is repeated here, where these limits are Sancho's human self which, once acknowledged and accepted, enables him to become an intimate part of reality. His newly discovered essence becomes one with the Sancho who existed in a latent state as the governor. He has achieved normality and the salvation or completeness that this implies. The question asked in stanza 2 of section IV ("what is he now?") is answered here:

> —Heme aquí, Sancho soy.   (444/216)

As a complete and self-knowing man, Sancho occupies a place which is both "native land" and "universe"; he has achieved the kind of eminence which is apprehended by the protagonist in "Luz natal".

His physical and spiritual concordance is not just passively accepted; he knows his mortal self, but is prepared always to move through time without being diminished by it, towards a future that is unknown but not feared, because it will be within reality:

> No armonía arcangélica,
> No hermosura celeste.
> Menos y más: ajuste verdadero,
> Partícipe del mundo,
> Partícula de veras insertada. (445/230-34)

The harmonious vision of the protagonist in "Las doce en el reloj" is repeated here:

> Mirando el horizonte
> La vista es siempre centro
> De círculo,
> Y gracias a sus límites
> Sancho es Sancho con fuerza
> De perfil y destino,
> Con tranquila adhesión. (445/235-41)

Sancho's limits are not just those of Creation, they are also his personal limits as an individual which have been accepted through his experience of crisis. He is thoroughly known to himself – "perfil" (character) – and has a future which is his alone – "destino" (destiny) –, a present and a future reality which is serenely accepted as a minute part of the harmony of Creation.

In the penultimate stanza Guillén chooses to juxtapose both a natural and a divine cause as possible creator of this harmony. Either can be accepted in this "Tiempo de historia", for though man's perception of harmony is only fleeting, it nevertheless has lasting benefits:

> El universo entonces,
> O la divinidad,
> Traza en torno el gran círculo perenne.
> Conmovedor instante.
> La criatura acepta:
> Humilde criatura. (445/242-47)

The structure of the last two lines quoted above is important. Acceptance and humility are vital aspects of man. Once they are acknowledged, each man can become the "maravilla rarísima" (rarest marvel) that Guillén has made of Sancho.

As in "Lugar de Lázaro" and "Huerto de Melibea", Guillén

has used for this poem source material which is faithfully reproduced. Each source, however, is re-created with a new significance
for the present-day reader. Sancho's disillusionment is converted
into self-knowledge, and as such represents once again à route to
absolute existence. In "Dimisión de Sancho" the noise of the
surrounding world (the attackers) contrasts strongly with the silent
struggle which eventually leads to discovery of self and the additional
benefits of future security. That phrases and statements reminiscent
of *Cántico* recur so frequently in this poem is no accident. The generic
protagonist of *Cántico* and his experiences are symbols of the
potential in all men to be the same as he. Sancho, a real character in
spite of his fictional provenance, is made by Guillén to represent in
Clamor what was described in *Cántico*:

> Maravilla rarísima
> De la humildad. ¡Oh Sancho!   (445/248-49)

"Las tentaciones de Antonio"

The final pillar poem of *A la altura de las circunstancias*, "Las
tentaciones de Antonio" (The Temptations of Anthony, *CL* 491-
505), is preceded by a quotation from Antonio Machado:

> . . . por mucho que valga un hombre, nunca tendrá valor más alto que
> el valor de ser hombre.

The emphasis on the value of human-ness in Machado's lines is
reflected in Guillén's poem, which begins and ends with the word
"hombre". The poem traces the efforts of Anthony to achieve his
vocation – that of being human. Both "Dimisión de Sancho" and
"Las tentaciones de Antonio" are illustrations of symbolic roads to
self-knowledge, and while Sancho's road is disillusionment, that of
Anthony is the temptation to become either supreme through the
destruction of others or solitary in mystic communion with God.
Anthony represents two aspects of man's character which tend to
isolation, and these are portrayed as dreams, indicating that all men
have the potential to become destructive or eremitic. His struggle is
thus with inner forces which tempt him away from that essential
"coexistence" which Guillén exalts. Sancho, on the other hand, has
come to terms with human beings who wish to destroy man's innate
need of companionship by alienating him with their cruel mockery.
The struggle with self and surroundings which these poems exemplify
is thus a vital road to being "equal to circumstances".

Gullón attaches no particular importance to the dual nature of Anthony's dreams, as both symbolize one fundamental temptation – the renunciation of reality.[34] However, Costa's understanding of the significance of the dreams is more useful as it recognizes each as of equal importance. The first, the desire to destroy, is interpreted as "vitalismo puro" (pure vitalism) or an instinctive self-interest which has no ethical basis. The second, the desire to live in isolation (which is desolation for Guillén), represents the abandonment of earthly, human characteristics.[35] These two interpretations lead to the conclusion that each individual must strive to avoid the instinct to overcome others and also the desire *not* to become involved with other human beings. Both of these imply that the individual is not actively promoting his characteristics as a social animal within the world of man's making, the only thing by which man's survival as a human being is assured.

"Las tentaciones de Antonio" begins with a man asleep. It is a sleep in which the weariness of the past day still affects the subconscious mind and causes tempestuous dreams and inner turmoil. In these dreams reality ("las hilachas triviales de aquel día" [the trivial threads of that day]) and the future ("lo jamás vivido" [what has never been lived]) are confused, and Anthony is "inquieto siempre y desasosegado" (always uneasy and restless). Thus there is an immediate contrast with Sancho's sleep in section II of "Dimisión de Sancho", where turmoil of a positive kind makes of that sleep a "great calm". Sancho is unconscious of anything, whereas Anthony's memory is still active, though "deforme" (abnormal), and conjures up "imágenes aéreas" (flimsy images).

The second stanza begins with the single word "Antonio", paralleling the start of stanza 1. However, Guillén goes on to question whether it really is Anthony who dreams. Just as in section II of "Dimisión de Sancho", Sancho is not named but referred to as "that man", Anthony in sleep similarly loses his identity and becomes a symbol of mankind. He is described as both a spectator and participator. He enjoys and suffers, watches and acts in these adventures invented by someone who has no conscious knowledge of the reality of sleep. His eyes are closed and thus vision of the real world is lacking. An uncontrolled inventor is creating a world of shadows, rather than the clear shapes of illuminated reality:

[34] R. Gullón, "Jorge Guillén: *A la altura de las circunstancias*", *Insula*, 208 (1964), 10.

[35] Costa, p.162.

> Y anulado en los ojos,
> Ve alumbradas las sombras?
> Antonio presta voz a sus deseos,
> Libres ya con sus máscaras.   (491/20-23)

His subconscious desires are freed in his tormented sleep, and appear in the guise of phantoms. This poem then begins by elaborating a change from the daylight of normality to the darkness of subconscious wishes.

Section II introduces the "Guardian Demon" and section III the "Guardian Angel". Both are custodians or aspects of Anthony's psyche and are not constrained by the conscientious participation, or "coexistence", that daylight requests of men. In section II Anthony discovers a part of himself: he is reborn as a destructive aspect of his own nature, which emerges from deep within his subconscious.

Stanza 3 sets the scene of this character's new world. It is quite remarkably like a horror film: the time is midnight, a full moon shines, a castle stands out in the moonlight. Anthony steals furtively away, so engrossed in his own intent that he does not hear the eerie howling of a dog. The description of this stanza is there for a purpose, for stanza 4 states that midnight is a propitious time for transformation into other beings. All the characteristics of a werewolf legend are here, as Anthony removes his clothes and takes on the "furor y forma" (frenzy and shape) of his other self. Physical nakedness is accompanied by a further denuding, whose turmoil and confusion symbolize the change to an animal's form and instincts. The person who suffers this "atroz angustia de un desorden / Que todo lo enmaraña desde dentro" (atrocious anguish of a disorder which entangles everything from within) faints away, as did Sancho, and in the peace and silence is discerned as an animal who awakens. In this poem the verb "desvanece" (fades away) means that Anthony's human nature has disappeared and knows nothing. The animal is a wolf, who remembers no details of its past, and in fact has no consciousness of itself as a wolf. The question "¿Sabe este lobo ya que es 'este lobo'?" (Does this wolf know that he is 'this wolf'?) serves to remind the reader of the earlier queries as to whether Anthony can possibly be the man who dreams. The point is that knowledge of one's identity means that one has responsibility for one's actions. In this fantastic situation, where man's desire for supremacy by means of destruction is envisaged, the symbol of that desire, the wolf, has no knowledge of himself as a responsible being. He merely acts suddenly and instinctively:

> ¿Sabe este lobo ya que es "este lobo"?
> Si acaso,
> Desde aquella conciencia —remotísima,
> Sin relación de espejo con figura.
> Sutil figura en rachas:
> Prender y devorar. (494/79-84)

Until the last two stanzas, this section traces the exploits of the wolf during a whole day. He stalks carefully in the darkness, all his instincts alive. In the quiet stillness of the forest, he is aware only of his need to concentrate on the sounds and smells which will yield his next victim. Stanza 10 relates the speed and viciousness with which the wolf attacks and devours a wild creature and in so doing achieves tranquillity. He has no moral conscience; all he is aware of is the satisfaction of a driving hunger. Guillén suggests that the gentleman who is the Anthony of these dreams does have an awareness of his actions, but sees them as a pleasure which needs to be fulfilled:

> Sensible a distinciones,
> Sintió como deleite
> Su crimen —necesario—
> A estilo de tortura. (495/121-24)

The animal continues placidly but attacks as soon as it hears a further noise. The human being is left wounded, and the wolf, no longer interested in the basic need (hunger), trots off, again with no awareness of his unnecessary violence. A whole day passes during which the wolf follows his instincts, with no need of any aim or final destiny.

Guillén refers to the creature as "the lycanthrope", indicating that he is a manifestation of psychic imbalance in subconscious man. It is now night again; the moon illuminates a peaceful, natural setting within which the wolf lives only to destroy. At midnight he comes across the dell in the wood, where branches hide some clothing, clothing which symbolizes identity:

> Ropas de identidad, ineludibles.
> Entonces ...
>   No miréis. No habrá testigo
> De la crisis horrenda. Sufre el lobo.
> Temblor. Trasformación. Sopor. Caída.
> Trascurren transiciones inconscientes. (497/167-72)

The transformation from human to wolf and back to human being is envisaged as the "atrocious anguish of a disorder" and a "horrific crisis". As such there is no detailed description of these transformations, other than in terms of disorder, confusion and suffering. However, the fact that Guillén sees the change to the form and attitudes of a wolf in terms of a denuding of human characteristics, and the fact that he refers to the wolf as the lycanthrope, are sufficient indication that the poet is using psychic imbalance as a symbol of man's potential to be destructive. His description of the wolf is long, accurate and extremely effective, even more so when one reminds oneself that the creature is an aspect of all men's character. This first dream is a warning to all that destruction of one's fellow men can be caused by lack of responsibility with regard to the rights of others to exist.

Anthony's return to his former state is indicated by the symbolic donning of clothes. But the section stands as a reminder that rapaciousness of an existential kind lurks in the depths of man's mind, as an ever-present temptation to self-preservation in isolation. The subject of section III is the temptation by "the Guardian Angel". The beauty, silence and harmony of Creation seem to Anthony to be visible symbols of God's presence. In order to be part of that harmony, to feel the presence of God himself, to know the Truth, he has to go through a process of loss of identity, as well as loss of mortality:

> Para trepar hacia la suma cumbre
> Necesita olvidarse,
> Abandonar perfiles, accidentes
> Que son de Dios y no son Dios y sólo
> Tierra, Tierra de paso.   (499/206-10)

His desire for "lo que no pasa" (that which never changes) brings about loss of contact with the world. Man tends to reject the world only in adversity, even though such adversity reveals the substance, or reality, of the world to him. These lines seem to imply that man has a use for God only when circumstances are difficult; when all is harmony and light, man happily leaves behind reality in the hope that he may enjoy union with the source of that harmony. If he suffers disaster and pain, he interprets it as the punishment for wickedness, and he does not see that adversity is merely the opposite of harmony and is, therefore, a real, substantial part of his experience:

> Se desvanece el mundo,
> Aunque tanto nos duela si es adverso,
> Y el dolor nos descubra sustancial
> Su fondo, su castigo.   (499/213-16)

In his desire to reach God, Anthony, now called Brother Anthony in recognition of his new role, avoids contact with others in order to achieve the final requirement: loss of personality. To claim "Yo soy" (I am) is wrong: "Sólo Dios sea" (May only God exist). At this point Guillén asks the first of several questions which indicate his mistrust of mystic desire because it eliminates the most important aspect of human life: "¿Ser hombre es un error?" (Is it a mistake to be a man?). The man who wants such an inhuman experience is described as having "mínima humanidad" (minimal humanity), because he betrays his "ley terrestre" (terrestrial law). In this situation Anthony in fact suffers, because without emotion ("Sin lágrimas inútiles, tan físicas" [without useless tears, so very physical]) he remains in an entirely cerebral state:

> En un orbe mental Antonio sufre,
> Cuerpo aún, criatura
> De carne, de memoria.   (500/232-34)

Thus the process which Guillén describes is, firstly, loss of self within time; secondly, denial of personality; and thirdly, loss of emotion. The next stage is to eradicate memory because to that is allied mortal existence, "historia convivida" (shared history). By describing memories as "intrusos torpes" (sluggish intruders) and existence as "ansiedad de historia convivida" (anxiety of shared history), Guillén makes clear his belief that this mystic desire for isolation is a negative and destructive aspect of man. Anthony has to remove all vestiges of his mortal and emotional existence as an individual, and in the following quotation the repeated use of negatives and of verbs which imply destruction emphasizes the implications of that process:

> Hay que abolir, raer, desmemoriarse
> Creando la tiniebla en que no flote
> Ni emoción ni noción,
> Ningún objeto ya, ningún afecto
> Que lo salve, ningún postrer vestigio
> Del eje en cuya ronda
> Se ilumina y persiste el gran embrollo:
> Cese el yo personal con su apellido,
> Triunfe un caos sin nombres.   (500-501/238-46)

The persistence and strength of the desire for absolute isolation in man is shown in the next stanza, where in spite of all the destruction which has already been part of the pseudo-mystic's experience, Anthony still survives, albeit as a "fantasma de piltrafa" (weakened phantom). Now he has to subdue reason, for God is "un Centro inasequible / Para la inteligencia, / Sólo Centro amoroso" (a Centre unobtainable for the intelligence, only a loving Centre).

Now that Anthony has reduced himself to only a minute impulse towards this infinite experience, Guillén goes on to describe him in images which again clarify the poet's attitude to such inhuman desire:

> Se arroja a su delirio
> Como si naufragara,
> Sin prudencia, sin brújula,
> Dócil a un solo impulso:
> Él mismo es quien se mueve,
> Fatal.
>   Dios lo permite.   (502/269-75)

The next three lines form the second question posed by Guillén as to the validity of succumbing to this temptation:

> ¿Al finito le estorban todavía
> Su peso humano, su porción concreta,
> Sus contornos, su porte?   (502/276-78)

The words "finite", "human weight", "solid reality", "outlines" and "bearing" all stress man's human and, therefore, mortal reality. These are, in fact, the gifts which should not be cast aside in favour of something which reduces man to a solitary, non-participatory entity. The result of Anthony's abandonment of human-ness is a great void, "la tiniebla ofrecida al más cruel / Amor, al más celoso" (the darkness offered to the cruellest, most zealous Love). Union with God requires the total negation of man's world:

> El diálogo posible necesita
> Soledad de universo destruido.
> Se agrava la inmersión
> Por esta hondura del más nulo océano.   (502/283-86)

There ensues more negation of the essence of man, who is seen by the Divinity, "el amoroso destructor" (the loving destroyer), as a sinner, guilty for being a physical and spiritual reality ("culpable / De su cuerpo y su espíritu" [guilty in his body and his spirit]). This kind of suffering is gradually reduced and the disciple sees light in the darkness of the void, experiencing the life-giving air of God, "un aire / De cumplida esperanza respirada" (an air of fulfilled, respired hope) (p.504).[36] Anthony has achieved mystic union with the

[36] The text on p.503 of the Barral edition should be on p.504 and vice versa. Page numbers are given as in that edition.

Godhead, and after his suffering and annihilation, it is an experience that is relished in all its glory. As Costa says, Guillén's description here is reminiscent of the works of San Juan de la Cruz or Santa Teresa, mystics whom Guillén is in no way criticizing with his presentation of the desire for mystic union as a negative aspect of man's psyche in this poem.[37] The love that Anthony experiences is "sin conceptos, / Sin fondo inteligible" (without concepts, with no intelligible depth) (p.503), and as such is an isolating love, one which draws him away from his terrestrial reality and causes not "co-existence" but "disincarnation". He becomes self-sufficient, and, worse still, inward-looking in his isolation. He has achieved participation in divine love, has become a "God-man" and as such wishes only to maintain that state:

> Amémonos, Dios-hombre.   (503/333)

The final three lines of this section show to what extent Anthony has become inhuman:

> La criatura ha superado el límite.
> El aún vivo no esperó la muerte.
> Ay, la felicidad es ya absoluta.   (503/334-36)

This temptation is here revealed as the desire to be immortal and, as with Lázaro, Guillén implies (by the insertion of an insignificant but highly revealing exclamation, "Ay") that such an achievement is not human. Anthony is merely a "creature".

In section IV Anthony awakes from his dream, and as always with Guillén, his awakening brings him back to reality. This simple phenomenon of human life is seen as a conquest of reality and as such is one of the victories achieved unconsciously by Anthony in this poem. In the clarity of day he can say, "Tentaciones: basta" (Enough of temptations). During daylight he is able to see all that surrounds him and his conscious mind is filled with reality, in contrast to the manifestations of a subconscious which is "dark" and, therefore, unbalanced. Guillén goes on to say that it is difficult to share life with other human beings, but if one lives responsibly, if one becomes involved in human life, then other people can become participators, with the individual, in the destiny of man:

> No, no es fácil
> Compartir la jornada con los seres

---

[37] Costa, p.162.

> En torno, muy capaces de ser algo
> —Todavía futuro— si la hora
> Circunstancial se eleva hasta niveles
> Bien convividos de figura humana.   (505/344-49)

When the restored Anthony gets up, his action is seen to be involved in the world of reality. "Se yergue Antonio" (Anthony gets up) recalls the description of Lazarus after his return to earth ("Lázaro erguido"). The former's natural return to reality through waking from sleep is another kind of resurrection, and the light of reality shows him his own being, the essence of which is seen to be the effort to make his physical form ("bulk") into a human reality ("person"):

> El semblante que Antonio reconoce
> Como resumen de una tentativa
> No acabada jamás: el casi logro
> De esa persona que ese bulto anuncia.   (505/354-57)

It is important to remember that Anthony achieves only partial success; the poem does not suggest that, through his experiences, he has become the ultimate manifestation of humanity. The temptations stand as examples of the lengths to which man can go in his efforts to make himself supreme. They lead to the destruction, or to the desolation, of "coexistence". The real vocation of man is one that does not bring about any such negative result:

> La vocación no induce a descarríos
> Diabólicos ni angélicos.   (505/358-59)

The use of the word "vocation" is important, because of its etymology. Stemming from the Latin "vox", its employment in this context suggests that it is, above all, man's command of language and ability to rationalize which makes him a superior animal, as was seen in the poem "Vida extrema" in *Cántico*. If man follows his calling he *will be* human. The final words, "Antonio / Sueña a diario con su fin: el hombre" (Anthony dreams daily of his aim: to be a man), bring the poem to a fitting end by recalling the way in which it began. Guillén has shown some of the experiences that being human entails. He chooses to depict them by means of dreams, where Anthony gives in to his subconscious desires. The use of the verb "to dream" to describe the character's daily activity is also most effective, for here, in daylight, the "dream" is a means to self-knowledge, rather than an escape into potential inhumanity. This, of course, is the way in which Antonio Machado frequently uses the word "dream", and Guillén hereby acknowledges Machado not only as the initial source for his poem but also as the origin of a significant area of its resolution.

As the final poem of structural and ideological importance in *Clamor*, "Las tentaciones de Antonio", with "Dimisión de Sancho", exemplifies Guillén's vision of man within a world which is the creation of mankind. Man suffers disillusionment (Sancho) and temptation (Anthony) and can make of both of these experiences a route to self-knowledge. Sancho learns to accept his "essence" and becomes thereby a part of the reality of harmonious Creation. Anthony, tempted by the desire for supremacy, accepts the "vocation" of consciously striving to be human.

Conclusion

Clamor starts with an outcry of anger and pain, *Maremágnum*, at the world that man has made within Creation. The two poems "Luzbel desconcertado" and "La hermosa y los excéntricos" are concerned with abnormality, both mental and sensuous, and yet provide the antidote for these in a recognition of Creation and heterosexuality respectively. The second part of *Clamor*, . . . *Que van a dar en la mar*, sees man face to face with death, natural and accidental, although the overall tone of the poems is not that of *Maremágnum*, but rather one of serenity and stoicism. "Lugar de Lázaro" and "Huerto de Melibea" are poems where love, life and death are the major preoccupations, but in each it is the place, which is the setting for the individual lives, which is exalted. Lázaro expresses a desire that life after death may be the same as his terrestrial existence, and Melibea dies secure in the knowledge that life can be re-created by love. In *A la altura de las circunstancias*, having faced the disorder of life and the fact that it inevitably ends, Guillén turns his attention to the final phase of man's striving – the effort to live courageously in the world, to learn from experience, and to be human. "Dimisión de Sancho" demonstrates self-knowledge as a route to harmony and "Las tentaciones de Antonio" shows that same exercise of self-knowledge as a constant source of potential for mankind.

These three phases of man's existence are summed up in the dedication of *Clamor*: "A mis hijos / A la posible esperanza" (To my children / To possible hope). Man's hope must lie in the belief that a desire to exalt and preserve our human nature may be the guiding principle that continues in succeeding generations. As long as there are human beings, Guillén implies, there is the possibility that our essential nature will be preserved.

At the beginning of this chapter the widely divergent attitudes of critics towards the content of *Clamor* were mentioned. The conclusion of Frances Day Wardlaw's unpublished thesis presents a very clear exposition of the differences between *Cántico* and *Clamor*. While her comments on *Cántico* tend to underemphasize the beauty and contemporary validity of this volume of poetry, her denial that *Clamor* is only "social poetry" can be strongly supported. She points out that such poetry is confined to the specifics of contemporary problems and is thus a poor description of the poems of *Clamor* which, she rightly claims, are universal in focus:

> While Guillén's secular, existentialist perspective reflects contemporary patterns of thought, the theme itself is not contemporary. Furthermore, although particular examples of contemporary life are present in *Clamor*, they are clearly a springboard to more universal concerns. Guillén's interest rests not on the contemporary issues themselves but on the problems of meaning they raise.[38]

The six pillar poems discussed in this chapter, created from either biblical or literary sources, effectively categorize the significance of such human problems as pride, abnormality, the desire for immortality, death, humiliation, and self-sufficiency. Moreover, Guillén's use of various different protagonists in each poem creates, according to Debicki, a distance between the reader and the characters portrayed. Because of this distancing, Guillén prevents his poems from becoming an indictment of human life:

> El libro contiene una actitud conceptual, crítica del mundo moderno; si ésta se presentara por medio de un solo protagonista generalizado, que expresara terminantemente la actitud del poeta, *Clamor* nos parecería un sermón demasiado directo. Al particularizar y distanciar a sus protagonistas, y al presentar voces muy variadas, Guillén se salva de tal peligro.[39]

> (The book has the critical, conceptual attitude of the modern world; if this attitude were presented via a single, generalized protagonist, who expressed categorically the attitude of the poet, then *Clamor* would seem far too trenchant a sermon. By individualizing and distancing his protagonists, and by presenting very varied attitudes, Guillén avoids this danger.)

In addition, the fact that the protagonists are all originally symbolic

[38] Wardlaw, pp.133-34.
[39] Debicki, pp.269-70.

or literary figures, created by man himself, is an indication that we can find our own *exempla* in our past creations, exactly as Guillén has done.

The structure of *Clamor* is like *Cántico* in its symmetry, but has an important poem, "El acorde" (Harmony, *CL* 15-19), as an introduction to the three sections. The tripartite format of this poem echoes the actual structure of the book itself. The first section celebrates harmony between man and Creation. The second elaborates the chaos and confusion of man's world, but relates these things to specifically human causes:

> ¿Es venenoso el mundo? ¿Quién, culpable?
> ¿Culpa nuestra la Culpa? Tan humana,
> Del hombre es quien procede aún sin cable
> De tentador, sin pérfida manzana.   (17)

> (Is the world evil? Who is culpable?
> Is Guilt our guilt? So human,
> Guilt comes from man even now with no link
> To a tempter, no perfidious apple.)

Section III celebrates life as salvation from chaos. When the individual's life seems insupportable, the universal life-force of Creation will be a constant inspiration:

> Y cuando más la depresión te oprima
> Y más condenes tu existencia triste,
> El gran acorde mantendrá en tu cima
> Propia luz esencial. Así te asiste.   (19)

> (And when depression most oppresses you,
> When you curse most your existence,
> The Great Harmony will keep in your summit
> Its own essential light. In this way it helps you.)

This final section thus sees human life as a phenomenon similar to Creation.

The three sections of the introductory poem of *Clamor* foreshadow all that will be developed in the ensuing pages, and these are then read with the knowledge that the faith in life so characteristic of *Cántico* is still the fundamental premise of the work. Ricardo Gullón suggests that *Clamor* is a muted *Cántico* since its last word is "silencio" (silence). The word "silencio" is indeed the last word of the final poem, but Gullón has mistaken Guillén's concept of his *oeuvre*. *Clamor* does not end until one has read and understood the final dedication. It is preceded by a quotation from Salinas:

> Mientras haya
> alguna ventana abierta   (*CL* 550)
>
> (As long as there is
> An open window)

These words should be seen as the last of *Clamor*, implying as they do that as long as there is a window open on to Creation, there will always be the possibility of interpreting man's world as a part of it: the "accident" within the "essence". The final dedication, "A / Pedro Salinas / en su gloria" (To / Pedro Salinas / in his glory), is in the same format as the first dedication of all the editions of *Cántico*: "A mi madre / en su cielo" (To my mother / in her heaven). If it is the mother, the life-giver, to whom the hymn of joy in praise of Creation is offered, then it is to the friend and fellow poet, Pedro Salinas, that a poet's view of man's life, with its desperate need of human friendship, is given. That the dedication of a work published in 1963 should be to a man who died in 1951 is a final affirmation of Jorge Guillén's belief in both human life itself and triumphant coexistence.

CHAPTER 5

CONCLUSION

¿Cómo concluir?
Hartura no es posible ...

One of the most remarkable aspects of the poetry of Jorge Guillén is that it is the result of a conscious decision to create a unified work. The progression of thought and ideology in the five volumes of *Aire nuestro* is not dependent on chronology but responds rather to an *a priori* ordered vision of the world. When that vision is organized into coherent units, it bestows additional order and harmony, both aesthetic and intellectual, upon the very world it seeks to elaborate. It might be argued that such rigour is indicative of a predetermined plan and that, therefore, the poetry in some ways lacks spontaneity; the reader may suspect that the poetry is simply made up according to the emotional focus of the particular volume. However, Guillén himself has indicated that this is not so, never more clearly than in the distinction he makes in the following lines:

> Valéry took a rather perverse pleasure in discoursing on the "manu-facture of poetry". This phrase would have sounded in the ears of that group of Spaniards like just what it is: blasphemy. "To create", a proud term, "to compose", a sober, professional term, do not imply manufacture. *(LP* 209)

This distinction, in fact referring to the composition of individual poems, is particularly relevant to Guillén's creation of *Aire nuestro*. Just as words are guided by the controlling intellect of the poet into a coherent context, the poem, so Guillén's poems are similarly organized into equally coherent volumes. Speaking of *Cántico*, he makes a reference which was the starting point of the present work:

No imaginaba yo el libro como una serie de textos mezclados caprichosamente, sino como una unidad orgánica, como un edificio.[1]

(I didn't imagine the book as a series of texts mixed together capriciously, but as an organic whole, as a building.)

Guillén began the construction of his edifice, logically enough, with foundations – the 1928, 1936 and 1945 editions of *Cántico*. In 1950 he erected the scaffolding, and the thirty-four "major poems", selected from all the editions of *Cántico*, are that scaffolding, presented to us visually in the index of the volume, and providing us with an initial key to the composition and development of his great work. A similar process occurs with *Clamor*, where in addition the poet indicates the ideological pillars of the work with the six individual poems which each comprise a subsection of the volume. In *Homenaje* there is no distinction made, nor is there in *Aire nuestro*, the tripartite volume of 1968, because the building is now totally self-supporting. The scaffolding has been taken away, and the architect's design now stands in its own right, an integral whole. The cornerstones and lintels supporting doors and windows are still visible – as the extended poems of *Cántico* and *Clamor* – but they are clearly integrated with the rest of the building and function as ways in to the thematic richness of the entire work. Moreover, the internal organization of each book is remarkable. Guillén always took great care with the typesetting of his poems, so that the individual lines and stanzas are framed in the centre of the page. Clearly he was concerned not only with poetic form and thematic content but also with the aesthetic appearance of his creations. Everything concerning his poetry, in short, constitutes an effort to create form, order and harmony. A detailed examination of twelve of the major poems from *Cántico* and *Clamor*, although they represent only a fragment of Guillén's work, nevertheless shows the value of structural control as a means to introduce thematic relationships. The stimulus of close reading and analysis of such texts inevitably leads to an awareness of the coherence and unity of these first two volumes.

Aire nuestro is the overall title of Guillén's five-volume opus of poetry. It was first used for the tripartite volume of 1968 and appears on all five separate books as published by Barral Editores. What is it that makes *"Aire nuestro"* a suitable title for over sixty years of creative endeavour? The juxtaposition of "air" and "our" can only mean human life in the context of the surrounding world, and thus

---

[1] Couffon, p.13.

life is seen to be the fundamental theme of Guillén's poetry. This is amply demonstrated in the poems from *Cántico* and *Clamor* which have been analysed in this book, and the six major poems selected from each volume represent on a small scale the primary concerns of the individual books. In *Cántico* "El diálogo", "A vista de hombre" and "Las cuatro calles" show three important aspects of life: friendship, self-affirmation through the experience of personal crisis, and the vicissitudes of urban life. "El concierto" stresses the value of man's creative ability in the sphere of music, a microcosm of potential universal harmony. "Luz natal" considers the nature of the individual's inheritance from his forebears and emphasizes the supreme ability of the human being – the power of speech which endows him with reason and the possibility of communication. "Vida extrema" takes these ideas further and demonstrates that language bestows on the individual a personal artistic ability which, though frequently ignored, is nevertheless a supreme, even sacred, talent. The six pillar poems of *Clamor* are significant because they reveal the lasting value of man's past artistic creations, represented by the mythological and literary figures who stand as *exempla* through which to approach the difficulties which are an integral part of life. Lucifer symbolizes the sterility and ultimate futility of the nihilistic attitude which seeks to deny order and harmony; the Queen of Nations represents female beauty and symbolizes heterosexuality as the true destiny of human eroticism; Lazarus lends dignity and lasting beauty to transient life; Calisto and Melibea are eternal lovers; Sancho Panza's renunciation of ambition and vainglory symbolizes true humility; Anthony's awareness of the power of subconscious desire suggests the need for reason to be allied with external reality in order for man to understand himself.

These twelve poems are a sufficient indication of the complexity and intricacy of this fundamental theme of life in the context of the world, both Creation and Society. But *Aire nuestro* itself constitutes a world which is the result of another creative force, the art of the poet. Thus *Aire nuestro* portrays not merely life in the context of the world, but also life in the context of art, an art which structures, defines and informs. Man's ability to create is also clearly revealed in the twelve major poems studied in this book, and this ability centres round his powers of speech and reason. In *Cántico*, dialogue is to be found in all spheres of the poetry, on the simple level of communication between individuals, and also at the more complex level of personal involvement with circumstances. Man uses his reasoning powers for the purpose of self-affirmation, for coming to terms with society and its ills, for participating in the creation and recreation of music, and above all for giving expression to himself and to reality. In the six pillar poems from *Clamor* Guillén uses various instances of man's creative past, but in his recreations he gives us further insight into what these exemplary figures can mean for us now. We see that Creation and Woman, in "Luzbel desconcertado" and "La hermosa y los excéntricos" respectively, remain steadfast in the midst of the "Sea of Confusion" (MacCurdy's translation of *Maremágnum*)[2] which is the reality of man's society. Love bounded by mortality is revealed in the poems from . . . *Que van a dar en la mar*, but in "Lugar de Lázaro" and "Huerto de Melibea" love as an enduring force is affirmed. The "lover" is strengthened and ennobled by his experiences, so that the harshness of mortality is transcended. In *A la altura de las circunstancias* Guillén presents us with two figures whose powers of reasoning ultimately set them on the road to self-knowledge. Neither character is offered to us as an example of the "perfect human being", the presumed result of acquiring self-knowledge: Sancho and Anthony function rather as individuals whose attempts to come to terms with circumstances demonstrate a profound respect and reverence for the human condition – that condition which requires from us all humility and active involvement with reality.

That *Cántico* and *Clamor* are complementary volumes is clear. "Luz natal" and "Las cuatro calles" are works which anticipate the "Tiempo de historia" of *Clamor*. Similarly, the six pillar poems of this second book reaffirm the convictions expressed in *Cántico*. But the composing or structuring does not stop there. Just as "Vida extrema" is a preparation for *Homenaje* in its exaltation of the enduring value of the aesthetic processes of art, so too are the pillar poems of *Clamor* in their use of mythological and literary sources from man's compendium of experience. This third volume of *Aire nuestro*, *Homenaje*, emphasizes above all the value of artistic creation for both poet and reader, the "friend" to whom so much of Guillén's poetry is dedicated and who collaborates with him in the "task" of living and articulating:

> Se funden cadencia y luz:
> Palabra hacia poesía.
> Que se cumple acaso en ti,

[2] See G. Grant MacCurdy, *Jorge Guillén* (Boston: Twayne, 1982).

> En tu instante de poeta,
>   Mi lector.   (*H* 517)

> (Cadence and light fuse:
> Word into poetry.
> Which is fulfilled perhaps in you,
>   My reader,
> In your moment as a poet.)

Homenaje is the central volume of *Aire nuestro* and it is most appropriate that the heart of Guillén's work should be concerned with the ever-renewable and inexhaustible themes of life and art.[3] He consciously aimed not only to preserve the art of the past, but also to demonstrate that man's creative endeavour is an eternal symbol of life. His belief that the poet is a "portavoz" (spokesman) and "porta-conciencia" (conscience-bearer)[4] has relevance to his admiration of creative writers of previous generations, as well as to his efforts to make his own poetry a meaningful record of one man's appreciation of life:

> Un poeta no es más que renovada incarnación de esa energía creadora que nunca se interrumpe.[5]

> (A poet is no more than the renewed incarnation of that creative energy which is never interrupted.)

The duration of the composition of *Homenaje*, from 1949-1966, is important for it spans the preparation and publication of *Clamor*, as well as including work which Guillén produced in the 1920s, a notable example being his translation of Valéry's "Le cimetière marin", first published in Spain in 1929 and much admired by Valéry himself.[6]

Of the fourth volume of *Aire nuestro*, *Y otros poemas*, composed over the years 1966-1975, Guillén wrote:

> ... confirma y completa toda la obra anterior —sin necesidad de título monosilábico. *Y otros poemas* son poemas según *Cántico*, *Clamor* y *Homenaje*. Hay que insistir en beneficio de la claridad.[7]

[3] See MacCurdy, pp.146-60.

[4] Jorge Guillén, "Poesía integral", *Revista Hispánica Moderna*, 31 (1965), 209.
[5] ibid.

[6] See Jorge Guillén, "Valéry en el recuerdo", *Plural*, 3 (1971), 18-20. On page 19 of this article, Valéry's letter to Guillén, dated 22 July 1929, is reproduced. After exclaiming "Je m'adore en espagnol!", Valéry goes on to ask whether he can hope to see further translations of his work. This question bore fruit, for Guillén includes in *Homenaje* not only translations, but reworkings of various of Valéry's poems in different metres. See *H* 410-23.

[7] Letter to the author dated 17 December 1979.

> (... it confirms and completes all the earlier work – without the need of a monosyllabic title. *Y otros poemas* are poems in the manner of *Cántico*, *Clamor* and *Homenaje*. This must be emphasized for the benefit of clarity.)

In the Introduction to this book reference was made to the subsection of *Y otros poemas* entitled "Al margen de *Aire nuestro*", where Guillén reviews poetically the works already published. This subsection begins with a quotation from Wallace Stevens:

> *the great poems of heaven and hell*
> *have been written and the great poem*
> *of the earth remains to be written*   (*OP* 340)

Guillén follows these lines with typical modesty, claiming that to try to represent the complexity and variety of earthly life is a "desmesurada tentativa" (impudent intent). However, critics and readers of Guillén's poetry do not concur with him, for his work is indeed an exaltation of the Earth and man's existence upon it.

The cycle of *Aire nuestro* closes with *Final*, composed during the years 1973-1981, but which Guillén was in the process of correcting for a projected second edition before his death. In the dedicatory poem at the beginning of the volume, we find the following lines:

> Es posible,
> Si el director-lector lo pretendiese,
> Decir daccapo.
> Lectura abierta a novedades.   (*F* 9)

> (It is possible,
> If the director-reader so wishes,
> To say *daccapo*.
> Reading open to new ventures.)

Title and dedication here testify to the creation of a work where the harmonization of the various themes and recurrent motifs once more gives coherence to the whole. The reader of Guillén has a final opportunity to discover poems which further clarify and complement those of the earlier volumes. Fittingly, *Final* ends with the words "Paz, queramos paz" (Peace, let us want peace) (*F* 349), an exhortation to all men actively to desire harmony.

It has not been my intention to give anything but the briefest of comments on the later volumes of *Aire nuestro*, but from these observations it can be seen that the informing principles dealt with in *Cántico* and *Clamor* shape the poet's entire work. Not only does *Aire nuestro* refer to the air which gives life, but also to the air – or song –

of poetry, which orchestrates words, thoughts and emotions into a symphonic appraisal of human existence and endeavour.

The poems from *Cántico* and *Clamor* discussed in this book demonstrate not only the essential concerns of each volume but also, implicitly, the overwhelming coherence of Guillén's work, described by MacCurdy as "diversity within unity".[8] The enduring value of the poetry, now and in the future, will depend on us as readers – another "diversity" linked by intellect, emotion and above all *attention* to the unity that is *Aire nuestro*. The entire work is dedicated *A quien leyere* (To whoever may read), but more than this, the poetry was actually composed and organized with us and for us, as the poet makes clear in the second dedication:

CONTIGO EDIFICADO PARA TI
QUEDE ESTE BLOQUE YA TRANQUILO ASI

(Built with you, for you,
May this work, now serene,
Thus remain.)

These majestic and rigorously structured phrases exemplify the purpose of Guillén as a poet: to use words in a context of coherence, or "bloque" (the poem and the volumes of *Aire nuestro*) – words set down with the intention of communicating with the reader who, in his individual "moment as a poet", participates in an act of attention and recreation of infinite value.

Much has been said about the importance of the many dedications throughout the five volumes of poetry. But the last words of Jorge Guillén to "all who may read" are not to be found within the covers of *Aire nuestro*. Those who consider the epitaph on his tomb in the English Cemetery in Málaga will find that Guillén has provided them with a simple and moving key to the richness, variety and essential unity of a life's work:

AQUI YACE UN ENAMORADO DE LA VIDA

[8] MacCurdy, p.161.

APPENDIX:
ENGLISH VERSIONS OF
TWELVE MAJOR POEMS

DIALOGUE

The day was a companion through its closeness:
Sphere of existence
Which latent attentiveness
Recognized thanks to incisive
5   Tracks, familiar shadows.
Colour participated willingly:
Good weather.
Thus the highway,
So normal, was suitable:
10   Route for good dialogue.

Hills rose up
With their whites and greys
So pure
That they were only horizon.
15   Areas of practical labour were in between:
Pine grove, vineyard, possessed land.
Oh, but we possessed nothing!
Dialogue,
Thus so free, proceeded at full pace.

20   Walking and talking, talking ... No objective.
Just this crossing of two voices
In air
Which unceasingly opens before us
With limpid transparency.
25   Us? It is neither spoken nor thought.
Friends:
Two equal voices.
For love, for emphasis!

A hurried phrase rushed headlong
30   Dominating, rising,
Although time,
Pleasure,
And a breadth of atmosphere ready
For the voice, so central at that moment, were

35   All gently floating.
That which is so shapeless
Among the mutterings of the many, came out into sunlight.
Thought, in the air, was ours.
From you,
40   From you it was born, dialogue of two people.

The hills,
So separate, lacking greenness, humble,
– Who treads them or flies over them? –
Spread out, and come very close, in curves
45   That give access to
Terrestrial sky.
This ruggedness of the horizon is pure.

Ruggedness? Is it really?
We talk, in accord,
50   Peace is warmer.
Our walk enjoys the unadorned,
Ripe transparency of so much valley.
We converse, I understand.
He is so in tune with me
55   That he succeeds in being what he is:
A friend.
And shared inclination examines
The various sights,
Double light clarifies some inkling
60   As it flashes,
There is language even in the pause
Which gathers it up silently,
Reveals its suspected shadow
As having purpose.

65   He is my friend. I am his friend.
Unobtrusive custom!
Adult perception
Pays attention through discriminating viewpoints
To our joint
70   Youth,
A perception so faithful that could
– Without gesture, without visible
Tears –
Be moved to emotion. Perhaps it has been moved?
75   Unseen
Something remains unconfessed.

May all the world, so impatient,
Flow into dialogue.
May thronging dialogue

80   Be improvised, flexible,
      Towards the distance of an interrupted
      End. How to conclude?
      Weariness is not possible.
      Are not the replies in union
85   Or do they not rush
      Unhesitating to their rightful situation?
      Walking, walking and talking . . .

      Highway towards light.
      Day and more day upon the word,
90   Which yields,
      On course towards sure silence.
      Eyes take pleasure in
      Recognizing, in delving into experience.

      Does the instant of novelty seduce?
95   More newly seductive is
      The bulky transparency of the atmosphere,
      The veteran greenness of the distant pine grove,
      Fortified by its density,
      Some mud walls, solitary in their rural
100   Untidiness.

      Still without voices,
      Dialogue does not stop moving on,
      Does not stop prospering
      In the clear plain
105   Where our destinies
      Deepen their own liberty,
      At ease in our tireless
      Coexistence, wrought
      Always by attentiveness.
110   Attentiveness which gradually becomes tenderness,
      Only happiness by living,
      Coexisting. The free hours are ours.

      The train.
      And it passed with its jot of rage.
115   The city offered itself above the valley.
      The return was pleasant.
      Small birds, without prestige
      – For what? – so exquisite, were unaware of
      Our role as passers-by
120   From the buzzing
      – Oh wind in the open country! – of the telegraph poles.

      The hills, so identical
      To our vision of their beauty,

Told us we were right.
125 We walked, we talked: friends
In friendship, without objective.

Attentiveness flowed. It had a channel.
The world hovered,
Unknown and light, over our voices.
130 Morning flowed through the dialogue.

CONCERT

Time is divided in resonances.
Ah! A world arises
Which has value, imposes itself on me, subjects me
With its need.
5 Thus it is. Justly,
According to this strict delight,
It must live in the air:
A world
Where I am able to breathe with
10 All my silences in harmony.

Submissive to that flow of will,
I listen.
My perception is my soul.
I coexist
15 With this convergence of energies
In resolution.
What is it saying, what does it suggest?
It suggests itself, shows itself,
Identifies with its own complete being.

20 Absolute of instants,
The one for the next already imminent.
All its being in the flow of
Sounds placed at intervals.
And everything slides free,
25 Coexists sure and pleasurable,
– What expectation, what tension, what heights! –
While in my memory,
Confine of my pleasure,
A monumental totality remains.

30 In tune the spirit,
From on high it listens,
Stronger and more acute

Than when below,
Amongst frowns and noises.
35   A man effortlessly renewed listens,
Now deep within this grove of harmony
Which surrounds like air:
It fuses with my existence.
With my very existence?
40   Is it I,
My ordinary self,
Who lives with the pure firmament?
You belong to me, music,
Superhuman exemplum
45   Which a man offers up to man.

Discord is not possible.
Chance can never erupt, never crackle
In this circle:
An orb in the hands and mind
50   Of a maker who fashions it completely.
Oh music,
Supreme reality!
It is the very unfolding
– Hear – of a firmament
55   – You see it – which gathers us in.
No sounds occur
Outside. Now, where are we?

(Music and good fortune: a room
Of friends.
60   The afternoon is the great setting.
Linked by means of the windows,
Profound,
Devoting itself to participate,
Participating,
65   Without hearing it heeds us.
Perhaps the ultimate universal brotherhood
Culminates here?
Very limpid atmosphere,
Tree grove in distant balconies,
70   Walnut wood-grain in the shades
Of that furniture, silent bench,
A general, companionable mood.
This present time assured.)

Where, where are we inclined?
75   A summit sustains me
– In any place. What does the rhythm require?
It responds not to its eagerness, it is not, with all
Its unavoidable beauty, self-sufficient,

And it turns and returns in supplication,
80 Perhaps searching for me.
The soul rushes headlong to that rhythm,
Which is soul.

Oh Goodness! It is revealed.
I am aware of it without thought, without vision,
85 Revealingly,
By no more than contact
With my being,
Which in rhythmic harmony delves into its life,
Its dominion or its melancholy,
90 In this being now so complete,
So sure that it belongs to all.
No secret!
The succession of sounds,
Never in solitude,
95 Without the break of oblivion,
Goes on linking up the great ensemble
Where the listener, participating and alert,
Continues incognito.

Controlled alertness.
100 Music, power!
And it entrusts its heights to me,
Fills me to overflowing with its faith,
Sets me up in its splendour,
Over the last conquerable space,
105 Leads me into wave upon wave of creations,
Beside the most fresh impulse of joy,
Exposes me face to face
With the great and evident reality,
And with its certainty inebriates me.
110 Triumphant harmony!
It persists in majesty,
Beautifully it is spirit.
It is spirit, in all its immediate
Abundance.

115 I breathe in glory.
Because so much is raised above me,
Perfection superior to all life
Controls me.
Oh music of man, and more than man,
120 The final dénouement
Of audacious hope!

Sound, music, sound,
Raise me to the edge,

125   Carry me off into the heart
       Of the happiness which you raise
       In my daily life.
       Exalted into the concerto
       Of this culmination of reality,
       I too share in your victory:
130   Absolute harmony in human air.

IN SIGHT OF MAN

I

       The city, offered in panorama,
       Becomes grander before me. Promising its essence,
       Already immensely simple,
       It is not scattered in its tumult,
5   But reduces the incidental to detail,
       It presses on with its destiny. Who does not revere it?

       Thus so tiny,
       The streets are kept for silent passers-by.
       There is a car
10   Which changes its lights into greetings
       To the strays in their darkness.
       Harassed pavements! There are disputes
       Of lights.
       In a vista of highways
15   Which travel far, darkness lies face down.

       Is it raining? One does not see the water,
       Which is only divined in the purples
       And reds which the pavement,
       Without illusion, really does forge.
20   Those beams of light illumine it, light sent
       In the night to temper its elemental rigour,
       The dangerous chances of its dice.

II

       Contradiction, disorder, rumpus:
       People.
25   The river is a black mass
       Which to my eye does not move – but it does run
       Majestically without decoration, without waves.
       In the mist the civil tower intensifies
       Audaciously.

30   Indefatigable pulses acclaim
      – Fullness and contour
      Of luminous letters –
      The fame
      Of the latest marvel.
35   Thus shining it begs
      The favours of all and of the wind:
      The wind in the streets launched into
      This ascension of gradations
      Which rise from river to firmament in the night.

40   Very nocturnal and enormous,
      These buildings of flats, flats, flats
      – With their angles sharply
      Incised by day –
      Become lighter. In conformity
45   With their destiny the now tenuous façades, so
      Brightly lit in so many gaps, resist.
      It is so frequent
      The intimacy of light opened towards obscurity:
      That interior light
50   More hidden beneath its tremor!
      And the wall beats,
      Solid in its substantiality riddled
      With clear pockets
      Of energy as if it were a sword
55   Set only to shine.
                        Perhaps there are lights
      Which colour the edges – in suburbs – of the vista,
      Beneath a reddish sky
      Without a single star?
60   With my window I too respond,
      Vast splendour, to the city. Who made it
      Terrible, who made it so beautiful?
      The city indivisible: thus it is.

            III

      May the window save me: my retreat.
65   Well examined, united,
      The population consoles with its sea-like impulse.
      Newly astonished, I admire again
      How all responds to him who questions,
      How amongst many chances one chance
70   Unknowingly opportune is of use to the best of men.
      Here is the city: sounding between its bridges.

      Meanwhile, ay! I, wearied, perceive the configuration
      Of so many corners and streets which tumbles around me,

Laborious, insignificant, ordinary,
75 So alien to my wishes, lost in uselessness:
This life which I earn
With scarcely a complaint.
Solution? I take refuge
Without flight right here, inside this contraption
80 Which surrounds me with its forgetfulness.

IV

Space, vast night, more space.
A remote room,
Remote from myself in the palace
Of everyone, of no one. Constant
85 Company?
Solitude? A certain presence,
Never cold, is unexhausted.
Oh crowd, which is mine also,
Which is I also! No, I will not be the one to be afraid,
90 One among so many.
There is nothing accidental which can surprise me.
(Essence will always be a marvel to me.)
It is winter. Naked beneath blankets:
Man.
95 You? Me as well. And everybody.
Confusion, crime, lawsuits.
Oh rain upon mud!
People, more people, people. (And the saints.)

This is my solitude. And it grieves me:
100 Solitude of brotherhood.
The blackness of night is now green
Near the sky, which is always close by.
How much sky, by day, is lost to me
If I give myself to the city,
105 And in thousands of pressures divide and confuse myself,
Together with the restlessness
Of the cables round about!

Solitude, restoring solitude.
And yet,
110 Even in the tardiest and unexpected withdrawal,
Do not abandon me, bitter world
– And so stupid that it knows not
Its prodigiousness.
Oh world, fill my attention, which I extend
115 Ceaselessly to you from this height
Fortified by darkness,
And thus never obscure.

Live in me, great city, for great you are. Weigh
On me with your noble gifts. The soul grows unharmed,
120   It endures in itself.

                    V

Winter is overcome.
When all's said and done, is not weariness something tender
Which awaits, which reclaims
Calm in solitude?
125   And the drama ...
Let all continue in obscurity.
Now let the darkness of a respite suffice me,
May my head find repose.
Unique solitude, oh sleep, sure
130   Transformation! Modestly the
Angel begins to serve me.
Little by little the harshness of the world
Slackens off. Is it temporary respite,
Shall I lose out?
135   I will gain. Growing forgetfulness
Will negate all devastation.
Long pause.
            So much, new!
And I will awaken. It will not be what it has been.
140   (Will the wounded really suffer in his yesterday?)
My existence will have thrust its roots
Into this profound being to whom I owe what I am:
Him who so trusted you bless, great sleep.
Everything, tomorrow, everything will lure me with its
                                    incentives.

NATIVE LIGHT

                I

The plain is illumined so broadly
That the horizon scarcely delineates it,
Finally, as a valley.

Horizon of hillocks
5   Where stripped bare there appears
–Never-ploughed peaks –
A piece of universe.
Desolate? But no.
It endures with so much eagerness

10   That even its coarse eternity attracts:
        Grey limestone which humbly bides its time,
        Grey of a clarity
        That were almost human.

        Ceaselessly revealing itself as the planet,
15   This silent hill
        Becomes for me a vista
        Which is revealed by means of its name:
        Hill of Saint Christopher.
        If with its shape it surrenders to me,
20   With its light it offers me help.

        Oh light of the universe,
        For me so original
        In the joy of full blown
        Revelation!

25   The light of this Castile
        Imposes on me my destiny:
        To be now and to live
        Within the return of each minute
        Which requires that I breathe
30   Facing a world which defines me so completely.
        Persisting in the law of life
        I enjoy shaping myself,
        Clear cut in presence of a limit,
        That of a creature raised
35   To its own peak: a creature
        Of generations.

                        II

        Blood has run
        Like rivers in search of other rivers.
        And unending they surge forward and run,
40   Run till they are lost,
        Renewed, recently launched through the crossroads
        Of a network which is intricate,
        Hidden away the edges of
        The incessant wood.
45   From where and whither?

        Eternity too
        Which outdoes time and its machinations,
        Outdoes all sterile digressions,
        All cataclysmic opposition,
50   All the energies and ideas of man,

Eternity of summer-spate rivers
Which are a single river like the sea.

Or more than the sea? It continues, passes on,
Fiercer than in its guise of death.
55   Life in the manner of life.
Generations of generations,
Gardens in layers,
So much countless new life towards the sun!

And amongst the creatures,
60   Once ... Ah, me. Me?

Me adjusted to my limits:
The person that I am, here, on this hill,
Beneath this heaven
Not chosen by me.
65   My thanks!

          I too am here. A gift,
Gift for one who,
Ah, merited nothing,
Who was nothing and nobody.
70   I owe to you and to you
My gift of assenting life
Amongst so many beings,
My phrases impelled
By words which are from your mouths.

75   Noble history, untouched liberty,
Sustenance of native land.

You, my great source,
You lit the spark sufficient for me
To feel being as good fortune,
80   To raise in myself anxiety for my work,
Love for my child.
Your energy reaches me like a
Link with all that is steadfast,
Ceaselessly sailing the current
85   Which has neither beginning nor end.

Oh noble father,
Always a crescent of help,
Quietly steadfast wall between this
Terrible world and our happiness,
90   With so much squandering of yourself
Fighter in a fight
That is a supreme game,

Soul already ceaselessly in line,
Ceaselessly tempered in the spirit of
95   Noble man.

The earth, with the sky, awaited me
Beneath your tutelage,
Hand tended towards the as yet
New, hopeful creature.

100   Between destiny and your love arose
– Oh supreme abundance here! – Spain.

III

The differences are slight: a whole world.
A certain impulse of the soul,
An undefinable fibre
105   Which displays spirit,
A certain walk. With that bearing,
That inflection – so unique – of the voice.

And the word. The word all ours!

A shared existence irreducible to concept,
110   Maybe the creation of many,
Close to their heavens,
– Mobile heavens never stilled –
But the definition of nobody.
Reality, reality
115   In iridescence, in mind.

Between walls and towers see the air:
An air of early-morning plenty
Which will also be heat
Even amongst shades and shadows.

120   And who can shut you in,
Movement of fire?
Have you to resign yourself to be ashes,
The problematic ashes of death?

Meanwhile, History ... Where?
125   History which is in my blood and my veins,
In this breath
Which is breathing life into my present words.

Yellowing ruins?
And the impulse which comes from you,
130   You who still live

In this pulse which marches on alone
Without me, so much mine, me myself?

Me, beneath my words
Resounding with pathways,
135   Through my own liberty
Towards the as yet unknown future,
Towards afternoons of expectant light,
Of a hue which is never solitary.
Will it be my hand
140   Which may perhaps give you colour,
Trembling, indeterminate afternoons?

Something was which is and will be:
Unknown, filial,
Youth which never ceases.
145   Oh native land, the precise name
Of our will, of our love!

IV

The continuous land undulates.
It is the native planet.
Minuscule, visible,
150   It is spherical for all,
And spins round with everyone.
Oh shared anxiety, oh united native lands!

Complete roundness
For our two hands.
155   Piles, bulks, precipices
And dust, dust, dust
If not charred wood and smoke.

Or earth for water?
Water of a full tank
160   Which daylight makes transparent,
Water raised to trembling
By drops of rain,
Saline water of the swelling surf,
Oceans, sea, a single sea.

165   Amongst sand and foliage, along shores,
Amongst wind and flame,
The assent, the "no" of the animal with choice,
Who already chooses to be human,
With such capacity to be a man.

170   He too is the other one, now on the stage

Of fiesta and imminent power.
Look at his face.
From the bull-like head,
The speckled lion's mane
175   Over shining skin.
And a summer-like smile which illumines
Mouth, teeth and voice,
An enchanting voice which now,
Suddenly, darkens,
180   Raging against the air.
Scandal, power, struggle, crime,
And an abstraction disguised by a uniform,
The multitude around their enemy,
Reasons and more reasons, dead and more dead.

185   How the human moment swarms!

History is not in isolation.
Separatists? United.
Terrible company,
Sweet and consoling company!

190   Listen: a man talking.
Spirit is manifest.
Speech is communal:
A loving invasion of clarity.

V

May not one single experience
195   Be denied us in the turning of the planet.
Beautiful precision!
Native grace: Spain.

That sharp skyline of the street,
That ceramic sparkle
200   Of a dome,
This murmur of conversation on
Street corners, all understand me.

Here I am part of this valley,
A poplar on the riverbank,
205   The tangible ambience of the plain,
The still warm wind
On those ears of corn.

So much vivacity
Spread all around
210   Which the heart draws together: my treasure!

And the granite desolations,
The bareness which reveals these contours ...
Is it perhaps my bones
Which better correspond
215   To that arcane call,
For me helpful and well-disposed?

With its sounds and increasing clarity,
Already the depths of morning
Lead me once again to my memory.
220   You surrendered, silent glance,
Withdrawn reticence which does not conceal.

And if there were nothing left amongst us
But civil ruin?
Ruin, yes, perhaps, but in the living sun.

225   Through duty? Through instinct which knows aright
Through the custom of love,
Through the childhood of then
Beneath this maturity now uppermost,
My roots, most innocent, are loyal
230   To you, earth. Only thus endures
My meridian earnestness.

And the frown on your face this day?
And so much such corrosive depression?
You alone, earth, exist, harsh, smiling,
235   For my love, for my will,
For belief by creating you.

Destiny? There is no destiny
Encoded in ciphers of wisdom.

Problem! Dusty
240   Problem of the inert,
Prophecy of those of blinkered sight,
Cowardly apocalypse.
Problem, no, problems
Cleansed of their lachrymose vagueness.
245   Let the dead bury their dead,
Never hopefulness.
It is mine, it will be yours,
Here, generations.
How many, and youthful too,
250   Will tread this hill whereon I tread?

Hope rooted in the captive
Tide: through time, time.

I entrust my hope to this planet
– In its actual configuration of earth.
255   All my being aims at
Full accord here.

Here, so green the water goes towards more water,
Always into the future, its infinity.

VI

Freshness gives refreshment:
260   Freshness of Castile at the meeting
Of the two rivers, of double greenness.
Tumult of riverbanks,
Fronds beside currents.
There are murmurings of skies shedding light,
265   Close, friendly.

And pine groves with deep fragrances
Of flowing energy,
Of preserved power.

And new wheat fields rise up without brilliance,
270   – Later so welcoming to the light –
New fields with the early stems
Which become green and grow tall.

The leaves of poplars still green:
Leaves with impatient life
275   Which must in yellowness find serenity.
Spring the invader!
This plain which eyesight embraces,
Ceaselessly dominant,
Tends towards the wholesome heavens.

280   Walls and the solace of blessed sun.

The greys of the luminous hills
Come alive with more colour,
And the air swells about me into native light,
Into this which makes me what I am.

285   This hill on the horizon balances me:
Saint Christopher modestly pure,
A summit offered as solace
From nobody for everyone,
Local eternity.
290   And the chalky earth
– Enduring without furrows –

Refers us to its familiar
And untrampled meaning,
A never ancient planet.

EXTREME LIFE

I

There is much light. The afternoon is dependent
On man and on his potential companionship.
Very clearly the passer-by feels, thinks of
How much the afternoon trusts in his love.

5   ... And another man passes by. Never alone,
Attentively he looks, goes along slowly.
That afternoon is not to be left incomplete.
It raises up its palace for the attentive man.

Has everything been seen? The afternoon yet offers
10   Its variety: the immenseness of one droplet.
Always there trembles another depth in this creek
Which the most familiar diver can never exhaust.

Inextinguishable life! And the attentive man
Ceaselessly entering within would like,
15   While so much movement envelops him,
To consummate fully his own true afternoon.

Ay! Time swollen with the present passes by,
Will be left behind. The street is fleeting
Like time: soon to be razed flat.
20   Will everything go adrift?

II

The humble passer-by. Reality surrounds
Him, humble in its acceptance.
So many truths! Let the task be.
If one is to live to the full, one must articulate to the full.

25   What is so lived but unfinished
Needs a metamorphosis,
Demands the supreme encounter:
Incarnation in its permanent state.

Let speech be! It is not only thought
30   Which is not reconciled to wander unclarified.
The one who in the afternoon breeze purified
His joy or pain wants to be more.

Did that action end? It is not complete.
It was thought and contemplated. That is not enough.
35   More impulse in the action is given and renders complete:
Form of plenitude which is precise and pure.

Form like a force at its height,
In the splendour of its just dominion.
The end result stands – neither beautiful nor ugly.
40   It is fulfilled through itself, beyond gratification.

The look-out man is attracted. Look: he expresses himself.
How is he not to find those heights
Where a soul imprisoned in flesh is raised
When the entire desire matures in the sun?

45   Ambience of a plateau. The word
Spreads its revelatory virtue.
There will be no better clue that opens up to us
The obscurity which not even its master explores.

Disputes, brazen voices,
50   Crowd hurled round the corner.
Darkness moves towards clarity.
World, who can divine your meaning?

Revelation of the word: may it sing,
Rise up, define its meaning,
55   May what is most profound pulsate in the sound,
May its essence illumine what now is never dead.

May more life be thus imposed by life alive
For ever, enduring to its extreme
Concentration, incorruptible above
60   Where a choir in flames never burns.

The cycle of that deed reached its end,
A deed purified in its correspondences,
Clarified and cleansed in spite of
Its colours, united in whiteness.

65   Soul outside the soul! Outside, free
Of its mist, it is like a thing
Which offers density in its material
Quality: it espouses the hand.

Feeling is transcended. It is an object.
70   Without losing its purity, before the general
Gaze it remains, all compact
With a destiny visible by its outline.

The orb does not dominate its mystery.
There it is, unmovable and fabulous,
75   But there it shines. So many signs
Of light it sends us in our pit.

Fugitive time does not escape.
Conduct was fulfilled. Peace: it is a Work.
That sea, not the blue plain of a map,
80   Recovers so many waves in our voice!

And it is another sea, another new foam
With a tremor now discovered
Which enraptures the spirit and takes it
On the high seas without a pathway to an easy port.

85   And the voice is inventing its truths,
Ultimate reality. Is there nothing similar
In details? Oh prudent one: do not be angry
If outward appearances do not attend the naked form.

Thus self-evident, the hour becomes serene
90   Without denial of its illusion or its bitterness.
Now blood no longer runs in veins,
But the pulse is transfigured into rhythm.

Rhythm of breathing, rhythm of vowel sounds,
Power is so profound that it rises up and sings.
95   Because I really exist, I really speak:
Air is harmonized in my throat.

Oh heart now harmony of language,
Oh illumined mind which is led by
Spring itself with its virgin
100   Fragrance to its central intersecting zenith!

The breeze in foliage sounds like foam:
Rustling noise in oscillating
Movement through waves. So much real
Perfection awaits the passing of the attentive man.

105   Matter is already substantive magic.
Inexpressible secret – with its own style.
Does such shapelessness cause pain? May its depth
Survive painlessly. Word in suspension!

110
Word which hovers in safety and floats,
Through the air word with volume
Where its note, always new, reappears
While the years are absorbed into chance.

115
Everything is intensified into the word.
So much energy flows in so light a
Body! Last action, last defence
Of this existence which has courage to persist.

120
Those warm siestas of summer
Are thus with their fervour more intense.
More cold is accumulated in this cold clarity
Of the song than in tacit winters.

Beauty does not deceive: it multiplies
Our abundance. It is not an ornament for
Our thirst: wine is inside a barrel.
Is a foul concoction more real?

125
Necessary poetry. Suddenly,
That reality then sacred,
Through the transparent afternoon,
Strips bare its essence for us. Who wouldn't sing?

130
Here it is. A rhythm beats. It is listened to.
This beginning in small solitude
Wants not solitude nor aspires to struggle.
Ah! Of probable attentiveness it dreams.

135
Nothing more than the attentiveness of a good friend.
He was born already, he will be born. Glory is faithless!
Better is the good silence which by itself
Safeguards timeless minutes.

140
Minutes in a train, amongst poplar groves,
Not amongst the erudite, undoubtedly at home.
There, reader, where you may give yourself
To that deity who harmonizes your spirit.

Then you will create another universe
– As though you had conceived it –
Thanks to him who was so immersed
Within his most daring task.

145
Is man already his name? May the work
– Itself – hurry on and still endure,
Growing amongst tacks and capsizings.
It is in alliance with so much moon in passing!

This requires the great Affirmation: patient tenacity
150   Which will never give in to the most grave Negation.
Vanity is superfluous. Correctly,
The assault against the cemetery.

— My knowledge will be salvaged in my future.
And if death pardons nobody,
155   May my words have value as a magic spell.
The individual will not die completely.

In the vibrations, in the sound
Of that cadence for ever spoken
My stubborn attempt to exist always will
160   Remain alive. Therein will be my happiness.

III

Yes, may the sovereign spark, in whose
Fervour the afternoon was more ample, endure.
May the beaming face of that summer always shine.
There was a witness of the unsmirched blue.

165   The witness goes along now beneath the sky
As if its beauty were pointing out to him
— With a radiance which is already solace —
The initial richness of a phrase.

The city in collaboration stirs up
170   All its fires and raises more heat
Over the whitish grey of the ashes.
Bedazzled balconies give off sparks.

Whitewash on a wall. The day is dependent
On luck to exalt its progress.
175   Something more, something more! And it is sensed
With great faith: it will be what it was not.

Impulse towards an end, already a complete pulsation,
Changes into creation which entrusts to us
Its inexhaustible atmosphere of newness.
180   Grace of extreme life, poetry.

THE FOUR STREETS

Four streets link up:
Culmination towards a stronger life.
Oh city, never silence
Their restlessness. It is your centre
5   Of luck.
Oh struggle in the hubbub,
Which hurls into so much
Confusion so much smiling
Service: a glance which
10   On passing is already an amusing
Way in to a life,
A phrase heard perhaps
By that passer-by who enjoys,
Laughingly,
15   That tiny
Variation of the unmastered spirit,
Iridescence of an enchantment
Which is air. There is no conductor
Who can direct this disordered
20   Orchestra. So much
Murmuring now lends
Sufficient background to the shout,
Which is not dispersed and lost!
An orb in its hullabaloo, but never damned,
25   At ease in this ambience
Enveloped by a good, evening finale
Which illumines its chaos with gilded
Greys between two lights. The sunset
Says no sombre farewell above the red glow.
30   The sun, behind the rooftops
– Visible face to face
Like a yellow moon –
Ends in a dust cloud of
Many suns.
35   A carriage-top shines
With silken smoothness,
And the smoother control rolls limpidly along.
Oh triumph! And yet,
The atmosphere shares its sweetness with all.
40   Why is there in some men so much bitter silence
Which reveals their character?
The peace is now tangible. There are no accomplices bent
On dissidence. Peace triumphant and ever onward!
Cars, more cars whose skidding
45   Subdues and muffles
Its victorious accent.
Now a horn becomes impatient:

Its blare insists.
Has the balance been broken in a second?
50 Beneath the evening, sad
Perhaps inside, how will the world be?
A world in essence beats, fabulous,
While, ay!, the city
And its towers keep up their relentless pursuit against time.
55 A truth beats
Amongst accidents, noises
And ills,
Scuffles and lucre.
Even the red dusk clouds are wounded
60 By terrible torrents
Of numbers with zeros,
The zeros of those men.
Those men! Along these streets they pass and do not hide
Their names. Look at them! No, no blushes!
65 Someone up above, from his window,
Sees the red horizon melt away.
Sumptuous reality? As everyday
As that reality which is happening now.
All is coexisting with that weather vane.
70 Destiny: the sun sets. A bell
Deepens, completes
The faith
Of some in the superhuman evening.
Through the clouds spreads a vein
75 Of purple,
Which also favours the street. There are balconies
Which are happy knowing of that floating
Leisure. For everyone its golden splendour is
Turned silver with variations
80 All the while becoming greyer. Even commerce
Gives in the shop windows a relief of jewels
Already magical in their abundance.
Oh possible caprices
Facing the final light of rapture!
85 Idols in their niches
Await a freer
Space.
May the dusk, pure on the palace windows,
Reverberate with even more heat.
90 Already that half-seen hand enhances its topaz:
Topaz with influence on beauty,
So widespread that it is in tune with
Clothing, hat veil, person.
Ay! Manly, after her will go a sigh
95 With its darkness. The loving night begins
Obliquely to tend towards

Whispered intimacy in the depths,
Denser now
With sustained hope.
100   Undoubtedly some well-fed horse comes
Smugly along with his rider,
The reins relaxed.
... And night is there – beneath the immense
Future, of such immediate tremors.
105   Life goes passionately on,
Even though here it retains its profound, perpetual
Rage and rapture. Streets at the very crux of the network!
Through the city there wanders a jumpy
Light which tremblingly shines over the darkness.
110   Listen to the cat, perhaps clairvoyant,
Which on the balcony recovers,
Noisily, in the far distance, the solitude of the wild.
But this passer-by, with no one beside him,
Who goes in an orderly way along the road,
115   Is he not also in anguish,
Perhaps even more pursued?
Order. In order! Groups, sparkling metals.
Amongst the arrogance in the streets
Potential martial drum-beats are perceived.
120   Steel!
There is so much brilliance that it is now sinister.
Not even the breeze is unaware of it.
Before everybody is shown,
Ah, the governing Void.
125   Nothing after all. And in the breast,
An anguish common to
All, gathered together on the edges of nothingness.
This world of mankind is badly made.
Is it chance without calculation,
130   Subtle error
Which is degraded in more disorder?
In the four streets there endures a tenacious noise
Which in persisting resists,
And is convincing.
135   Beneath so much discordant, grim, sad
Caprice
The noise continues resounding beneath the sky,
Also a tyranny, and admirable: it does not lie.
Living immortal breeze, fierce desire!

LUCIFER DISCONCERTED

I

LUCIFER I, I.

I too dawn
With this sun, which only the cockerel announces.
As no one suspects my arrival,
5   A cockerel is sufficient.
Stupid sleepy corners!
There too the streets entrust themselves,
Abandon themselves in sleep to the surroundings
Watched over by someone. Him, perhaps?
10   But does it matter to Him
Whether these unfortunate beasts – men
And cockerels –
Rest, cackle?
Chanted adulation will suffice Him.
15   Oh, vanity of God!
Let them accuse me of pride: I prefer it.

That mountain is very ugly.
Redundant its peaks. Stupid mist.
And just where is harmony?
20   Confused ostentation
Disorders everything.
It would have been better for Him to have conformed
With us, his angels, and the sky.
This crude abundance,
25   Always a chaos which is badly disguised ...
Can a creator have good taste?

Delirium of grandeurs,
Vanity, vanity.
I was the first – as everyone knows –
30   To discover His motive.
For this he hurled me from Paradise.
He forced me to be an eternal wanderer for ever,
The first universal wanderer.
(Doubtless a privilege.)
35   I sinned. Did I? I saw clearly.

And these men, who now awaken,
Imagine me to be powerful like a
Fallen, perverted god,
Raging dumbfounded,
40   And thus head of an infamous country.
God didn't want to understand me. They don't understand me.
Men. They re-create me as human,

In their most uncouth form.
I, who am an angel, inevitably the angel
45 Of supreme light,
As though I were a man satisfied
By the fire,
The sacred fire of expiation,
As if I were an executioner who rejoiced
50 With this cruelty of
Civilized people!

Yes, you, you who cannot hear me,
You,
Unsuccessful creation
55 Of your Creator.

Hell is yours,
Admirable men.
Amongst your sabres
You are eternal evil.

60 "Praise God"
Chant the cauldrons
Who inflame the wild creatures
Of His Majesty.

May greater splendour
65 Illumine the believer.
The greater the kindling, the more people
To see more clearly.

May the blessed flame
Purify the evil-doer
70 Because it is the gift
He most needs.

Hell is Earth.
Saint Vitus' Dance!
A single cry is heard.
75 War, war, war!

Above the sleep and peace
Of so many unfortunates,
Unfortunate ones now, I am the one who
Hears this cry, ceaselessly latent.
80 Dawn now uncovers the city:
Old rooftops with ochre tiles,
Shelters of
Foreseen evil.
Is there anything more monotonous

85   Than trickery and guile?
And they think that I am evil,
I who never deceived:
Cause of my situation.
Alone I drag myself through the outskirts
90   Of that my native land.
(I am always aware of it nearby.)
I faced up to the Supreme One.
I was unique then. I, I. Alone.

         II

And who listens to me,
95   Figure without importance
For the ignorant?
So angelic am I,
So subjected to my category,
So unmentioned by the Other,
100   That I can do nothing amongst men.

That man, in this flat,
Will be faithful to me. I suspect his rhetoric,
His logic.
Alone, as alone as I, he cannot accept
105   Elegant compromise.
There is no dialogue.
Nobody would approve it. It offends him
To continue his existence, totally
Abhorred.

110   The world lies deserted.
The worthlessness of everything
Corrodes their souls,
Their aims.
Even if nothing happens to this human being,
115   Life
Is fleeing from his breast.
Unbreathable horror:
He turns to the light and sees so complete
An emptiness that he is suffocating, trembling.
120   Vision of the great emptiness. Ecstasy is pure.

The window murmurs
Its temptation. The air now so limpid,
So profound, does not lie.
Logic intoxicates.
125   What to do – spit? Blaspheme? Blasphemy in action.

The window is open.

The logical man
– His desperation so luminous –
Wants to hurl himself through ...

130
                                       Perhaps he hesitates?

No. It's all over.
                   Arrow towards darkness.

This noble suicide
Has as much reason as a madman.

135
In the presence of the unrivalled Musician,
How Harmony is breaking apart!
Pray, pray to God. It's His consolation.

          III

We are all afflicted by the very mistake
Of the Spendthrift:

140
This divine superabundance
Of unnecessary worlds.
Works, works, stupid weakness.
What is the purpose of perverting
Nothingness, a supremely perfect marvel?

145
I, I am the strongest of all.
I could if I wanted ... I don't want to!
Adhering to this impulse
Which has no issue inebriates me.
May the impulse endure in me, latent,

150
Invulnerable, limpid.
I am more than my works,
Finalized and yet unborn,
They spread ceaselessly
Towards my power as the perfect one.

155
           Honour to the unwritten work,
                To the power
           Which never sentences to death
                Its stalactite.

           Hold back imminent pleasure:

160
                The greater your enjoyment.
           Truth kept in a well
                Is not refuted.

           Honour to him who keeps his source
                Pure.

165
           Unshadowed he will continue triumphant
                Facing the future.

Keep watch over your silences until
　　They become gold.
Never reveal your treasure:
170　　　Be a pure soul.

Honour to the sterility of the
　　Affected one,
Unshakeable in his Infinitude.
　　Be silent, silent!

175　But these crowds
Who in failure work and scurry,
Deceiving themselves ...
Mortal: with pleasure let them be born to you.
There will come out to receive you with their flowers,
180　Their plagues and their atoms,
Three or four policies in search of
Your happiness,
Elegant stupidity
And its multi-headed monster,
185　The crusade and its crimes,
Two distinguished civilizations
Which offer you on their altars
The glorious privilege of sacrifice,
Chance, injustice,
190　Their masks,
And round about, misery,
Constant misery with its stench
Of corrupt spirit:
God's fiasco.

195　And me? Leave me in peace. I demand nothing.
From nobody can I bear worship like the Other One,
Always in vile expectation of chanting and dirge.
And if some invoke me,
It is not I whom they invoke. I am no caricature
200　Of God,
I am no grotesque shadow of His light
For nights of witchery. Idiots!
My light is mine, mine. It crowns me
With faith, with certainty. I am Lucifer
205　With my constant, sure splendour,
Which covers the city.
And the noise of the streets in the centre
Forms at last a constant movement in discord
Which, fortunately, breaks the Harmony.

IV

210   Harmony, gilded
       Prison.
       Is it not the greatest scandal?
       What I hear shatters me,
       Stupefies me
215   With its idiotic chorus, its so superfluous
       Harmony, its inertia.
       All, all as one, prostrate,
       Passive,
       In order to extol the glory of the most silent!

220   Let the slave sing,
       Let the harmonious slave sing,
       With a harmony well-subjected to a Master,
       The Master of music,
       The music of a subjugated orb.
225   And all sounds false, stupid, poor,
       Or worse still, blandly pompous.
       The correspondences
       Of hoped-for sound,
       These intolerable symmetries!

230   The ray of an intelligent light,
       If it illumines well, will break the whole thing,
       Will open up the prison.
       Will make a way for the ever non-conformist.
       I feel happy in this hullabaloo
235   Of the city.
                   Bedlam,
       Contradiction, contrast, midday
       Sun above the noises.
       I am the angel of unlimited light.
240   I, I myself will denounce the great darkness
       Of order,
       I will rip asunder the fictitious ties,
       I shall hurl forth the truth
       Against the sacred fraud.

245   Oh Criticism!
       You certainly move an extraordinary orb,
       Beyond the unanimous heaps
       Of canticles and decrepit masks
       In temples,
250   In princes' mansions,
       In prisons,
       Beneath this midday
       Of condemned shadows.
       Amongst the windows

255 That man has fashioned,
The mind is what invents the universe.
Uncontrollable rocket
– Beautiful, fleeting –
It shines, burns in light and passes away.
260 Spark! It will extinguish itself.

Against the buzz of praise
I listen to a movement
Of bold hearts who dominate
The crisis.

265 The fear of the faint-hearted,
Venerable coyness,
The complaint of the feeble,
The chorus of extras,
Will not avail.

270 Clamour!
Doleful clamour of the most oppressed,
Unlamenting clamour of captains,
Clamour of many, many so lost
That they know not of all those who are
275 Already lost, their own crowd,
Clamour with dark rage or raging
Clarity,
Clamour in the archangel's trumpet,
Clamour, clamour. And all these
280 Resound beneath the firmament,
And become more light: the most pure.
Light it is which illumines,
Without divine deceit, the truth,
The great truth which imprisons us not.

285 Whistle at the emphatic tenors,
Never sleep in the waves
That the nightingale offers you,
Don't be seduced by these trills
From honeyed throats,
290 By the upturned eyes
Of the poor chap in ecstasy:
His cell is his dungeon.
Down with Harmony,
The cowardly murmurs which do not reach
295 The one who never listens,
The Cruel, Impassive One.

The Great Confusion of these streets is pleasant.
The city,

An invented attraction,
300   The republic of the agile.
The Great Confusion vibrates, adapts itself,
Absorbs all.
            Does it triumph?

Everything is sliding between wheels
305   – And no longer grinding wheels –
Of speed for speed's sake. No, there are no aims,
There are no believer's objectives
For the speedy car.
Between proud walls, cars, cars
310   Desperately dedicated
To haste:
Vain speed. And so incredulous!

                    V

What to do but wander round, in passing,
A little less solitary among inventors?
315   There, unequalled, strutting about, is
One who calls himself "a great poet".

GOVERNOR   With the unanimous vote
            Of our city, we offer
            Our warm tribute
320   Of admiration to the distinguished poet
            Par excellence, master
            Of all his contemporaries.

GREAT POET   (Ridiculous! Only of you!)

GOVERNOR   In our country, a leader ...

325   GREAT POET   (What does a country mean
            To one who travels the universal
            Roads of the world?)

GOVERNOR   It's not possible to have heard
            Him speak for four minutes,
330   Even if only on record,
            Without acclaiming him. Foremost
            Figure in the labyrinth
            Of today's art.

GREAT POET   (Imbecile! No one has ever suffered
335   Greater insolence. Me, me!
            – The foremost of this supremely
            Wretched century?)

GOVERNOR	See him pale,

GOVERNOR   See him pale,
                 Overcome by the ecstasy
340   With which his people receive him.

GREAT POET   (Oh! If you don't shut up, I'll scream.
                 He wants to offend me, he insults me.
                 Reduced to "my people",
                 To the dimensions
345   Of its ridiculous stature!)

GOVERNOR   After such an ovation,
                 The Maestro will say a
                 Few words to us.

GREAT POET   Help!
350   I don't know what's happening.
                 (My patience hasn't been able
                 To stand the homage.)
                 I'm ill.

GOVERNOR   Divine
355   Countryman!

GREAT POET   Oh God! I really
                 Am ill. I am no superstar.
                 I cannot speak. I will not speak.
                 (Oh insolents. They have contrived
360   All this against me. Foremost
                 Of my country – what a mockery,
                 Foremost of my time, nothing more!)

GOVERNOR   Gentlemen, we are not worthy
                 To listen to the great poet.
365   Applaud him: he is a suffering
                 Captive of this fervour.
                 Look at him. Seen and not seen!

Poet, great poet, creator,
He cannot tolerate even the praises.
370 They never reach the secret height
Where his image dwells,
The image he alone perceives in his mirror.
He tries to be divine.
His works – immortal! The dreamer
375 Has to accept his failure as complete.
What has just been concluded betrays him:
Substance in which spirit is never made flesh.

VI

What boring moments
Beneath this weary afternoon light!
380   Weariness more visible in the rays
Of sun, so thick while it lingers,
Already picture varnish,
On sunny surfaces.
The public, anonymous
385   Painter is revealed improvising
Sketches of
Badly made reality.
What intelligent person is not repulsed?

This young man is. His window
390   Offers him this "landscape", pretty chaos:
Unavoidable its disorder.
It was inevitable. If he has already "meditated on the world",
For ever inferior to such a spirit,
This spectator in the embrasure will have to
395   Prefer his own repugnance.
Repulsive symptoms are insinuated.
He philosophizes long and hard.
Does the window suggest heaven and earth,
Creation corrected
400   By its most famous residents?
Useless.
Anguish torments the lucid
Mind beside the window.
His eyes squint. Ah, unhappy man,
405   In his nausea only thus is he superior
To the stormy end he guesses at!
On the paper, the pen.
Beside the table, the washbasin.
                              (Cigarette
410   Smoke.)
              Vomit?
Not exactly. More and more pages
Over which the pen passes in consolation.
More glory in such boundaries.
415   (And yet
His anguish is real.)
Neither does this bother him now.
Good-bye!
And off he'll go to the café, which isn't far away.
420   Metaphysical revulsion is overcome.
Creature! By being submissive
He'll end up by strengthening the orb
Which he yet denies: he contributes with his work.
Traitor!

VII

425 I seek myself in myself. Who more unassailable?
     Girt with splendour, myself all splendour,
     How could I bear the darkness
     Of this "Inferno", its depths
     Dark with human troubles,
430 Supremely human troubles,
     At the simple level of dismal villainy,
     Of earthly justice?
     Me, a man of law? They,
     Oh yes, they delight
435 In these barbed-wire fences
     Of unquenchable "concentration",
     Hatred by law of the hell-fiend who judges.
     No! I have no such "camps".

     And what to do but wander amongst the circuits
440 Of these surplus planets,
     Who are bored as well? The stars follow
     Their eternal orbits
     With a tedium we all share,
     And I more than all others.
445 Canticles do not deceive me.
     I manipulate my reflector.
     It is not resisted by the most self-satisfied sun,
     Whose round emptiness
     Explodes in my hands.

450 If this universe is not justified,
     Why does it affect me, resplendent
     In my own light?
     I confess, a certain pain eats away at me.

              It grieves me that the stars
455   Move round with no knowledge of me,
              It grieves me that the world
              Has no affinity with me.

              It grieves me that some mountains
              Perhaps may be
460   As beautiful as men
              Perhaps see them.

              The more You illumine all
              By day and night,
              Less does my light guide and
465   Illumine me.

It grieves me that You exist with such
Power and esteem,
Grieves me that I am not
You.

470   It grieves me, ceaselessly
Grieves me
That You exist, oh Being
With such presence.

And this pain – who knows, love as well? –
475   Overwhelms me
Like an addiction.

Sad the choirless angel,
Far from the heights where he used to admire.
For me there is no place that can be mine,
480   And in these suburbs
I am lost without any tasks to complete.
I am not even the tempter. I am accused of it.
Man is free. Let him choose,
Decide, risk all.
485   So divine a gift routs all my ruses.

But this Creation ... Falsehood. Chaos
Facing the Other One and His order,
Against universal dictatorship.
And is it not better this way: that all should struggle
490   Beneath inviolate intelligence?

I cannot disguise my discoveries.
The Other does not allow it.
He obliges me to live at the very heart
Of my clear-sightedness,
495   And the more it takes on the more it destroys
Within the depths of me,
Which want to be a greater angel
Beyond my own self,
Beyond the atrocious limits
500   Which chain me to myself and humiliate me.

The light of this modest setting-sun
Wanes in the streets
Of the city, chaotic yet guileless.
(Strange:
505   These first lights,
Electrical fantasies,
Opposing the dusk even so adorn it.)
Venus is shining. The society of stars

Is announced, such faithful stars who proclaim
510   The glory of Him Who Is.
Venus, farewell.
          Glory?
                    No. I deny it.

No, no.

BEAUTY AND THE ECCENTRICS

          I

Sodom. The afternoon is festive beneath a sky of
few clouds, friends of that leisure, of that light
so lavish as leisure itself.

It is the relaxation of many subordinated attentions, a
5   pause in the almost tangible reflections which settle
beneath the foliage.

How superfluity is a companion! So much colour
suddenly auspicious, a border which stands out even
more for the leisurely passer-by.

10   Time of substantial frivolity which does not rush to its
end but which is entertained by circumstances, bound up
with events.

Festive presence! Body and face are more real, for
they are not veiled beneath slavish services. Everything
15   is alive.

The town is everything: rooftops in groups, branches
spread with their shade, glimpsed hallways, stalls with no
purchasers, the market.

The crowd, with the density of a multitude, because it is
20   free and unites its various groups in pleasure, bids
farewell to the visiting Queen.
                    Queen of Nations

And the Queen passes by amongst bearded ancients,
clothes that belong as much to the air as to woman,
25   rosy-cheeked adolescents, shouts.

All united in general uproar: people. People who crowd
in close as the Queen of Nations goes by. Queen by right

and by quality: her beauty.

Necklace, rings, ear-rings are scarcely noticed and
30   encourage attention towards the bearing and power
which represent her radiant being.

Her head erect and her face never haughty, in the
distance always straight-backed, she smiles as though
knowing each individual.

35   Illumination which leads to her eyes, between green
and grey. If her stature is so commanding, how is she so
graceful, when so emphatic in her power?

Pride.
       What bloom on her skin, with its irrigation of
40   blood-sap, so animal, so vegetal!

Attracting the attention is her shape in naked simplicity,
although fully dressed – or because of it: everything
attracts to her person, to the immediacy of her.

Immediately feminine beneath her own destiny, so
45   dedicated to man, the Queen attracts because of what
she is, the culmination of the world.

Enchantment culminates in a shape which is already love:
beloved with a lover and of a lover. Through and beyond
his absence, she exists for her resplendent King.

50   And how else other than in song, the silent song of those
lips, can one tell of the eternal pathway that she who is
so destined follows to a man?

               II

My mouth directs all my hope
Ceaselessly
55   To its wonderful end:
The most real.

Hurrying in flight I go towards our secluded place,
Towards your voice, your law,
So as to live as flower to root,
60   Petals to your plant.

My hair curls and my arms stretch
Towards you,
Secret magnet of the endless
Instant.

65 My breast knows well where it goes
With the sun,
Knows well in whose hands there will be a perfect nest
For my heart.

Now my destiny is just this ecstasy
70 Of our health:
I want no other good fortune
Than you.

III

And the Queen progresses amongst the curious, the
enthusiastic, the hostile who cluster round the retinue
75 in warm and jostling confusion.

Like Hortense escaped from her garden, a young man
gesticulates, rapidly, rhythmically, in front of an adult with
the air of a very erudite sage. They smile at each other.

That other man, the talkative one, laughs suddenly: a
80 fleeting sunshade, which has just welcomed his companion, the dominant one although so young.

This sixty-year old, shaven and robust, with vehement
jaws and already despotic hands, is not isolated. Looking
the procession over he follows up his hopes.

85 That very beautiful face with the abundant, curly hair,
rather like a wig, who is it? Proud, magnificent, he is an
author, as it were, of his own form.

He stops there, a spectacle. The blue of his tunic, like a
great sapphire ring! Everyone admires him with the
90 reverence due to Androgynous Perfection.

The sweet warmth of June, with no chaffing excesses,
gives pleasure. Why exert oneself in the sparkles and
shadows of imminent summer?

From a doorway lean out a woman and her brother, or
95 is it her sister? Emulation at the same level: similar
eyebrows above oval eyes.

And the same lips – thick and generous – must serve two
distinct voices. What are they saying? They hardly
murmur, with dignity they are attentive.

100 A small individual, very much alone, walks along,

well-guided by his star. But it can be sensed that he is
timid on the threshold of mere contemplation.

The retinue is held up.
                                    Ah, Queen of Nations, woman
105   beautifully destined for man, more beautiful than flowers,
more beautiful than the sea!

IV

Time hangs more ample and more profound. The Queen
is drawn to distant things! She says farewell, she goes,
she will have left. Benevolent Queen!

110   Her eyes, very wise, distinguish or sense many people. A
crowd? A single abundance of hospitality? Him and him.
Her and her.

Yes, that woman. Complacently fat, with a brazenness
that softens her elegant lineage, covetous, she calculates
115   seductions.

The Queen puts waist and torso into perspective. With
what bold hopefulness these two girls look over the most
desirable Queen! A delight which is already atmosphere is
                                    more persuasive.

Fig-trees with motionless leaves announce the farm la-
120   bourers' fields. Leaves above a wall, with fragrance from
invisible flowers, conceal a garden and solitude.

An opportune moment. For whom? For that girl: loud
clothing, and sandy-coloured hair. Her sight fixes on the
Queen, a dream across her vision.

125   Now on the move, the cavalcade is approached by a forty
year old woman of noble, horsy looks. Her powerful neck
permits no submission ... or submits very willingly.

The horse-faced woman, blushing, so close to the Queen,
contains her imperious impulse and turns her eyes, now
130   hard, away – while she succumbs.

Why is there this roving disquiet? In this girl, for example,
who starts violently. That bejewelled circle enquires.

The uproar of that group trails with it an allusion that
all women understand. Two less noisy girls kiss beside
135   a whitewashed wall.

Triumphant above everyone, the unchallengeable Queen
seduces with waves of attraction ... which seek out him
who awaits them.

Oh King of Nations!

V

140   See the Queen who goes in beauty, beauty by grace
and by destiny, towards her purest seclusion.

There is a palace which awaits with all its great
mirrors the two figures of triumph.

A royal chamber of intensity, with the value and secrecy
145   of a mine, which, I am sure, watches over the supreme
treasure.

It is the Couple, two lives in a single movement onwards,
double heartbeat inventing a single happiness.

The gifts and desires of those disposed to the pleasure
that unites return towards this summit of air.

150   A harmony added to the heavens by pervasive
glory ignites two pulses in perfect accord.

Oh earthly and heavenly Watchmaker, with what sage's
detail you gave rigour to this luxury,

The ever-necessary luxury of this invasion of life in
155   life, pleasure in a tumultuous avalanche,

Spoken marvel towards a crisis of transformations:
more world, mature world!

The woman, so feminine, gives of herself, her arms open
wide, to those of the strong fervour which never dies away.

160   Oh coherence of body and destiny, great animal unity of
leaders who would take up the struggle

To be at the same time so human and so exposed to
creation, creation now and in the future only before gods!

Two lives become more profound because of humble,
165   everyday pleasure. How long the minute,

How short in duration the simple line which, being
infinite, denies the termination point!

Towards her King goes a Queen. Resounding stars. Man
in his love is a musician.
170   See the Queen.

            VI

The Queen presides over and controls the afternoon, in
its submissive or rebellious thronging, and all because of
her virtue: woman beautifully destined.

A street corner. Young men. Firm, delicate, agilely
175   prepared for action. Bracelets on their arms are not
out of place.

They receive the sun on their faces and they shine, resplendent, simple, voracious pink cheeks, like a bed of
sunflowers, inoffensive and happy.

180   Contrast: this bearded one who hails many, affectionate,
sociable. Suddenly, a laugh uncovers some startingly
white teeth.

And behind the beard's mass emerges, a momentary
flash, the revelation of a girl, her eyes wide open. And
185   . . . then the man reappears.

Bangs, shouts, widespread curiosity which also shines in
the brilliant afternoon. Two others. He speaks to her:
"They are so lost!"

Two boys slide by, absorbed, each keeping his arm
190   round the friend's waist. And the Queen? She
watches.

Another outline: this one goes along holding something
bulky on the palm of his hand, high above his head. As
if he were dancing at a slow pace.

195   Some glance falls on the Queen, on her breast, and
reveals indifferent eyes or a face of contradiction.

There are rejoicings which join with the cheerfulness of
the clothes on young girls and young men, and even
some of the gardens stand out more green.

200   There is the aroma of jasmine, more sharp among many
flowers, of roses displayed on fences.
                                    The stamens of those
iris await the bees.

VII

205
A warmth of blues and purples floats through these
shadows of spring tinged with summer, and even the
smallest shrub is the passer-by's companion.

That man – with a child – is happy, in agreement:
Queen in all her authority when he respects the
supremacy of Enchantment.

210
Dominion of the most estimable woman: constant gift,
joyous energy in participation with clarity, tower of
splendidness!

This girl and the other one, both dark-skinned, pass by
and weigh each other up. They offer no other resistance
215
than their stature, which is the protective kind in the tall
girl. (She doesn't hide it.)

A motherly figure, decked out in dark clothing, with the
dignity of authority, very correct, and with never a wicked
thought, loves the younger girl with paternal affection.

220
This lady, so courteous, in blue and red silks, walks
along, very friendly, disoriented, or with successive
orientations; she smiles at men and women.

One woman with an allure defined by its links with
someone male, moves away, now alone, towards her
225
passions. (No encounter has brought her to life.)

Now, two silent women. Within what refuge of melancholy – such is their abandon – will they remain
consoling each other, far from love?

230
The farewell intensifies on the outskirts of the city.
Concluding pleasure. The height of ceremonial crowns
the final homage.

Oh true, gracious woman, centre of rays of grace,
so like the sun! All around her a vibrant profundity
unites the clouds with the earth.

235
A route opens up.
                    Queen of Nations, Queen of everything
and everybody, how beautiful and natural.
                                    The farewell ends.

VIII

240
The beloved goes towards the lover,
Who dreams so much of her.
Earth will shine in the star-studded
Sky.

Nothing hidden divides the days,
Thus so foreseeable.
245
Profoundness in the obscure hours,
The pathway so shared.

Grief and joy
Are understood, tempered and adjusted.
The noble gift is daily reborn,
250
A pathway to greater happiness.

The night of the world
Will point to supreme joy.
The naked instant
Will be enraptured in its light.

255
Amongst inferior attempts
The already fabulous, greater reality
Is fulfilled:
At last its dazzling brilliance.

IX

And the city is left to itself, in its light, which goes down
260
towards the west. And the crowd disperses, not captivated
by the Bride-Queen. And the Bride-Queen goes im-
patiently after the Groom-King, through vineyards
which welcome and serenade her.

A blackbird – see him leap, it is a blackbird – crosses
265
under the oak tree's branches. An old man on a bench
perhaps neither contemplates nor meditates, vaguely som-
nolent because of the passing time, which slips away from
him. Is everything returning to everyday life?

These are the details of life, and they succeed each other
270
bringing the weight of custom to this moment: this
one, which is the last – and already the one which
follows. All these couples, for they are couples, more
or less, pass by in their own way.

Ah! Young girls and young men, men-girls in transition,
275
towards what future, what horizon? Crossroads of a crisis

which is never, or scarcely ever frivolous, but painful,
ardent, difficult, tough, towards what ever-unfulfilled
end?

280   Look at this pretty hand, which corresponds in
slimness to this swan-like neck – which is neither swan
nor ... But what is it? Look at that face, pockmarked
and weather-beaten. A great man?

And yet, around his mouth, what a delicate and unexpected appearance, smiling, being affected and finally
285   hiding away in the big voice and hollows of his rough
cheeks. Everything is and is not. But what is it?

Two young boys are playing guilelessly in a corner. The
transition is slow and pleasant. What's happening? Nothing. A spinney gets darker beneath the cirrus clouds
290   that sunset will set on fire. Nothing, almost nothing.

Sunset of celestial fire? No. Not punishment. The
couples move about within their own flames. Amongst
their flames they fulfil themselves and are consumed.
Approach, there is no hint of hell – the couples,
295   indolent or impetuous, are lost.

The couples are getting lost in their colony, so remote
from the Metropolis, so dependent on the Metropolis:
humble, fertile provider. Oh, solitude of solitudes,
impossible endeavour, solitude in solitude!

300   Charming, stupid, furtive, cynical, triumphing and failing,
drunk with triumph in their frustration, forced to be
resigned so as to accept each other. And that man,
how valiant! And that woman, how self-denying! So
many, so many ...

305   So many in these streets, which are still so rural. And as
the sky dips down its low clouds, the spread towards
tilled and fertile lands is reinforced. Noise of unbroken
Nature: rustles, murmurs, chirps.

And voices of the eccentrics beneath a sun getting ready
310   to set. There the secondary city extends, persists and
is worn away with its particular things.

                                        Some strangers are perceived.
Are they angels descending on Sodom?

THE LAND OF LAZARUS

I

The agony ended. Now he rests.
The air bade him farewell. Now there is no breath
To mist over a mirror.
No, there is no struggle to breathe with difficulty
5   In order to keep the last vestige
Of that happy concordance
Of being with complete being.   The body is vanquished:
Its abandoned substance all alone,
10   Flesh as sad as a sad bulk
Which beneath the sun knows not and will never know –
Because so opaque – of penetrating light.
Without the stubborn durability of stone,
Into stone the body is turning.
15   Alas! It will become slack, a future heap,
An indifferent and disintegrated heap,
Earth in the earth or in the air. Dead.
Suddenly, distant. Where? Where?
The grieving circle of the living
20   Surrounds the absent one. Somebody lies there
Who is no longer himself: involuntary betrayal.
After death there is no possible
Fidelity. The body still
Has a face which becomes distant,
25   Which thus belongs to no person. Alone, alone.
The sightless eyes must be closed.
Oh, corpse, oh ever strangest corpse,
So obviously incongruous to everyone!
The immobile figure sinks into rigidness,
30   The nose hard, and without memory
The entire face which was still vibrant
When ... There is no shared measure for this
Timeless calm and the variable restlessness
Of these unique coursing hours,
35   Which tremble in the hands of the living.
What is the world for a departed Lazarus?
The soul moves in solitude.
                                It stirs out of sleep,
Grey, a refuge of tired trembling.
40   The shadowy, distant peace, which the dead man
Perhaps intuits, presides over him.
They must be clouds ... No, no they are not. Soft
Swathes! But, are they soft? Nothing
Can be felt. What exists outside? Outside, now,
45   To realize space is very difficult.
If only a presence would make itself known!

On the most indistinct of stages
The present time of that world floats obscurely.
The present? Intimations of
50   Unknown, further depths are insinuated.
Something continues: certainly consciousness is salvaged,
Consciousness of some end impossible
To elude or negate.
                    And who is conscious?
55   Someone – Lazarus – knows. How surprising,
To arrive at oneself in this distress,
A catastrophe of simple solitude,
Alone, without bones, without flesh,
Without the body's companionship, without speech,
60   Nothing more than a spirit in essence!
Monstrous solitude – is it harmful, painful?
There can be no pain in this state.
                            Everything is lost.
And there endures – there still endures –
65   This inability to recover his form,
Lazarus hardly existing and remembering,
Aware of himself as minimal on the outer edges,
Tattered remnant of a past.
While affirming himself the dead man begins
70   With the discovery of deficiency. Solitude
At the very heart of the displaced soul!
Displaced now – if it is "now" –
From his own refuge, he wanders, searches,
With neither boundary nor sign, without direction.
75   He who was Lazarus seeks himself in his name,
And amongst the mists, amongst the darkness
– Oh bosom of Abraham! – identifies himself,
Formless, so much an ex-Lazarus in Limbo,
Dwelling of the neutral ones and of the just.
80   And annulled, he resists: pure shadow
Of no sun. The living deadman goes up
– Or descends, neither pathway nor height –
In that unrecorded region.
What do the Earth and men matter
85   To Lazarus?
                  So distant is the already distant
That it is submerged, extinguished in oblivion.
Fatal, obscure shipwreck. No one weeps.
All remains amongst corporeal brambles.
90   All expired in the dust and passions.
Unreachable Nearby! Not even longing.
Eternity devours recollections,
Roots speckled by fertile humus,
All traces of activity, of movement:
95   Perhaps the living are as dead for the dead man,

Spirit amongst spirits of the just,
Men no longer, initiates prepared for
Heavenly fulfilment. On the floor
Of the Globe – tiny, lacking details,
100 With neither graspable shapes nor horizon –
Roam the ants, the living
Who are almost always unaware of the absent ones,
Hardly entwined in the mesh
Of this eagerness, this light, this foliage.
105 Oh life which slides amongst the breaths of those
Who passing through time survive together!
Lazarus accepts.
                    What terrible
Purity, what permanent calm,
110 Spirit in peace which awaits the Son!
The Son will come. Is Lazarus awaiting Him?

                    II

Then the Lord decided
To attend to Lazarus, so indistinct.
            "Our Lazarus sleeps deeply.
115   I shall awaken my friend."
The Son of Man is followed by
Those who follow Him in all things,
As well as the wanderers with
Neither faith, compassion nor fearlessness.
120 They go to Bethany,
Where Lazarus is alone
Amongst the linen bands
Put around him by others,
Free in light and air,
125 Light from sorrow to grief.
Faithful Martha approaches
Him who presides over the repose
– Or the anxiety – of the dead,
And her face shows relief.
130 "Lord, whatever you ask of God
He will give abundantly to you."
                    "Your brother will come alive again.
                    He will walk towards you with me.
                    I am the resurrection.
135   Whoever earnestly believes in me
                    Will not die.
                    I am the life, the truth, the way."
The Man's words reach the heart,
And His feet stir up the dust
140 Of a highway chalky white
In the perfect afternoon.

Mary arrives
With the elderly and the young boys
And this sorrowing group
145 Who strengthen the depths
Of mourning soon to be
Changed into great amazement.
Martha, Mary, the people
Weep in their sorrow,
150 And the Son of Man weeps
In silent lament.
"How He loved him", they say,
All pressed close and much moved.
"Come, Lord", murmurs an old man.
155 The Lord dominates the circle
Of expectation and moves
Slowly towards the distress
Of that cave in which he who was
Lazarus endures, now hardly
160 Lazarus, a form with no soul,
A form in total stillness.
The Son of Man asks for
The gloomy, sickening
Enclosure to be opened up.
165 For four days that corpse was
In the bosom of the earth,
Pathway towards his final annihilation.
And the Son of Man exclaims,
Raising His eyes to heaven:
170   "Thank you, Father. You are the Father.
             Thank you for hearing me."
And crying out towards the tomb:
             "Rise up. Come out yourself."
Then the buried man
175 Leaves his own horror,
Bound head to foot
In white cloths, following
The sacred word
Which demands resurrection.
180 Word which that Voice is
Eternally launching
– Eternally supreme
Over deity and man –
Towards the children of men
185 So much in need of love.
Love which is as unavoidable
As the splendour of the sun
At midday, stronger
Than the desperation of
190 Man hunting man,

Catching no glimpse of You, Lord:
For all, the hope of
Total consummation.

III

Lazarus is now living as the new Lazarus
195   After his adventure.
Modestly he smiles amongst his family,
To whom he has nothing to tell.
Did he know? What did he know? Does he know?
His knowledge has no words,
200   No recourse to shared, human
Terms.
Do they question? He says nothing.

It is confusing to return from danger,
To emerge from catastrophe.
205   But to live is always something familiar,
And one learns quickly to live again.
To breathe again
Is humble pleasure.

In the window Lazarus
210   Does not represent the role of the once-dead.
Here he is, natural,
With Martha and Mary,
With no otherwordly paleness,
Lazarus with jobs and chores
215   In this home which knows him well,
Which clarifies him and sustains him with sweet
Support and companionship.
There is no greater wholeness:
To be in completeness – with all his roots –
220   Amongst the words which are his homeland:
These streets, streets full of noise
Which is music.

And Mary's voice,
And Martha's silence,
225   Which is also heard,
And carries weight.
Everything is simple and tender
When the two women
Direct at Lazarus an attention
230   Perhaps already absent-minded amongst customary activities.
The house,
And in the house the table,
And at the table the three of them taking bread:

Volume of joy
235   Shared round tablecloths
Or pinewood table-top.

Nor is our Lazarus often alone,
Neither does he seek solitude for his soul,
Happily aware of his dependence
240   On his fellow man.
With him Lazarus' heart
Is revealed,
Thus he knows himself. Coexisting
With loved ones
245   His existence as a man is deepened:
A man in this his belovéd Bethany.

The pleasure of being there,
There, on the ground crossed
By feet and eyes which remember,
250   Beneath the shady tree,
Shade which is so amiable,
Beside the flower which smells from afar.
That elm with widespread embrace,
The cypress tree in its row,
255   Ever peaceful for the contemplator.
And like a surprise the attacks
Of jasmine, of orange-blossom:
Aroma with a beating depth,
So intimate,
260   Of afternoons with jasmine and orange-blossom,
Living in moments of fragrance.

With no awareness of pleasure
– Continuous activity, that of everyday life –
Lazarus gives himself up to the current
265   Of incessant life,
And always on awakening
The virile freshness
Of the sun in the wind over coursing water
Is renewed for him.
270   The relationship with these sequences
Of transparent abundance
Is convincing.
And Lazarus moves around
According to
275   His spontaneous rightness,
Humbly at ease:
Intimate part of the place given to him by God.

That place, the soil

Of clay
280 Whose redness so delights the traveller,
Or the one who is aware of it without travelling
Like Lazarus there,
Seated on a bench
Of stone,
285 Companion for its master when weary,
Or when simply at peace,
Beside the passing hour.

An hour which, fortunately,
Also escapes the one who was resuscitated,
290 Good navigator along his own river,
Adjusted to the transient mode,
Waves, white hairs, farewells,
With his own brief existence.
And this swift dusk,
295 Here and already dying away
In the dense rays which rise
And fade away
Before Lazarus erect.

Everything is familiar with hidden marvellousness.
300 That living man, who was in the grave,
Does not cause anxiety,
Neither does he himself take on airs
Because he is the one who has returned
From the depths.
305 Lazarus, with no noticeable surprise,
Takes on
Inevitably a life
Where Lazarus is Lazarus
Day after fugitive, terrestrial
310 Day.

Days beyond harm with his two sisters:
That tenderness which is never expressed,
Which keeps them together.
No pomp,
315 Just the usual companions,
The Son,
His words, His silence,
His Grace.
Everything is being woven into the network
320 Of wrinkles
Where the time-span of that man
Will come to an end:
Well-sculptured time-span,
The face of

325   Patient Lazarus.

       And Lazarus, so real,
       In spite of that gloomy descent,
       Lazarus with no visible
       Legend,
330   It being now hardly remembered,
       Greets people, lingers,
       Caresses that mongrel
       Who suddenly catches his attention,
       Works,
335   Prays in the temple, sings.
       Thus completely Lazarus:
       Earthly creature of his God.

       Sometimes,
       During a pause in his chores,
340   Talking to himself,
       Sleepless on his bed
       In the nights, at times long and clear,
       Lazarus goes back,
       Slides downwards.

345   Peace is not enjoyed by the man who remembers
       For himself, deep within, the inexpressible.
       Unique in his return from beyond the grave,
       He questions, compares, suffers, fears,
       Commends himself to God,
350   Implores.

                  IV

       LAZARUS

       Submissive to your greatness,
       Here You have, Lord, Your servant,
       Always astonished
       At the miracle: I see it
355   As a light which never ceases to
       Cause bewilderment.
       Although the world is unaware of it,
       I stand in a privileged place
       Before this world which knows nothing
360   Of all that silence taught me.
       Atrocious silence! These noises
       Spread round about me
       Sound now for me
       Above that secret depth
365   With the appearance of impending danger,

Which I ceaselessly, hesitatingly,
Consider.

Lord:
The tumult of this carnival
370   Goes through my ears to the soul
Of this Your servant and all my being
Rejoices when dawn
Uncovers once again the earth,
And in the dew of the meadow
375   The most fragile first-life trembles.
If the morning wind
Blows amongst sun and grass,
My happiness rises up to You,
You who made everything.
380   You it is who presents to me
The hubbub of riverbanks,
And beneath moving shadows,
Love of this complete life.
To the swarthy travellers
385   I owe all the news
Of countries which You,
Lord, also watch over.
But only here do I live in earnest.
My centre is this street
390   Where Your servant, Your poor Lazarus,
Is Lazarus in very truth.
Between mind and flesh,
My fervour and my frailties,
And thanks to so many strong
395   Shapes which show themselves to me,
I am – because I exist.

Here I am me,
Myself: flesh and bones.
I will lose nothing, will I?,
400   When once again
– A second time – I undertake the great journey,
For me one of return,
To the final homeland.
I hope for everything from the Son.
405   I must come alive again
With my spirit and my body:
The promise has to be fulfilled.
And if You wish, in heaven
Where at last ...

410   Forgive me.
Yes, I am committing a sin.

And at this very moment
Remorse pierces me.
Lord, I know. It is not here,
415 But There where the kingdom is
Which You reserve for man
Destined to be a perfect
Enjoyer of the divine
Vision. I do desire it.
420 Me.
    Me? Who?
        Is it this Lazarus
Of hopes and efforts
Who between each breath
425 Respires with breathing
Compulsorily and necessarily
Attached to the air, in
An atmosphere where there are rivers,
Mountains, heathers,
430 And young and old men
Who – seeming like me –
Know how to come alive
Each morning?

        If I were
435 An inhabitant of Your Glory
For me let it be earthly glory.
More summers, more woods,
And beaches beside the sea,
And in times of inclement weather
440 Fire: may the firewood crackle.
If through Your mercy
My happiness were dependent
On You, Lord, and if time
Didn't make and unmake me,
445 What would impel my hands?
What would impel my resurrected flesh?
What would I be like, this being who,
Mortal, still dreams of You? My
Immortal being, would it be mine?
450 Shame
Afflicts me because I cannot even
Conceive of Your Eternal Life,
And humiliated I confess
To confusion, to impotence.
455 May the sacred sublimeness
Be like Bethany,
And may blessedness
Salvage the modest fortunes
In which a man comes to be

460   The man whom You, You create
       In so human a form.

                                   I am mistaken,
       Lord. I only perceived
       With sufficient clarity
465   What Your Israel
       Treasures up in the profound
       Vaults of our faith.
       Never remote or lost,
       Your servant continues at the mercy
470   Of Your right hand, Your light.
       I only believe in Your power,
       And I wouldn't like to trust
       In my anxiety, my thirst,
       My most stupid anguish
475   Which hides my insignificance,
       So very shameful. My place ...
       Is this one where I am who
       I am while towards heaven
       I am pushed by something almost cruel,
480   A requirement of heaven,
       Supreme place, supreme good,
       The revelation of the Son,
       And the soul follows after Him.
       May His light be my guide.
485   I want to believe in His truth.

MELIBEA'S GARDEN

All for life

Fernando de Rojas

NIGHT

From the instant in silence, forces depart towards obscurity,
Forces which increase by desiring,
By forming their future:
The authority
5   Which midday will preside over.
       Murmurs ... The murmurs come back again. They are guided,
       Between the rooftops and foliage,
       By this clement moon
       Which I attracted to my kingdom

10   So that it might still smile.
        And coming to life again in calmness, with pleasure it lingers
        Over what it illuminates as if it were fountain
        Of a love which announced that of dawn.
        All, all moves towards an object
15   Now
        As yet more desired than known.
        Is its secret revealed to nobody?
        See how this young girl,
        Whose voice is a spark of light,
20   Gives meaning to darkness.

        MELIBEA, LUCRECIA

        M   He whom I so hope for
             Always seems late in coming,
             And even the stars suffer
             With my body's anxiety.
25   What will he do without me in this world
             Which so hides him away from me
             If for me when alone all
             Is undone in the wind?
             Still he doesn't come. Sing, Lucrecia,
30   Sing, relieve my trouble.

        L   Flowering branches, stars,
                  Live with me
             Because you will all be more beautiful
                  If my lover sees you.

35   Even the ripple of the fountain
                  Never tires
             Of turning and returning so elegantly
                  Because he is aware of it.

        M   Is that footsteps I hear?
40   No, it's not him.
             Without music time passes
             More slowly.
                       I too
             Will sing.

45   L   Isn't it him?
                       Let's sing together.

        M, L Time as yet not mine,
                  Do not detain my lover,
             For you will pass at our side
50   Like a great river.

Rapture will be fulfilled for us
In such a way
That all of life will leap
From embrace to kiss.

55   And the night will be so clear
If Love touches it
Oh!, as though God illumined it for us
In my mouth.

L   Waiting is better thus.
60   Your very voice gives you strength.
Shall we carry on?

M   Let me say by myself
How I am transported.

So as not to shout out I will sing
65   Of my pleasure
In an earthly heaven when
I give you my faith.

And together, ah, happy at last,
What you say to me
70   Soft-voiced is always true.
Stars, sing.

L   Listen.
There's nothing to be heard.
To protect your love
75   Everything becomes deserted.

M   And he will arrive, already I see him
Coming down our pathway,
Alert, covered up, determined,
Towards my eyes on the threshold
80   Of fable and firmament,
Where Love will protect us
– Safe within the garden –
With the joy of glory
Which will keep us eternal.

NIGHT

85   The voices and the silence of the Earth
Are fused in an expansive
Murmur which has a hidden source.
Enamoured yearning thus does not miss
Its goal.
90   A goal perhaps eventually ill-fated?

No one knows – meanwhile that supreme goal affirms itself,
Bringing with it a tumult
Which knows nothing of good and evil.
So swiftly the arrow goes to its centre:
95   Divine expectation!
The two lovers, within
Their future star,
Will bring together the galleries of their rich mine,
And working together will find their present
100   Happiness
Is like an eternity which matures between them.
Oh fugitive perfection, stay a while!

MELIBEA, CALISTO

C   Melibea!

M   Calisto!

105   C   Although every night
           You see me arrive at the same hour,
           A great remorse of slowness
           Pains me each time.

M   Here!
110   Now you are here,
           Your presence is real,
           Real, real, real.

C   This voice, this voice ... Oh, my good fortune!

M   What did you do during the day?

115   C   It doesn't matter, I don't know.
           During daylight hours I don't know whether I exist.
           Probably I wander about like a phantom
           Which thus suffers from hardly existing.
           Can I really exist if you do not exist,
120   If you are not in very truth before my eyes,
           If my hands search for you
           In the daylight and do not find you?

M   My love, my love, find me now.

C   Always you are at the end of corridors which are
125   Dark in the sunlight,
            And with neither sight nor hearing, numb
           Within my own darkness,
           My head against the wall in front of me,
           I sink into a suffocation

130   Where I hardly breathe,
                      Hoping for the night which will drive me
                      With a force, though mine, yet not mine,
                      No, for it's so incredible,
                      Towards your arms. And your mouth.
135   This very mouth.
                                  Silence!

        M   Listen.

        C   No, be quiet, be quiet.

        M   What are you saying? I can't hear you.
140   Tell me clearly, nearer to my ear.

        C   Your ears.

        M   There, there as well?

        C   The moon illumines your hair
              And this softest of earlobes
145   Which is another god – to be revered.

        M   Oh! Oh!
                      The moon now . . .

        C   Leave her be amongst her clouds.
              They are hurrying away.

150   M   I will not pass away.
              Together with you in the instant
              Which will never stop!
              Take me to a garden of sure shade:
              Shade which will unite us for ever.

155   C   Where can such a garden be, Melibea,
              Which can be possible for us?
              At times a wave snatches me up
              –Though I reject it –
              An oceanic frenzy that carries me off toward more water,
160   More water . . .
                          of oblivion.

        M   Oh, you are mad, mad!

        C   No, not mad. Almost drowned,
              Still resisting, I struggle.
165   Unless it be that I live
              By shipwreck, always coming to grief.

Here I can breathe.
                          The breeze. Very slight,
        It scarcely moves the leaves.
170   And this so pleasant warmth in the night,
        Warmth for us, within us!

M   Find rest in me, with me.

C   Ah, to sleep – or die – upon your breast,
        Not to waken in the sunshine of the outsiders,
175   To sink down gloriously together!

M   I sustain and will sustain you.

C   Nothing sweeter for my head which
        – D'you understand – is unbalanced
        By ceaselessly dreaming of this port.
180   My port, my refuge!
        How it fits my reverent lips,
        How it quenches my thirst!

M   Oh God!

C   No, it is not quenched.
185   This joy which returns, returns, returns,
        Always its own source.
        What are you saying?

M   Nothing.
                                    Take me.

190   C   Melibea!

M   With you.
        Without you there is no Melibea.
        With you I have life, I know myself, I feel
        My blood like a river which is a gift.

195   C   Treasure of so many
        Treasures! Here I am a king.
        I lose myself in your wonders.

M   Love, regale me, love,
        Encircle me with enveloping words.

200   C   Melibea, you, you ...

M   Are you accusing me?

C   No, I'm naming you, caressing you.

M   Melibea is for you,
          For your desire, with your body, your soul,
205   Earth and heaven, my law, my salvation!

C   Oh if only there were no world
          Other than this garden!
          Oh Melibea, my own, complete garden!

NIGHT

          The garden, gathered in
210   Beneath voiceless shadows,
          Deepens in this oblivion
          Which the world reserves for it.
          Moon amongst the clouds: do you no longer know us?
          The garden now is no more than softest
215   Grass
          Which alone has true knowledge of the great recondite pulse,
          While the blurred branches, offering
          Their profusion to the darkness,
          Fuse in shapelessness
220   So as to join forces with the
          Invisible, but human, earth.
          Nobody can be seen in the unlit
          Density,
          And whatever is contemplated denies
225   Its details to him who strives to
          Understand that which is most obscure. Neither do I see
          Moonlight tremble across windows.
          Triumph openly, greater circles!
          So strong in its element,
230   Love, so capable of inspiring love,
          – If all doesn't demolish it with the
          Sudden violence of the hidden knife-edge –
          Spreads far this discreet
          Peace.
235   Oh crisis like ecstasy, culmination of the world
          Which in its complete harmony
          Centres and reabsorbs it!
          Love: the planets orbit around this garden.

MELIBEA, CALISTO

C   Oh wonder!

240   M   For ever and ever!

C   Yes.

              Melibea!
                       Only Melibea,
    I want no other horizon.

245   M   Life? Only with you.
                            Are you sleeping?
                                    Sleep.

      C   What joy like this!

      M   The moon
250   Leaves the clouds behind and to us
    Consecrates her great and precious innocence.

      C   What joy like this, almost
    Awake, free and stretched out
    As though to die!

255   M   No, no, never death! Now there is no death.
    Look into my eyes.

      C   Such green eyes! Would I were a poet!
    No. Speeches are useless ... You inebriate me
    With your absence and your presence.
260   Awesome is your very presence,
    Dawn itself.
    Oh, no horizon other than your body!

      M   Take it. It is yours.

      C   And even better than a horizon,
265   Which can never be touched. Objective!
    Goal of my life – or of my death.
    How can I accept the coming dawn
    If my own dawn is hidden from me?

      M   You are mine in daylight, I never lose you.
270   Also this cypress tree gives me the shadow
    Wherein I keep you safe.

      C   Look at your cypress tree,
    Perhaps sad.
                    What freshness! Now it is tapering sharp
275   In this breeze.
               It must be getting late.

      M   I don't know. May your warmth beside me
    Last and last!
    Warmth illumined

280   With the light wherein I live,
           Where such hope promises us
           Our immortality.
           Within your arms time does not exist.

      C   Time leads me relentlessly to the day.
285   Empty day beneath the empty sun!
           And I am lost in the air breathed by others,
           Other ignorant people
           Who do not know of you.
           And what suffocation there is in waiting,
290   Far away from your knees
           – Here, here they are
           Oh, to obey me!
           And I desire them so much
           That I could destroy them.

295   M   Is this love? Calisto,
           Harsh Sir, be silent,
           Don't darken the night. Be still!
                                            Look at me.
           I am more faithfully
300   Naked for you – beneath my clothes –
           Than the moon up above, so naked,
           Giving herself to the garden.
           Here you have me plainly before you,
           My worth given willingly,
305   All innocent in your arms.

      C   Softest whiteness with its rosebuds.
           This one. Let me ... And this one. My own garden!

      M   You it is who's created it. Oh God! I am yours,
           Because you caress me,
310   You give me your worth, your eternal being.
           What atrocious deprivation
           To live, without your glance, in cave or crowd!

      C   Through caves I drag myself along,
           Without air to breathe amongst the people
315   Who separate us from our night.
           And the heat of a light that could not illumine me
           Burns me.
           Mine the cruel furnace. And I waste away
           Always despairing, always desiring you.
320   How can I avoid dreaming
           Dreams of rage where I destroy myself
           Or search for you
           So as to hold you close

325		Till I lose the strength To hold you, exhausted? Exhausted, mad, dead.
	M	My love, you are raving, stop it. Do you want to cause me pain, Am I not with you?
330		The night is yours: it offers you everything. My clarity is yours, you control it. Ah! Your forehead burns me.
	C	I am the one who is burning. And you, you, wonderful girl ...
335		Do you hear something? What's that noise?
	M	People passing by.
	C	Perhaps they'll bother my servants ...
	M	Bah! They'll look after themselves. Don't get up.
340	C	I'm going, for they need me. Someone is attacking them.
	M	Farewell to our happiness!
	C	There's no danger. The ladder's near the wall.
345		Good!
	M	Don't rush. Careful! You're going without your armour.
	C	Wait. I'll come back.
	M	Alas! I'll call Lucrecia.
350		These moans and cries ... Oh capricious Fortune. I was so happy that I'm afraid.

NIGHT

	I cannot hear clearly the murmur of this fountain. Some people's destiny runs so inexorably
355	To its climax That suddenly into the silence is hurled The expectation of the world.
	Is all the divine order Undone?

360   Is it snatched away in the wake of some fate,
        Messenger of a chaos which could
        Negate,
        By means of a single creature,
        The remaining harmony?
365   A human being hurries.
        Where to? What end awaits him?
        Rigour.
                And then ...
                        What?
370   A being, who then was alive,
        Is no longer.

        MELIBEA, LUCRECIA

        M   I don't understand. What's happened?
              What are they saying there?

        L   The voices
375   Confuse me.

        M   Calisto, dead?

        L   He fell from the ladder. Clumsy!

        M   Clumsy, no. Mad for me!
              How awful!

380   L   Don't cry, don't weep.

        M   Is it possible for this glory
              To have been destroyed in one blow?
              I hear this horrific noise,
              And these fierce, lying words
385   Pierce me.
              Do they lie? Oh, my voice
              Is breaking. I cannot weep.
              Where are you, Calisto, where?
              Neither on stones do you lie
390   Nor do you know yourself.
              I don't know myself either,
              Lost in the clamour,
              Unbreathing in your air,
              No longer dependent on your night,
395   Your day, your sun,
              Your eternity. There is no one
              On God's earth
              Poorer than I, there are no pleasures
              With you, nothing exists.
400   Only this double exile,

For I am not here,
Beside this bronze door
Which hides its secrets from me,
Secrets which are splendours for Calisto.
405   If they are yours, they shall be mine!
I must climb the tower
Which will enable me to see straightaway
The refuge which hides you,
I must fly towards you,
410   Plunge into the vast gold,
Live in revelation
At the summit of the great order,
Saved, oh yes, for ever,
My mouth on yours. Place me,
415   Calisto, my love, once again
In triumph within the circle
Which you will illumine for me,
Where you await me. Will fears
Detain me? What fears?
420   Forgive me, loved ones
Who remain in this house,
Supreme protectors
Of my virtue and honour.
It is God himself who selects me.
425   Oh! I shall have to leave you
Feeling the terrible cut
Which slices through me as well
And pains me much. My blood
Runs so much to its sea,
430   My yearnings so urgent
That I don't know how I still
Suffer here pain which is so
Far from my happiness,
Without rising up to the summit
435   Which will never be covered
By these stains which corrupt
The light of your paradise.
What light more pure, more noble?
To your love, to your garden
440   I come now, Calisto. Gather me in!

NIGHT

The garden is empty of love.
In accord, the cypress trees
Deepen their blackness, now funereal.
Solitude torments a still world,
445   And amongst so many set-backs,
Humans feel themselves even more mortal.
Has Love destroyed its lovers?

Were they lucklessly free,
Blindly nocturnal, pitiful?
450   Early morning comes over the meadows,
Over the dew once again so innocent,
So that the darkness of the earth can be
Reunited with the new urgings
Of Attraction – which persists in the fountain,
455   Ceaselessly sliding in clarity.
Who would not defend the one who loves?

SANCHO'S RESIGNATION

> *. . . the speed with which Sancho's
> governorship ended, was finished and
> undone, and disappeared as in shadow
> and smoke.*   "Quijote", II, 53

I

Shouts. All of a sudden shouts.
A tremendous din falls, crashes down
On the half-sleeping man.
And the pleasant night
5   Hurls onward with menacing fury.
"Master:
It's the enemies' attack!"

Trumpets and drums
Dominate the tumult.
10   Warnings, orders, the most frightening
Ringing of bells erupt in the air.
Absolute violence
Strengthens its grip.

The astonished Master,
15   Not understanding that uproar,
Investigates.
More shouts. Everyone shouts, hurries about,
Responds to the attack.
The Master, an impromptu
20   Captain, will guide them,
And already between two breast-plates
He stands – immobilized.
The rigid figure crashes down.
Adversity: the floor.

25   His ridiculous bulk is weighed down with relish by

The brutal weight
Of a mass with solely human viciousness:
Crude feet of animals
– Look at them – they can only be one thing: men.
30   And meanly they become cruel,
Obscene confusion of men,
On the Governor, brought so low,
Who lies in sweat and pain,
Alas, defenceless against the
35   Many kicks of the crowd.

Crowd? They are but few – of the many,
Contemptuous with jokes
Which scorn and humiliate
The presumed inferior,
40   Fallen there beneath the worst ones.

Knife blows are aimed
At the breast-plates of Sancho, no longer visible,
A tortoise
Which suffers and withdraws into its shell,
45   Ridiculous
Perhaps for the cruel
Eyes,
Who no longer see the man,
Now a phantom shape, a mere plaything.

50   The confusion and noise favour
Such a multitude of
Cruel, capricious blows,
Which through tiredness finally have less force.
The mistreated captain is a boat
55   Beached broadsides on the sand.
The monotonous surge wearies.
"Enough", says a voice.
Victory!

Victory is acclaimed, peace,
60   Relative peace spreads
Until it covers the body
Of the victorious Master.
Victorious?
            On his feet, now extricated
65   From the fastenings, he rejects the homage.
And aching, beaten,
His soul sorrowful in afflictions,
He asks the favour of a glass of wine
To ease his thirst. They give it him. And he drinks.
70   Pause.

Will the mockery continue? Many surround
The harassed man, who fades away.

II

Sleep of great calm,
Sleep like a crisis
75 Which moves and gathers up everything
– Still without light –
In earth, sunk
In deep, longed-for freshness.
The sleeper seems unaware of himself,
80 And without knowledge of that stubborn throb,
Entrusts his darkness – with stars –
To a supreme power.

The world moves round in widespread silence.
A supreme network
85 Holds creatures captive.
The dark foliage
Vibrates beneath the starry lights.
The still body of the sleeper exists
With a dignity which is
90 Submissive to unknown inspiration and numbers.
All is firmamental.

That man, lost,
Sleeps, sleeps, and finds himself:
Now he is himself.

III

95 What time is it?
                    "It is dawn."

And Sancho, distressed,
Looks towards the window
Where clarity is scarcely breaking through.
100 The greys
Are vaguely blue
Through the lattice
In noiseless air.

He wakes up in silence.
105 The man
Discovers himself
Slowly
While, once again,
The sun reveals the world.

110 And Sancho gets up and keeps silent, silent.

Such silent bearing
Causes respect, draws limits.
Expectation. The mute hoaxers
Let Sancho, who slowly and in solitude
115 Imposes himself, from his own spirit,
Do what he must.

IV

So, very slowly sets off
– No one knows where to –
The man, still buried in his silence.
120 Was there a kind of death?
Will there be resurrection
In this dawn-light?
Dawn is a spring.

He who was Governor – what is he now? –
125 Crosses the rooms,
Goes down
Followed by the others,
Limited now to being observers,
And in the smelly stable
130 Comes to a halt.

All await, circumspect. Sancho,
Sure,
Approaches, finally,
One who knows more about
135 His love, his destiny.

Faithful Dapple! Tenderly
He bestows a kiss of peace on the donkey's head.

V

The donkey, a companion – and why not? –
In toil and in labour,
140 In many long, shared hours
Of always mutual companionship,
The donkey,
Dapple by name and by colour,
Was waiting there, faithful,
145 Always ready to serve
With grave gentleness.

His master already feels his soul to be relieved

          Beside one who immediately restores him
          To shared life,
150   To his own existence
          As the real Sancho.
          In Dapple's eyes shines
          Daily truth.

          Tender, content, strong, careful,
155   Sancho prepares the donkey for departure,
          He talks to him as if the two of them,
          Already alone, were enjoying shared liberty.
          To set out on one's rightful road
          Is a joy to men.

                    VI

160   Images, recollections of the past
          With the force of the future,
          Return to Sancho's memory, moved by emotion.
          Digging, ploughing, pruning, layering vines,
          Vineyards, a sickle,
165   The oak tree's shade in summer,
          Sheepskin jacket in the winter . . .

          A man is this tapestry of insignificant
          Customs
          And things felt
170   Amongst impulses which are then alien
          To the fraud
          Of an unreal perspective:
          Island with no sea,
          Governorship, laws, wand of office,
175   Pointless vanity,
          Towers of an ambition which collapses around us.

          And there, in very truth, is brotherly Dapple.

          With him goes one who, with real clear-sightedness,
          Says farewell. Simple resignation.
180   "I was born naked. I leave naked.
          Move aside."
          "Oh not like this,
          Lord Governor!"
          "No second time round for these hoaxes.
185   The heights are not for me.
          Let the ant's wings,
          Which raised me aloft
          So that the swallows would eat me, stay here.
          Let me tread the ground

190   Again with a plain and simple foot,
This foot in its leathern
Sandal.
Now, let me pass, for it's getting late."

The listeners bow.
195   Respect bends their necks.
Is there anything he needs for his journey?
"A little barley for Dapple,
Half a loaf, half a cheese for me.
Farewell, farewell, gentlemen."

200   Weeping he embraces everyone.
They, filled with wonder, embrace him one by one.
The highway is straight.
Sancho urges Dapple on,
In freedom towards ... Who knows! – Friend Sancho ...

        VII
205   Dapple, almost joyous,
Trots along beneath a man who,
In spite of his tears, is happy.
Sancho has touched the earth,
So obvious, so pure. Sancho is Sancho,
210   In his place, girt about by his limits:
The reality which is buried deep within him,
A truly well-assumed plenitude.
Being embraces being, his being, the unique
Feasibility:
215   Health and salvation. There will be no greater glory.
"Here I am. I am Sancho."

There, from this point
Which is his own in his native land, his universe,
Before the everlasting depth
220   Which for Sancho too is expressed
As a Creation.

His being is in his true situation:
A simple, just harmony,
Beyond facile, passive
225   Self-indulgence,
No adhering to fleeting bonds,
And ready for whatever activity awaits him,
Though always entering an unknown
Future.

230   Neither angelic harmony,

Nor celestial beauty.
Less and more: a real concordance,
A tiny but perfectly established
Participator of the world.
235   Sight is always the centre
Of a circle
When looking at the horizon,
And thanks to his limits
Sancho is Sancho with strength
240   Of character and destiny,
With tranquil commitment.

Then the universe,
Or divinity,
Traces round everything the great, everlasting circle.
245   Poignant moment.
The creature accepts:
Humble creature.

Rarest marvel of
Humility. Oh Sancho!

THE TEMPTATIONS OF ANTHONY

> *... however worthy a man may be, he*
> *will never have greater worth than that*
> *of being a man.*   Antonio Machado

I

A man.
         Stretched out, he dreams,
Always uneasy and restless
Still feeling the weariness of the day,
5   Which comes back into his mind stirring up
Reality and future,
The trivial threads of that day
With what has never been lived.
And over his abnormal
10   Memory
Flimsy images
Surge and slide.

Anthony.
Is he called Anthony – this man who is still enjoying,
15   Suffering,
Spectator or actor,
Those adventures invented

By someone who knows nothing of his own
Real night,
20   And with his vision annulled,
Sees shadows illuminated?
Anthony gives voice to his desires,
Already free with their masks.

II

The demon, the Guardian Demon,
25   Tempts his body.

The demon promises the sleeping beast
Satiation,
And Anthony, as he dreams, discovers himself
Deep within himself,
30   He is reborn.

It's almost midnight,
And a round moon
– In the starless sky –
Shines down towards the castle,
35   Which Anthony leaves
With furtive slowness.
The walls, and their grey
Battlements, are left behind.
The gentleman moves forward,
40   Contains his trepidation,
Goes deeply into profound,
Distant, solitude.
Anthony doesn't even hear
The dog howling
45   At the face of the moon.

Midnight.

Now is the right hour for the return
– Necessary, terrible –
To his other being, to its frenzy and shape.
50   The man undresses,
And there,
In the usual place,
In that hollow covered by
Shrubs
55   – Surrounded by the pathless wood –
The clothes are left
Hidden,
Clothes which individually proclaim:
Anthony, gentleman, grandee,

60   Castle.

        The man is naked.

        Greater nakedness invades him, dominates him,
        Shattering his body, shaking,
        Trembling, aching and so very confused.
65   And with the atrocious anguish of a disorder
        Which entangles everything from within,
        Blindly the one who was begins ...
                                        Who?
        Someone, in a dead faint, knows nothing.
70   The silence passes over all like peace.
        The bulk of an animal sleeps.

                                And wakes up.

        A man-wolf? A wolf
        Who barely retains in his bad memory
75   Any remnant of a mute
        Past, remnant which practically smothers
        Mounds
        Of much murkiness.
        Does this wolf know now that he is "this wolf"?
80   If perchance he does,
        Knowledge comes from that very remote consciousness,
        With no reflecting relationships with a person.
        A subtle shape in bursts of activity:
        Capturing and devouring.

85   The wolf wanders and explores,
        He goes along through oak trees to a path
        Which leads to a road,
        He searches
        The shadows and patches of light
90   Between two lights, dawn and its chill
        Now imminent,
        He tenses ready for ambush:
        He needs some prey.

        A greyish fur moves and leaps.
95   Alert, alert! Too late.
        Our animal runs off. The fur flees.
        Beneath the sonorous light, the woodland rustles.
        Birds, still invisible, chirp
        – Judging by the sound they are blackbirds –
100   Accompanied by the whisper of foliage,
        Tremulous with the breeze and bird feathers.
        The wolf

Concentrates his attention,
Heeds the smells and noises
105 Which matter to him. There!

Frenzy. The victim falls
To the most agile ferocity.
In the already silent mass one cannot make out
What the vainly fleeing form was.
110 The bloody mash
Is churned round between teeth,
Becomes the substance of abuse,
Despoiled,
Final tranquillity. The sun sheds its light.

115 Instincts rest.
Did they enjoy
Destroying a living creature?
Hunger was satisfied.
And perhaps the very remote consciousness
120 Of the lethargic gentleman,
Sensitive to distinctions, felt
His crime – so necessary –
In the style of torture,
To be like a pleasure.

125 The wolf knows even less. He continues to roam,
He does not wait in ambush.

Is that pause leisure?

The animal walks on,
Goes down to a river, drinks,
130 Hears a noise as of a human being,
Goes towards it,
Hurls himself onto the noise.

The traveller shrieks, hardly struggles, lies
Wounded and groaning.
135 And the wolf loses interest,
Goes off slowly,
Quite natural, with neither memory nor fury.

Midday. Afternoon. Dusk.

The wolf is ever a wolf,
140 And with unswerving zeal turns the objective of
Any impulse into a victim.

The fields become dark,

And the wanderer – faithful to his origins –
Moves towards a return
145   Whose disposition and orientation is unknown,
And his footsteps follow at random
An unknown light.

The lycanthrope returns,
Dark in the darkness,
150   Which is illumined and comforted
With the familiar radiance
– Bound up with the land –
Of the moon: to everyone she shows
Her circle of peace.
155   The foliage hides
Many, silent birds.
An owl lights up his
Wise eyes. As the wolf comes
He flies away, he closes his eyes.
160   The hairy bulk at last
Stops.
        Silence. Solitude.
There is the hollow which safeguards
The clothes, well-hidden by confederate
165   Branches. All is anticipated. The moon,
Soon it will be the secret midnight hour,
Unavoidable clothing which implies identity.
Then . . .
        Don't look. There must be no witness
170   To the horrific crisis. The wolf suffers.
Tremors. Transformation. Stupor. Fall.
Unconscious changes follow.
A naked man gets up, starts dressing.
Anthony becomes himself, a gentleman.

III

175   The sleeper is tempted by an angel,
The Guardian Angel,
Always close to his spirit.

In the remote garden on the mountain,
– A garden of orange trees, cypresses,
180   Grasses and some flowers –
It is Anthony who views the panorama.

Ranges of bluish hills,
With their gentle, forested slopes,
Peaks of virgin height,
185   Scattered dwellings, turrets,

Mounds of greenness which lead to the river,
A valley crossed by the river and its banks.

Everything, entranced, sinks deep into the silence,
Powerful on high
190   While someone listens to
The voice of his Lord.
And so many excellent things
Felt and understood beneath an arch,
In a single rapture,
195   Utter the words
Of gratitude to the Father.

The Supreme One requires the most humble of men.
In his soul he takes his seat if there is room.
There too he shines with his glory,
200   His shattering truth.

If earth and sky announce his truth,
A single spirit of faith, of charity,
Intones it,
And God himself lives within him.

205   Anthony is becoming lost within himself.
To climb towards the supreme summit
He must needs forget himself,
Abandon characteristics, accidents
Which are of God, and are not God, but
210   Only of the Earth, transitory Earth.

"I want that which never changes."

In seeming sameness
The world fades away,
Although it grieve us so much if it is adverse,
215   And the grief reveal to us its substantial
Depth, its punishment.

Seeking remoteness,
By means of virtue, abstinence,
All contact avoided,
220   Anthony, Brother Anthony, turns his attention
Deep within himself
In order to negate that redoubt,
That final obstacle: his personality.

"I am." May only God exist.

225   Is it a mistake to be a man?

May minimal humanity
Suffice him who scorns to be human,
And, abhorring his terrestrial law,
May he acquire sudden fleetness in flight.

230   Without useless tears, so very physical,
With no ambiguous ecstasies,
In a mental orb Anthony suffers,
Still a corporeal reality, a creature
Of flesh, of memory.

235   (Recollection, recollection ... Sluggish intruders:
Existence, with the anxiety of shared history,
Clings to recollection.)

It is necessary to abolish, erase, destroy one's memory
By creating darkness in which
240   Neither emotion nor thought can float,
No object, no feeling
That can salvage anything, no last vestige
Of the axis around whose curvature
The great confusion persists and is illuminated:
245   Let the individual and his personality cease,
Let nameless chaos triumph.

Darkness! Grievous with horror,
On the edges of nothingness darkness almost overrides.
That battered man,
250   Weakened phantom, survives
And turns to his God.

And now love is everything,
Along harsh stairways
From this still-human abyss,
255   To a Centre unobtainable
For the intelligence,
Only a loving Centre.

No studies, no journeyings.
No spiritual exercises in the shadow of virtues.
260   Is Brother Anthony improved?
Is he genuinely good?

He wants to love, only to love the greatest lover
With the ambition of a poor creature
Lost in the world.
265   For this he raises up
His necessitous arms,
His insignificance, his faith.

The insignificant man avidly
Hurls himself into his delirium
270 As though he were being shipwrecked,
Without prudence, without compass,
Obedient to a single impulse:
He himself is the one who moves,
Fatal.
275   God permits it.

Is this finite man still hindered
By his human weight, his solid reality,
His outlines, his bearing?

Let the emptiness emerge, like an empty,
280 Available room,
Darkness offered to the cruellest,
Most zealous Love.

Possible dialogue needs
The solitude of a destroyed world.
285 Immersion in this depth of the most invalid ocean
Becomes more difficult.

Days, months pass by.
The loving destroyer hopes.
Virtues? Works? More horrific emptiness,
290 More punished humanity, guilty
In his body and his spirit:
A creature with his form. Creature!

At the end of the passage
The chink of light of a window is perceived.
295 Darkness can be seen,
Now a more merciful cloud.
If the Almighty grips tight, he does not smother.
An air of fulfilled, respired hope
Fills the throat.
300 What, who is happening?
God – with his creature.

Tender, intimate, sweet clarities
In widest space
Where love reunites the tiny being
305 With the most respected sovereignty.
Growing rapture absorbs all,
Rapture far beyond all words.
There occurs ... No. Silence.

A splendour,

310   Which illuminates the inexpressible marvel, gives warmth.
        The Creator of all things
        Is at last revealed,
        In revelation,
        And the mysteries are no longer mysteries,
315   And the loving soul
        Embraces its lover.

        Delight of everlasting pleasure,
        Of nuptial abandon,
        Of endless beauty.

320   Love governs.
        A soul, already divine,
        Fuses with Supreme Goodness,
        And, conjoined with him, in him is it united.

        Love! Without concepts,
325   With no intelligible depth,
        Love of God. He exists,
        And the soul, sharer in spirit,
        Is of God and is already God
        – With no timidity,
330   No terrestrial, contingent scruples –
        In perfect love.

        Oh disincarnation of the Man-God!
        Let us love each other, God-Man.

        The creature has overcome the limit.
335   Still living he didn't expect death.
        Alas, happiness is now absolute.

                    IV
        The sleeper gradually wakes up,
        He conquers reality, which already invades him.
        Mutual embrace. Enough of temptations.
340   Daytime demands perception which is flexible
        Which may ceaselessly impose its own control
        Comparable with the so precarious movement
        Of the moment and its impulse to a flight
        That has potential gifts. No, it is not easy
345   To share daily life with people
        Round about, people well able to become something
        – Still in the future – if the actual
        Moment is raised to levels of
        Human involvement which are well-shared.
350   Anthony gets up, moves towards the world,

Superior to his own self, always in the process
Of arriving ... At final achievement? The light presents,
Already like a truth in the mirror,
The face which Anthony recognizes
355   As the summary of an attempt
Which is never ended: the quasi-realization
Of this person which this bulk proclaims.
Vocation cannot lead one down
The wrong roads signposted by devil or angel. Anthony
360   Dreams daily of his aim: to be a man.

BIBLIOGRAPHY

1. WORKS BY JORGE GUILLEN

Poetry

Cántico, ed. C. Couffon (Paris: Centre de Recherches de l'Institut d'Etudes Hispaniques, 1962). A reprint of *Cántico* (Madrid: Revista de Occidente, 1928)

Cántico (Madrid: Cruz y Raya, 1936)

Cántico (1936), ed. J.M. Blecua (Barcelona: Labor, 1970)

Cántico (Mexico: Litoral, 1945)

Cántico, primera edición completa (Buenos Aires: Sudamericana, 1950)

Clamor: Maremágnum (Buenos Aires: Sudamericana, 1957)

Clamor: ...Que van a dar en la mar (Buenos Aires: Sudamericana, 1960)

Clamor: A la altura de las circunstancias (Buenos Aires: Sudamericana, 1963)

Homenaje (Milan: All'insegna del pesce d'oro, 1967)

Aire nuestro: Cántico (Barcelona: Barral, 1977)

Aire nuestro: Clamor (Barcelona: Barral, 1977)

Aire nuestro: Homenaje (Barcelona: Barral, 1978)

Aire nuestro: Y otros poemas (Barcelona: Barral, 1979)

Aire nuestro: Final (Barcelona: Barral, 1981)

English Translations of Poetry

Affirmation: A Bilingual Anthology 1919-1966, trans. J. Palley, introd. Jorge Guillén (Norman: Univ. of Oklahoma Press, 1968)

"Cántico": A Selection, ed. N.T. di Giovanni, introd. Jorge Guillén (London: Deutsch, 1965)

Contemporary Spanish Poetry: Selections from Ten Poets, trans. E.L. Turnbull, with Spanish originals and personal reminiscences of the poets by Pedro Salinas (Baltimore: Johns Hopkins Press, 1945)

Guillén on Guillén, trans. A.L. Geist and R. Gibbons (Princeton: Univ. of Princeton Press, 1979)

Selected Prose

"Anatole France", *España*, 303 (1922), 12

"Aire aura", *Revista de Occidente*, 2, 4 (1923), 1-8

"Carta a Fernando Vela", in G. Diego, *Poesía española contemporánea: Antología*, 3rd ed. (Madrid: Taurus, 1966), pp.326-28
Federico en persona: semblanza y epistolario (Buenos Aires: Emecé, 1959)
El argumento de la obra (Milan: Scheiwiller, 1961)
Language and Poetry (Cambridge, Mass.: Harvard Univ. Press, 1961)
"Poesía integral", *Revista Hispánica Moderna*, 31 (1965), 207-209
Lenguaje y poesía (Madrid: Alianza, 1969)
"Valéry en el recuerdo", *Plural*, 3 (1971), 18-20

2. SELECTED SECONDARY SOURCES

Alonso, D., *Poetas españoles contemporáneos* (Madrid: Gredos, 1958)
Barnestone, W., "Two Poets of Felicity: Thomas Traherne and Jorge Guillén", *Books Abroad*, 42 (1968), 14-19
Bates, M., "Guillén's 'Advenimiento' ", *Explicator*, 26, 1 (1967)
Blecua, J.M., *Floresta de lírica española*, I (Madrid: Gredos, 1963)
—, and Gullón, R., *La poesía de Jorge Guillén: Dos ensayos* (Zaragoza: Heraldo de Aragón, 1949)
Books Abroad, "International Symposium in Honour of Jorge Guillén at 75", 42, 1 (1968)
Burnshaw, S., ed., *The Poem Itself* (New York: Holt, Rinehart and Winston, 1960)
Cabrera, V., *Tres poetas a la luz de la metáfora: Salinas, Aleixandre y Guillén* (Madrid: Gredos, 1975)
Cano, J.L., "Machado y la generación de 1925", *La Torre*, 45-46 (1964), 483-504
Cano Ballesta, J., *Poesía española entre pureza y revolución 1930-1936* (Madrid: Gredos, 1972)
Caro Romero, J., *Jorge Guillén* (Madrid: Epesa, 1974)
Casalduero, J., *"Cántico" de Jorge Guillén y "Aire nuestro"* (Madrid: Gredos, 1974)
Castellet, J.M., *Veinte años de poesía española* (Barcelona: Seix Barral, 1962)
Ciplijauskaité, B., ed., *Jorge Guillén* (Madrid: Taurus, 1975)
Close, L.J., "Guillén and the Aristotelian Tradition", in *Studies in Modern Spanish Literature and Art*, presented to Helen F. Grant, ed. N. Glendinning (London: Tamesis, 1972), pp.45-64
Costa, L.F., "De la *Divina Comedia* a *Clamor*", in *Homenaje a Jorge Guillén* (Massachusetts: Dept. of Spanish, Wellesley College/Madrid: Insula, 1978), pp.143-63
Couffon, C., *Dos encuentros con Jorge Guillén* (Paris: Centre de Recherches de l'Institut d'Etudes Hispaniques, 1963)

Darmangeat, P., *A. Machado, P. Salinas, J. Guillén* (Madrid: Insula, 1969)

Debicki, A.P., *La poesía de Jorge Guillén* (Madrid: Gredos, 1973)

Dehennin, E., *"Cántico" de Jorge Guillén: Une Poésie de la clarté* (Brussels: Presses Universitaires de Bruxelles, 1969)

Diego, G., "La vuelta a la estrofa", *Carmen*, 1 (December 1927)

—, *Poesía española contemporánea: Antología*, 3rd ed. (Madrid: Taurus, 1966)

Gil de Biedma, J., *El mundo y la poesía de Jorge Guillén* (Barcelona: Seix Barral, 1960)

Gilman, S., Introduction to Fernando de Rojas, *La Celestina*, 2nd ed. (Madrid: Alianza, 1971)

González Muela, J., *El lenguaje poético de la generación Guillén-Lorca* (Madrid: Insula, 1950)

—, *La realidad y Jorge Guillén* (Madrid: Insula, 1962)

Guerrero Martín, J., *Jorge Guillén: sus raíces. Recuerdos al paso* (Valladolid: Miñón, 1982)

Gullón, R., "'Huerto de Melibea'", *Papeles de Son Armadans*, 4 (1956), 89-98

—, "Jorge Guillén: *A la altura de las circunstancias*", *Insula*, 208 (1964), 1 and 10

Havard, R.G., "The early *décimas* of Jorge Guillén", *Bulletin of Hispanic Studies*, 48 (1971), 111-27

Insula, Number dedicated to Jorge Guillén, 26 (1948)

Ivask, I., and Marichal, J., eds., *Luminous Reality* (Norman: Univ. of Oklahoma Press, 1969)

Lida, R., "Sobre las *décimas* de Jorge Guillén", in *Jorge Guillén*, ed. B. Ciplijauskaité (Madrid: Taurus, 1975), pp.317-22

Long, V., "Colaboración escolar: Las esencias en 'Más allá'", *Revista Hispánica Moderna*, 16 (1950), 369-77

MacCurdy, G.G., *Jorge Guillén* (Boston: Twayne Publishers, 1982)

MacLeish, A., "Jorge Guillén: A Poet of This Time", *Atlantic Monthly*, Jan. 1961, pp.127-29

Macrí, O., *La obra poética de Jorge Guillén* (Barcelona: Ariel, 1976)

Miller, M. La Follette, "Self-Commentary in Jorge Guillén's *Aire Nuestro*", *Hispania*, 65 (1982), 20-27

Morris, C.B., *A Generation of Spanish Poets 1920-1936* (Cambridge: Cambridge Univ. Press, 1969)

Paz, O., "Horas situadas de Jorge Guillén", *Papeles de Son Armadans*, 40 (1966), 209-18

Pinet, C.E., "The Sacramental View of Poetry and the Religion of Love in Jorge Guillén's *Cántico*", *Hispania*, 62 (1979), 47-55

—, "*Cántico*'s Threatened Eden: A Historical Perspective", *Hispanófila*, 79 (1983), 53-68

Pleak, F.A., *The Poetry of Jorge Guillén* (Princeton: Univ. of Princeton Press, 1942)

Prat, I., *"Aire nuestro" de Jorge Guillén* (Barcelona: Planeta, 1974)

—, "Estética de lo absurdo y del sentido estricto en *Homenaje* de Jorge Guillén", *Insula*, 310 (1972), 11 and 12

Ruiz de Conde, J., *El cántico americano de Jorge Guillén* (Madrid: Turner, 1973)

Salinas, P., *Literatura española Siglo XX* (Madrid: Alianza, 1970)

Sibbald, K.M., *Hacia "Cántico": escritos de los años veinte* (Barcelona: Ariel, 1980)

—, "Some early versions of the poems of *Cántico 1919-1928*: Progress towards *claridad*", *Bulletin of Hispanic Studies*, 50 (1973), 23-44

Siebenmann, G., *Los estilos poéticos en España desde 1900* (Madrid: Gredos, 1973)

Terry, A., *Two Views of Poetry* (Belfast: Queen's Univ. Press, 1964)

Wardlaw, F.D., "A Thematic Analysis of Jorge Guillén's *Clamor*", Diss. Duke 1977

—, "Jorge Guillén's *Clamor*: Harmonious Dissonance", *Kentucky Romance Quarterly*, 30 (1983), 77-86

Weber, R.J., "De *Cántico* a *Clamor*", *Revista Hispánica Moderna*, 29 (1963), 109-19

Weidlé, W., "La poesía 'pura' y el espíritu mediterráneo", *La Torre*, 19-20 (1957), 199-210

Wellesley College, Department of Spanish, *Homenaje a Jorge Guillén* (Madrid: Insula, 1978)

Whittredge, R., "The Poetic World of Jorge Guillén", *Romanic Review*, 29 (1948), 140-45

Wilson, E.M., "Modern Spanish Poets: Guillén and Quevedo on Death", *Atlante*, 1 (1953), 22-26

—, "Guillén and Quevedo on Death: Postscript", *Atlante*, 2 (1954), 237-38

Yudin, F.L., *The Vibrant Silence in Jorge Guillén's "Aire nuestro"* (Valencia: North Carolina Studies in Romance Languages and Literatures, 1974)

Zardoya, C., "*Clamor I*: Stylistic Peculiarities", in *Luminous Reality*, ed. I. Ivask and J. Marichal (Norman: Univ. of Oklahoma Press, 1969), pp.145-78

The most complete bibliography is to be found in O. Macrí, op.cit.

INDEX OF POEMS ANALYSED

Además, 67-68
Advenimiento, 29-32
Afirmación, 50
Aguardando, 64-65
Ahora sí, 34-35
A la intemperie, 54-55
Amplitud, 29
Anulación de lo peor, 55-56
Así, 65-66
A VISTA DE HOMBRE, 82-83, 102-113 (trans. 244-47)

Buenos días, 53-54

Callejeo, 28-29
Camposanto, 57-58

De paso por la tristeza, 43
Descanso en jardín, 52, 56
Desnudo, 15-16
DIMISIÓN DE SANCHO, 208-216 (trans. 306-312)

El acorde, 227
EL CONCIERTO, 82, 94-102 (trans. 241-44)
El desterrado, 35-37
EL DIÁLOGO, 82, 86-94 (trans. 238-41)
Elevación de la claridad, 18-19
El hondo sueño, 37-39
El horizonte, 17-18
El viaje, 34
Equilibrio, 67
Esos cerros, 29
Estatua ecuestre, 19-21

HUERTO DE MELIBEA, 197-208 (trans. 294-306

LA HERMOSA Y LOS EXCÉNTRICOS, 173-83 (trans. 275-83)
La hierba entre las tejas, 60
La nieve, 27
LAS CUATRO CALLES, 85-86, 138-49 (trans. 260-62)
Las doce en el reloj, 40-42
Las horas, 51
Las ocho de la mañana, 34
LAS TENTACIONES DE ANTONIO, 216-25 (trans. 312-21)

Lectura, 52
Lo esperado, 26-27
Los amantes, 46
Los nombres, 21-22
Los tres tiempos, 46-48
LUGAR DE LÁZARO, 183-97 (trans. 284-94)
LUZBEL DESCONCERTADO, 158-73 (trans. 263-75)
Luz diferida, 54
LUZ NATAL, 83, 113-28 (trans. 247-55)

Más allá, 32-34
Más amor que tiempo, 73-74
Más verdad, 60-63
Mayo nuestro, 71-73
Muerte a lo lejos, 43-46

Naturaleza viva, 26
Nivel del río, 58

Perfección, 39-40
Perfección del círculo, 24-25
Plaza mayor, 139-40
Pleno amor, 52

Redondez, 28
Rosa olida, 70-71

Sabor a vida, 58-60
Salvación de la primavera, 48-49
Ser, 66
Siempre aguarda mi sangre, 49-50
Sin embargo, 76-77

Tarde mayor, 74-76
Temprano cristal, 27
Tiempo perdido en la orilla, 27
Tornasol, 16-17
Tránsito, 23-24

Una sola vez, 57
Una ventana, 68-70

VIDA EXTREMA, 83-85, 128-38 (trans. 255-59)
Vida urbana, 56-57
Viento saltado, 29